MURDERED OR MISSING?

MURDERED OR MISSING?

THE ARLENE FRASER CASE

REG McKAY
&
GLENN LUCAS

BLACK & WHITE PUBLISHING

First published 2005
by Black & White Publishing Ltd
99 Giles Street, Edinburgh EH6 6BZ

ISBN 1 84502 044 8

A CIP catalogue record for this book
is available from The British Library.

Printed and bound by Creative Print and Design

CONTENTS

FOREWORD

All my life I have held firm views. Public school educated and one-time conservative candidate I thought the cops did a good job and could be trusted. In the UK we had law and order we could be proud of. Police states were other states – not this state. Criminals? Lock them up and throw away the key. If there had been a referendum on hanging, I would have voted in favour. In fact, hanging was too good for those convicted of crimes.

Then something happens to turn your life upside down.

My life has changed. Not by my choice or by bad luck. But by design. Not my design. Their design. Just because it suited them.

Now I'm on the side of those who complain of being jailed unjustly. The ones who claim police corruption. The cons who tell tales of being set up. My phone is bugged and I'm followed when I drive north. I warn my friends that this is my life now and, by association, their lives too.

Playing by the rules, I ask the powers that be why all this happened? Why it was necessary? They tell me they can't tell me. Or is that won't? But, if they think I'm giving up now, they can think again.

This is the true mystery of a friend of mine, Arlene, who disappeared on the 28th of April 1998.

It's also my story, all written by Reg McKay. The story of a changing life that started changing on the 28th of April 1998. And it's not over yet.

Glenn Lucas
Lincolnshire
April 2005

DEDICATION

To those who are left
When their loved ones go
Without message, trace or clue.

Reg McKay & Glenn Lucas
28 April 2005

MURDERED OR MISSING?

THE ARLENE FRASER CASE

WHERE ARE YOU?

28 APRIL 1998

He was a happy child. Anyone could see that as he walked with a half skip and an occasional jump, confident, relaxed, feeling safe. He was going home – to his mam.

It had been a long day – away first thing in the morning on a school trip. No lessons that day for Jamie Fraser. They had taken the train up the main line to Inverness. Everyone was excited and happy. Even the teachers were in a good mood. It had been fun.

That morning his mam had waved him and his wee sister Natalie off as usual. His mam and dad, Arlene and Nat, weren't living together and that made him sad. But they had made sure nothing much had changed for him and Natalie. They saw their dad most days and he was still their old dad – good fun, full of jokes, interested in what they were getting up to. And mum liked it that way. In fact she insisted they saw their dad.

The weather wasn't so bright that day. Big dark skies lumbered across the horizon, breaking into vicious, sharp, short storms. It was weather to take care in – stay indoors, wrapped up, safe and cosy. But he was too young to bother about weather. What did it matter to him? He didn't have a care in the world.

So off bright and early that Tuesday morning. Natalie left first out of Smith Street to the end of the road to her school. He followed a bit later. He didn't mind going with his wee sister but her school was close by and the way there was safe. Besides, he was big now, ten

1

years old, and Natalie was only five. Younger, much younger, but not too young to go the short distance to school on her own.

Jamie liked his home town of Elgin. It was small enough so that everyone knew everyone else. But it was big enough to have a good sports centre, swimming pool and a football team and you could follow almost any hobby you fancied. He had a lot of friends. A popular young boy. Just like his sister and his dad and his mam. He liked that. Elgin was a good, safe place to live.

But it had been a long day and the school trip had been even later getting back than they had planned. When the train pulled in at the station, it was almost 7 p.m. Way past his teatime. He was hungry, a bit tired and looking forward to getting home to his wee sister and especially his mam. But his teachers had given him a lift up the road as planned and he was home now.

Arriving at the smart house that was the family home, Jamie cantered down the path to the back door and pulled on the handle. Instead of swinging open as he expected, it remained firmly shut. He tried it again. It was locked. That was strange. His mam didn't have college or anything much on that day. Wait a minute, didn't she have an appointment with a lawyer or something? That's why Natalie had gone straight from school to their friends and neighbours, the Higgins. But Mam hadn't told him that she might be late. Not this late. She would have been sure to do that.

Jamie bent down and fumbled under the wheelie bin, his hand clutching at the spare key his mam always left there.

'She's probably left me a note,' he thought as he unlocked the door. 'She always does.'

'Mam,' he shouted as he walked though the door. No response. The boy went from room to room. Everything looked just as it had that morning when he had left for school. In each room, he wondered and worried a wee bit about what he would find even though he knew it was his home, a place he knew intimately. Somehow it was scary. Everything looked just as it always did. Except his mam wasn't there as she should be.

Back in the kitchen and living room, he looked for a note, the note his mam would always leave him. There was no note. But his mother, Arlene, had taught him well. He was too young to stay in the house on his own. So he would go over to the Higgins' house nearby and join his little sister Natalie. Besides, he got on well with Mark Higgins who was just a year younger than him. Just because his mam didn't leave him a message, Jamie would leave her one, just as she always told him to. Finding paper and a pen he wrote,

> I was home at 7.30 pm.
> You were not in.
> I am at Mark's.
> Where are you?

Jamie didn't know it but, within hours, the world would be asking the same question. Where was Arlene Fraser?

3

1

EARLY BIRDS

JUNE 2001

I should have been frightened. Early morning, not yet dawn, and the battering on my front door splintered the silence of sleep. At that time and place, it marked an omen of doom to send half-asleep people stumbling from bed down the stairs, acid dread flooding their stomachs. But not me. Wrong time and place for me.

I was awake and up already, dressed and in the kitchen ready for my cup of tea when they arrived. It was almost 5 a.m., a time I was accustomed to rising and a time when I was used to solitude. Not like most people. They'd be fast asleep in their kips. So who the hell was this who had the nerve to thump on our door at that hour when they expected us to be asleep?

Heading to the front door, I cursed under my breath hoping that the intrusion hadn't wakened young Maya still lying asleep in our bed. Maybe someone had forgotten their key for work and had called by to get mine. Fair enough but it's not everyone who is up at that hour.

Irritated, I rattled at the key and yanked the door open, ready to let rip with some sarcastic gibe.

'What the fuck?'

There on the step wasn't the errant work colleague, looking a bit sheepish and apologetic, but three hulking men in dark suits.

'Mr Lucas?' one asked.

'Yes.'

4

'Glenn Lucas,' he continued, waving an ID card, 'we are here to arrest you in connection with the murder of Arlene Fraser. I must warn you . . .'

The rest of his words melted into the morning air. One minute I was making a cup of tea, mulling over in my mind plans for a long day at work. The next I'm being lifted in a murder case. How would you feel? Me, I've dealt with crazy, risky situations in my life and never panicked. It's not my nature. Maybe I should have.

The cops came in and closed the door behind them. Big buggers they were and efficient looking – as if they could hand out the damage if it was necessary. This was the serious mob and no doubt.

'Read that,' ordered a cop shoving a clutch of papers into my hand.

Now I was wide awake. Fully switched on. I had been getting up at this time for so much of my life it was second nature. But even I was having difficulty in comprehending the enormity of what was in those typed sheets.

'Arlene Fraser . . .'

'murder . . .'

'withholding information . . .'

'search warrant . . .'

'rings . . .'

There was more, much more, but the detail simply wasn't percolating. All I had tried to do was help a friend. I had known for some time that the cops believed Arlene was dead – they had announced that to the world. But murder? No way. And me? This just wasn't real to me. Or maybe it was too real to comprehend. My eyes flitted across the print in what seemed like a long silence as the cops edged from foot to foot.

Suddenly they decided I'd had enough reading time. 'Is there anyone else in the house?' asked one copper.

'Yes. Yes, Maya, my girlfriend.'

'Aye, Maya,' one replied with a smirk. 'She's Russian, isn't she?' It was more of a statement of fact than a question.

I nodded, wondering what the hell that had to do with me being arrested.

'Where are you going?' barked one policeman.

'To waken my girlfriend,' I answered.

The detective shook his head.

'And you'll need to pack a bag,' said the cop. He smirked and went on, 'You're going to be away for quite a while.'

Here they were at my home in Spalding in Lincolnshire, saying they were going to take me all the way north to the cop shop in Elgin to interview me. And they were telling me – not asking me – giving me no option but to go. And so it started, the loss of freedom that goes hand in hand with arrest. I turned and glowered at them. This was now getting on my nerves and I was reverting to type.

Away for a long time? Arrested? I didn't believe him. Not then.

MISSING

28 APRIL 1998

Arlene Fraser was very late.

As the family became aware that something was far from right, the police were notified by her neighbours, the Higgins, and Nat Fraser went on the rounds asking people if they had seen Arlene that day, if they knew where she might be. No one had. No one did.

A picture slowly emerged. Early that morning, Arlene had phoned the school to check on the arrangements and timing of Jamie coming home from a school trip. It was a caring but unusual thing to do. Unusual for her, that is. The school staff were very efficient at informing parents of all their activities and Arlene was good at remembering. Still, maybe she had forgotten that time. When the school returned Arlene's call ten minutes later they received no reply. Arlene was already gone. It was around 9.40 a.m.

It was a day off college for Arlene. She was thirty-three years old, had decided to get an education and enrolled on a business studies course at the local Moray College. Tuesday was her only day off. On every other day of the week, her absence would have been spotted sooner by someone. Not that day.

Arlene did have two appointments though. The first was with her good friend, Michelle Scott, for lunch at 1 p.m. Michelle had nipped round to see her pal earlier than usual at around 11 a.m. – the way friends do. When she arrived, there was no one home. This wasn't like Arlene. She would usually still be doing her hair, choosing her clothes, taking advantage of the free time to make sure she looked her best. Slim and attractive with long brown hair, Arlene always looked good. Always.

Worried, Michelle tried the front door and was amazed to find it open. Arlene was very security conscious and would never leave without making sure her home was locked up tight. Now beginning to panic, Michelle went into the house and checked the rooms. No sign of Arlene. Nothing to do but go away and come back to go for that lunch date as planned.

At 1 p.m., Michelle Scott went back to the Frasers' house at 2 Smith Street, Elgin. Arlene still wasn't in. Michelle checked the house. Everything was there. In fact, too much was there. It was as if Arlene had just popped out. Michelle waited and waited but Arlene never showed.

Later that afternoon, Arlene had an appointment to meet with a lawyer about divorce proceedings against her husband Nat. They had had a stormy relationship for a long time but, just a month before, he had assaulted her so seriously she required hospital care. Nat had been charged with attempted murder and released on bail with a condition that he didn't go near the family home. All her friends knew it was the breaking point for Arlene in her marriage and she was determined to go through with the divorce.

Arlene never showed at her lawyer's office.

It had been a bad time all in all for Arlene Fraser. She had a car, a big Ford Granada, that she was very proud of. Just two weeks after the assault by Nat, her much loved motor burst into flames when it was parked in the driveway of their home. An electrical fault, the police said – just one of those things. But it was still worrying for her. Very worrying.

By the time ten-year-old Jamie arrived back from his school trip, his mother had been missing for over ten hours. He didn't know that. No one did. Finding the house empty and joining his sister Natalie at their friends and neighbours the Higgins' family home, Jamie still thought that his mother was just a wee bit late. Maybe delayed at the lawyers or maybe she had popped in to visit a pal. It was out of character for his mum but he wasn't worried nor was his five-year-old sister, Natalie. For the adults it was a different matter.

Arlene's house had been abandoned. Dirty glasses lay around, her wardrobe was full, clothes for that day left out ready to put on, none of her make-up had gone, her expensive watch lay where she used to leave it. None of this seemed right for a house-proud young woman who took great pride in her appearance. Their fears increased when they discovered that she hadn't taken her medication for the Crohn's disease she suffered from. She would never go without taking that.

By 9 p.m., they had alerted the police that Arlene Fraser was missing. Normally the cops would note it as a missing person report and do nothing much for a few days. Many adults who disappear come back again within a short time, especially one who had her fair share of marital grief to contend with as indeed Arlene had. That's how the cops would normally react. Not this time. The cops rallied the top brass and phoned the local paper, the *Press and Journal*. Everyone read the *P&J*. By the next morning, Arlene's disappearance would make the Stop Press column but soon it would be carrying headlines.

The police were worried. Very worried indeed.

Arlene Fraser wasn't late. She was missing.

2

CONNECTED

JUNE 2001

Sitting in the back of that cop car while I wondered why the hell I had been arrested, there was no mystery about what was troubling the police. Arlene Fraser was a friend of mine, well known to me for over eleven years through her husband, Nat, and she was missing. Had been for three years and more. That was the problem.

For much of my adult life I had worked in the fruit and vegetable industry, importing and selling. Still do. Some years earlier, I had lived and worked in the small town of Elgin in the north-east of Scotland, managing Harrison & Reeve, a well-known company in that trade. Arlene's husband, Nat, and his good friend, Ian Taylor, had worked for me there. These were two likeable rogues and no question. But then that industry is full of characters.

Nat was young, good looking and had an eye for the ladies. A keen guitarist, he played in his own local group, The Minesweepers, and had regular gigs in the pubs of the area every weekend. That added to his local celebrity, some would say infamy, as someone who did things his way and didn't give a damn.

Arlene was slim, beautiful and personable and, no doubt, when the two started dating, locals saw it as an ideal match. Or at least some of them did. Others were jealous of the good-looking twosome. That's the way it is everywhere but it's more obvious in small communities like Elgin.

Elgin claims city status due to the burnt-out remains of a

cathedral, the victim of Alexander Stewart, more familiarly known as the Wolf of Badenoch, in what people consider to have been the bloodier times of the fourteenth century – or so people thought. Now home to around 20,000 people and wedged almost halfway between Inverness and Aberdeen and ten miles from the sea, it is one of the largest towns in the vast rural area of north-east Scotland. Elgin is a thriving community with many small industries, bus and rail terminals. It is surrounded by rich agricultural soil, vast gorgeous wild country and is stacked full of entrepreneurs – just like Nat Fraser.

When Nat and Ian Taylor, who was nicknamed Pedro, decided to leave my company and start up on their own, I wasn't at all surprised. The handsome pair were inseparable and both were ambitious. By the time they left, our working relationship had moved on into friendship. So, I helped the two mates in setting up their new business. A bit of advice here, a forewarning there and a little analysis of the market were all designed to assist them to avoid the pitfalls that wreck so many new small companies within months. They were my friends and that's the way I am with friends – loyal. Was that my downfall?

Nat didn't stop his old ways. When he and Arlene married in 1987 and set up home in a bungalow in Elgin's Smith Street, I swear it was half-kitted out in goods that weren't exactly legit. But he wasn't alone in that. Most folk I knew around those parts were quite willing to barter for goods and ask no questions. Maybe it was something to do with old country traditions. Nat was just better at it than most but not the worst offender, not by a long shot.

Nat didn't stop his old ways in other respects. Out and about in their vans, delivering fruit and veg around the small rural communities, Nat soon developed a range of lady friends on his routes. Many of these lovers were married and were up for some daytime fun while their men were out at work – some were fishermen and spent most of the week at sea. These women were highly respectable and they felt safe in the knowledge that no one could know what went on in their isolated houses. One time there

11

was even the young wife of a vicar involved. Well you would be tempted, wouldn't you?

The worst thing I could say about Nat was that he had no hesitation in shagging someone else's missus while the poor bloke she was married to was grafting for his wages. I could say that but then, for too many years of my life, I was a prime shagger too. So this pot isn't going to call that kettle black or any other colour. Then again, he wasn't shagging my wife.

That's where Nat's local press started going badly sour. It was well known what he was getting up to with the lonely ladies. There was also a local legend that he was hung like a horse. Now that might make him popular with sex-hungry women but, of course, it had the opposite effect with ill-confident men who would happily see him in deep trouble. Not me. I liked Nat and Pedro.

Arlene and Nat's relationship was tempestuous. Always had been apparently. When their two kids, Jamie, the older and young Natalie, came along, some people hoped that the pair would quieten down. No chance. Nat didn't change his ways one bit. I knew Arlene, had been at her wedding, met her loads of times and, according to Nat, she handed out the grief just as much as he did. An intelligent, beautiful, feisty woman, once both kids were at school, Arlene had enrolled at college. It seemed to me she oozed the confidence of a woman in her thirties who had experience of the world and knew she could do better for herself. Good on her.

Nat didn't show any objection to Arlene's ambitions that I ever noticed but his relationship with her was, if anything, deteriorating rather than improving. Always a confident person, there was an added edge to Arlene, an extra assertiveness. She started going out regularly with female friends, often to boozy nights that ended with her coming home in the early hours of the morning. It was nothing that Nat hadn't been doing for years and he didn't seem to mind or didn't show it if he did. But still their relationship was going downhill fast to unacceptable depths.

In March 1998, relations between them finally fell apart and Nat was arrested for assaulting Arlene who ended up half-choked, battered and bruised. Any assault on a woman is wrong but, by all accounts, this was a particularly bad one and Nat was charged with attempted murder. Yet, from what I knew of Arlene and Nat, unlike other couples whose marriages are in trouble, violence had never been a feature of their relationship before. Something had brought their hostilities to this terrible head – but what?

The pair of them separated and Nat went to live with his business partner, Ian Taylor, and his family. One Sunday, I paid a visit to Nat and Ian en route to visit old friends up north. We passed a quiet day and, at night, we'd arranged to go out for a few drinks with another bloke. Just as we were leaving the Taylors' house, a long-term friend of Nat, a guy called Hector Dick, arrived with his wife, Irene. They had come to visit. Hector Dick preferred to stay with his wife and Ian's wife, Jane, and have a cup of tea. Nothing wrong with that but most blokes, particularly rough and ready types who fitted in with that crowd, would have popped out with the men for a pint. I didn't know Hector Dick back then but I remember thinking at the time it was a wee bit odd that he didn't join us. Before this was all over, I was going to think that there was a great deal more about Hector Dick that needed to be explained.

Staying over at the Taylors', I had the top bunk while Nat was in the bottom one in their spare room. We lay in the darkness and chatted as you do. I had never once asked Nat about why his relationship with Arlene had got so low as to result in an assault but that didn't mean I didn't care or want to help. 'If you like,' I said into the darkness, 'I'll pop round to see Arlene tomorrow.' In spite of Nat being my pal, I was a bit nervous about this, feeling like I was treading into a personal space without an invite. There was silence from below. 'You know,' I continued, 'try and smooth the waters.'

'No,' he sighed. 'Thanks, Glenn, but that's OK.'

So I didn't visit Arlene that Monday, thank God. For starters, I wasn't really sure what I would say to her. The soft-shoe shuffle really isn't my style and I might have caused more problems than I solved. That's how I felt at that time – slightly relieved that Nat

13

didn't take up my offer. But now, being arrested in connection with Arlene's murder, it was relief with a capital R.

The next day, Tuesday the 28th of April 1998, Arlene disappeared. The cops searched the Smith Street house numerous times after her disappearance and carried out full forensic checks. If I had visited the house that Monday, I would have been in big shit with my prints and DNA all over the shop.

Arlene had gone, leaving no letter, no message, no warning signals. That's how it usually is when someone simply decides to go. The house showed no signs of a struggle or anything sinister – just Arlene missing. For some reason, the local Grampian Police immediately sprang into action. Why?

The whole community started talking about Arlene vanishing in hushed tones. The common wisdom was that a woman didn't just up and abandon her young kids for no reason. That didn't happen in Elgin, they all agreed. Well, maybe not but it happened everyday everywhere else. What was so different about Elgin?

In the meantime, it had got messy – awful messy – but was it murder?

I should have anticipated the cops' visit to my home. The night before they arrived, Ian Taylor had called me from Elgin excitedly reporting, 'The shit has really hit the fan up here. The cops are everywhere.'

I found the news interesting but only that. It probably concerned my good friend Nat and his wife Arlene. It might involve some other folk I had known while I was living up there. So I was interested, as you are about local gossip and events, but what had it to do with me? Nothing. So I had gone off to bed. Believe you me, if I had suspected that there was to be a dawn raid the next morning, I would have spent that last night making sure I got my leg over with Maya. That's how I am. But I had a relaxed evening, went to bed, pecked Maya on the cheek, snuggled down and slept the sleep of the innocent.

When the cops fastened the handcuffs on me, it felt as if they had ripped the skin from my wrists. I grumbled that they were far too tight. I'm a big man – big boned – but not that big. Surely they could have been looser? Apparently not. They just left them where they were, a small torture in what was to be a long day.

They didn't allow me to see Maya. Not even to say goodbye. All I had was a bag with some clean underwear and some toiletries since I wasn't planning to be away for long. I had my doubts, mind you, when we hit the street.

A few other coppers had come into the house but there was a whole stack outside in three cop cars, a transit van and a people carrier. What did they expect, an armed siege? The scene seemed surreal to me. A movie set. Like they were playing cops with me as the robber. Except I wasn't the bad guy and I certainly didn't want to join in their game.

Now here I was, twenty minutes after they had rattled my door, handcuffed and locked in the back seat of a cop car, being driven north to be grilled. Soon I'd learn just how nasty this episode was going to be.

COME HOME

6 MAY 1998

Arlene Fraser had been missing less than a day when her family, the cops and the local community started looking for her. It was a mark of the strength of that small place, how the people stick together when the going gets tough. But would it work?

Almost immediately, Arlene's mother, Isabelle Thompson, and her married sister, Carol Gillies, travelled north from their respective homes in Hamilton and Erskine. They moved into Arlene's home and cared for her two kids, Jamie and Natalie.

The national media was now in attendance. Grampian Police's worried signals had been picked up loud and clear. Chief Inspector Laurie Stewart admitted to the press that they were 'totally baffled'. There was nothing like a mystery to attract the media, particularly when it involved a beautiful young woman who was the mother of two great young kids as well.

Arlene's family were bereft but hopeful. Her mother, Isabelle, said, 'We are all puzzled. We want her back and her children are desperate to hear from her.'

Her sister, Carol, was more forthright, 'Please just let us know you are safe. Just one phone call, Arlene, just one.'

The cops backed the family up. Chief Inspector Laurie Stewart said, 'It is totally out of character for Mrs Fraser to disappear like this. Her family are all desperately worried about her and we would urge her to

16

contact us.' As far as they were concerned Arlene was missing. She had gone like hundreds do in the UK every day – just upped and off without warning, explanation, note or phone call. They did what most families do in those circumstances and asked her to come home. The press printed their appeals and waited.

The police didn't wait though. Several times within seventy-two hours of Arlene's disappearance, a forensic team had hit the Frasers' home and searched it room by room. A squad of forty cops were drafted in and began house-to-house inquiries. They found nothing.

Five days after Arlene's disappearance, hundreds of local volunteers were drafted in by the police to scour the town, searching open land, sheds, farms, work places and lock-ups. Police frogmen were dispatched to drag the rivers, burns and lochs. A mountain rescue team was sent off up into the Grampian hills. A police helicopter hovered over the area looking for signs, any signs.

They found nothing.

Though divorced from her mother, Arlene's father, Hector McInnes, was quickly on the scene from his home in Preston, announcing he would lead the search of the area. Now there were around 300 people turning up every day to join in the hunt. But where was Arlene's husband Nat?

The cops weren't just quick in arranging a major search for Arlene, they were quick in their investigation. On the first two days after his mother's disappearance, young Jamie Fraser was interviewed twice for around four hours each time. And it was just Jamie and the police officers – no responsible adult was present, as is his right, and certainly not his dad.

Nat was busy in other ways. By day and night, Grampian Police interviewed Nat Fraser early on and repeatedly. It quickly got to the stage where he didn't know what any day would hold for him and he stopped planning anything. The interviews were long and repetitive, going over and over the last time Nat had seen Arlene, forcing him to retrace his movements on the day she disappeared and raking up the recent past when Nat had assaulted her.

Within days of Arlene's disappearance, Nat Fraser had formed the distinct impression that the cops believed she was dead and he was her killer. That's how it felt for Nat Fraser. But how could he know? He'd never had a wife who had gone missing before.

All the media quoted Arlene's sister, mother and father but not Nat. Having been charged with the attempted murder of Arlene some weeks before, the media weren't allowed to report on Nat or even to photograph him. There is nothing unusual in this since media coverage is generally held likely to prejudice any forthcoming trial. That's a form of protection accused people are entitled to under Scots law. But most accused people aren't at the centre of two high-profile cases at the same time, one of which, so far, was the mystery concerning what had happened to Arlene, his wife.

So, as far as the public were concerned, Nat Fraser wasn't having much to do with finding his wife. Yet Nat Fraser was involved in the search as much as anyone else – that is, when the police weren't interviewing him or telling him to stay away.

Why did they do that? Telling him to stay away was enough to set some tongues wagging. What if Arlene hadn't decided to go away? What if worse had happened? It's always the spouse you suspect first, isn't it? It's always the spouse.

The family issued more public appeals and Arlene's sister, Carol, spoke to the media again, saying, 'If Arlene is out there and has seen all this and it's putting her off getting in touch or if she is worried about the enormity of it, don't worry.' Believing that Arlene couldn't help but see what was going on back in Elgin if she was still in Scotland or even farther afield – the papers and TV news programmes all carried the story of her disappearance – Carol added, 'Problems can be sorted. Let us know you're alive. That's all we want to know. She can stay away. She doesn't need to come back if she doesn't want. But get in touch.'

It was an open offer – non-threatening and appealing to the missing woman to take care of her family's needs and the hurt of her children. It was exactly the right type of offer to make – if Arlene was missing. Arlene Fraser didn't get in touch. Either she wouldn't or couldn't contact her family.

Then the police had a change of heart. At first, when Arlene's car had burst into flames as it sat in the driveway weeks before, the police dismissed it, saying it had been caused by an electrical fault rather than anything malicious. But, once they had looked at the vehicle again, they reached much more sinister conclusions – the front seat had been torched. They didn't know if this had any connection with Arlene's disappearance, they admitted, but were keeping an open mind. No one asked the cops why they had made the first error. Everyone was too busy worrying about Arlene.

The cops had turned up the heat, getting a large squad of detectives to interview folk at bus terminals and train stations and stopping traffic on the roads. They wanted to stir the memories of the people who may have been passing by on the day Arlene disappeared. Their efforts proved fruitless.

By the 6th of May, a mere eight days after Arlene disappeared, attitudes were already beginning to change and folk were starting to think the worst. The area had witnessed the biggest land search in its history and people were remembering another name that had been on everyone's lips – Renee MacRae.

With her three-year-old son, Andrew, Renee had gone missing in 1976, her burnt-out BMW having been discovered in a lay-by on the A9, the main road running south from Inverness. That had been the last big land search in the area and it had proven to be a failure. The two were never found. Everyone now long believed that Renee MacRae was dead, murdered. That thought was already beginning to creep in to the minds of the good folk of Elgin about their neighbour, Arlene Fraser.

The police were the first to signal their fears publicly. Chief Inspector Laurie Stewart said, 'We are becoming more and more concerned. We have no clues and no sightings. She was a normal caring, loving mother.'

Arlene's family weren't far behind. Her sister, Carol, went public saying, 'We have been down every avenue – has she run off or has someone taken her?'

Arlene's mother, Isabelle, was more direct, 'The only avenue we

19

don't explore is the worst one. Our lives are just on hold at the moment.'
The lives of a few people were on hold. But for how long?

3

THE LONG ROAD

JUNE 2001

Driving north to Scotland is nothing unusual for me. I had spent long stretches of my life up there both while I was married to my first wife, Anne, and after we separated. It has left me with strong connections with the Scots, many friends and a few idiosyncratic links, such as my unquestioning support of Falkirk FC – well, someone has to. So the road from Spalding to Elgin is a route I'm very familiar with. I can even work out the times of driving to various destinations accurately and that includes keeping an eye peeled for speed cameras and copmobiles. I was bored stiff with the trip, the way you get when you've driven a road so often. But, one thing I knew, this was going to be one long trek.

I'd recovered my usual cheeky-bastard-don't-take-the-piss-with-me attitude. The police noticed and didn't like it. I suppose they expected me to be cowed, terrified and silent. We'd hardly left my home in Spalding when they established a good-cop/bad-cop routine with the driver staying mute throughout. What the good cop had to say is irrelevant. He was clearly just filling in time, by playing up to his mate and trying to soften me up in interludes between the bad cop having a go.

He started on me. 'You are involved in a very serious matter here, Glenn,' he announced. Right – as if I needed telling. It's not like I'm always being escorted to jail by a load of wankers in suits. They went on and on about how serious this was for me. How many

21

years I could spend in jail. Would it be six, ten, twelve or longer? they mused aloud. But it didn't penetrate my thick skull for one very good reason. I knew I was innocent of any crime and had faith that soon I would be scuttling back home with a signed apology. That's how I believed the legal system worked back then. These days I blush remembering my naivety.

'You'll be looking at some jail time for sure,' the cop went on. 'They take a dim view of men hurting women.'

I hadn't hurt a woman in my life. Not physically. I certainly hadn't hurt Arlene so why should I be worried?

'This is a serious matter. The most serious.'

Shit. They were pursuing a murder rap. Did they mean that I was being accused of actual murder? That was how they were talking. They'd shown me the paperwork at the house but I had been so staggered it hadn't penetrated my thick skull.

'Perverting the course of justice . . .'

'rings . . .'

'keys . . .'

That's what I remembered and it made sod-all sense to me. I'm usually a tough bugger and don't give in to bully-boy tactics. But their strategy worked. Here I had allowed myself to be handcuffed, arrested and driven away from my home and I was clueless as to the reasons. I hadn't put the words on that document together with what the world now believes – that Arlene Fraser had been murdered. They were tying me in with the murder investigation.

Fuck me. When that penny dropped, I was both horrified at the prospect that Arlene Fraser might have been killed and more certain than ever that I would be walking out a free man very soon. I break the law like many of us do – speeding, buying some dodgy goods, throwing an extra bottle of duty free whisky into my holiday suitcase – so hang me for what I've done but not for murder.

The more I spoke up for myself the more irritated the cops seemed to get. What did they expect? Fear? I had nothing to fear or so I believed. Was it my accent? Not only English but also a childhood in public schools had left me with what they would hear as an upper class, plummy voice. That annoys the hell out of some people, as I know only too well. But these were policemen, paid by you and me to defend the law and to find out the truth regardless of class, race or gender. Surely they would be above such prejudices? Well, they should be.

'Of course the system looks favourably on those who are co-operative,' they went on. 'All you need to do is tell us about Nat.' Nat was in the hot seat. That was their game.

I asked them what they wanted to know – his bad habits, his weaknesses, his good points, his hobbies, favourite songs, sense of humour, what type of grub he liked and stuff like that? That's all I knew about him. I was his friend, not his accomplice. Besides, I couldn't believe he could be guilty of murder, especially not of Arlene – not of anybody. A rogue with an eye for the ladies, there was something gentle – almost weak – about Nat. I couldn't imagine him killing anyone. Most folk who know him well think the same way.

'Glenn, you know what we mean. You must have realised he was up to something. He's a close friend of yours, isn't he? Very close.'

And that's how it went for mile after long slow mile.

'Nat . . .'

'Nat . . .'

'Nat . . .'

The bastards were really getting on my tits, to be frank. It might sound strange that I was starting to get aggressive rather than submissive and terrified. They were stating that I would be going away for a long time unless I spilled the beans on Nat. But I had no beans to spill and didn't think there were any beans. What I was certain of was that I had played no part in any murder. As far as I could see, these coppers were interfering in my life, disrupting it big time, putting me in danger and all for nothing – or maybe for some strategic reason that I hadn't sussed yet. Of course I was getting aggressive. Wouldn't you?

Hours later, having had no food or anything to drink all day, I was desperate for some refreshments. The detectives conceded and pulled in to a service station. If I had lost my sense of personal freedom earlier in the day, now I was about to risk public shame.

It hadn't occurred to me that getting to the toilet and sitting in the café for a drink would require me to be chained to a copper all the time even though they took that very precaution while we were speeding up the motorway in a car. I suppose, if I were a career criminal, such events would have become common occurrences in my life but I was a businessman and this was one walk I'd never walked before.

The service station was crowded – most are during the day. As we strolled across the car park, I could see heads turning to ogle at us. Since I was wearing tracksuit bottoms and a T-shirt and my dancing partner was suited and booted, there would be no doubt about who the bad guy was. Who could blame the public? I'd have done the same myself and probably speculated on exactly what heinous crime had been committed, absolutely accepting that the cops had lifted a guilty man, of course, as we all tend to do. We all trust our honest bobbies, eh?

I was in too great a need for a piss to hang about or concern myself with social niceties and headed straight for the public toilets with chappie in tow. As soon as we entered the gents, I realised there was going to be a problem. The jogging-suit bottoms I was wearing had no fly. That meant I'd have to pull down the elasticated waist to free the equipment and ensure the relief I so desperately needed. There was no way I was going to do that surrounded by all the weird sods you get hanging around service station toilets. Fuck that, I needed some privacy.

'I'm going to have to go in there,' I said to the cop, nodding towards the cubicles. The sour expression on his mug told me he didn't understand so, before he could say anything, I blustered, angry again, 'I am not standing in this bog with my trousers around my ankles for anyone. Right?'

He looked down at my legs, understood the problem and nodded, 'OK.'

The trouble was that, when I went into the cubicle, the copper refused to undo the cuffs and tried to come in with me. What did he think I was going to get up to? Swim down through the sewers? I'm a big bloke and he was no skinny sod himself. We would have been wedged together and me with my tadger in my hand.

'No chance, you bastard – they'll all think we're poofs,' I growled.

Now, I know he was within his perfect right to stand there and watch me take a crap, never mind a pee, if he wanted but I was humiliated, furious and fed up of having my personal liberties stripped away. In all fairness to the policeman, he agreed to stay outside but refused to unlock the handcuffs. There followed this ridiculous scenario with me standing over the bowl holding my manhood with one hand and pissing while my other mitt dangled in the air still attached to Dixon of Dock Green who was standing close to the door which remained half-open because of the chain between his cuff and mine. God knows how I managed to pee at all – desperation, probably.

Ordeal over, we headed to the restaurant and joined the other two cops. While we were sitting with a sandwich and a cup of tea, an exceptionally beautiful, sexily dressed woman strolled past. Serious predicament or no, the head of every man at our table turned and followed the cutie. Most blokes really are shallow sods.

'Is she a Cat One or a Cat Two then, Glenn?' asked one cop with a cheeky grin. My jaw dropped as the meaning behind his words percolated through the confusion of the day. They were terms I used chatting to pals about women when their missuses were within hearing. Category One was the tops and Category Two was acceptable but no show-off and so on. They could only have heard me use such lines on the phone since I wasn't on social terms with the sods. The bloody police had been bugging my telephone – listening in to private conversations – and for how long? Only they knew and they weren't for telling me. But what they were telling me, without spelling it out, was that they had been listening. Message received loud and clear. This was bloody infuriating but I didn't miss a beat.

'Haven't you ever had a Cat One then, you cunts?' I blurted. 'Because then you'd know.'

One turned away and rolled his eyes. Another blushed red though whether with anger or embarrassment I couldn't tell. The third just kept drinking his tea and staring into the distance. End of that conversation. But I was left with a problem. They had been listening in to my home phone and God knows what other type of snooping. I had nothing to hide, at least with regard to any murder, yet they were still arresting me. This didn't make sense to me. Not yet.

Back in the car, the rozzers started on about the theme that worried me most.

'Maya's a beautiful girl,' started good cop.

'Must be a big change for her living in England compared to Russia, eh?' continued bad cop.

'She's a lot younger than you, eh?'

'She'll be over here on a visitor's passport then?'

I now began to suss why they hadn't allowed me even to say goodbye to Maya before we hit the road. That alone made me fret for her well-being.

Maya is exceptionally intelligent and confident but she'd only been in England for a short time and didn't have much English. How was she going to cope with whatever that troop of cops congregating outside our house were planning? Most folk would struggle with such an unexpected invasion but she was a young woman from a country where, at an early age, you learned to fear the police. Now she found herself in a strange land and she'd have little comprehension of the lingo being used by the police. How would she manage?

I hadn't asked for this but somehow I was feeling guilty for bringing trouble into Maya's life. It was me they were after and she was caught in their net.

Maya and I had met through a mutual Russian friend in London in February of that year and we hit it off immediately. A short two-month courtship later and she had moved into my house and my life. So, although we'd only known each other for four months, I had already decided I didn't want to lose her. Ever. But she only had a visitor's visa and we intended to get that sorted out. Trouble was, so far, we had been too loved up to bother with such boring formalities.

'We could have her sent back to Russia in an instant,' said one cop, getting to the point. 'All you have to do is tell us about Nat Fraser.'

'I don't know anything about Nat and any murder,' I replied, feeling fearful for the first time.

'That's a shame,' the cop went on, 'she's such a lovely girl.'

'How the fuck do you know?' I demanded, knowing Maya had never met that cop. It annoyed me that he even dared to comment on her.

'Aye, a lovely lass and life's very difficult in Russia right now,' he said, ignoring me. He continued his line, 'A lot of poverty and terrorism. It would be a shame to send her back to that.'

'Well, don't,' I barked.

'Well, tell us about Nat,' persisted bad cop.

'I don't know anything about Nat.'

'One phone call from us and she's away.'

'She'll never be allowed back into England again.'

'You'll never see her again,' said the first cop. 'And you never even got a chance to say goodbye – shame . . .'

'BASTARDS,' I roared in frustration.

'Well, tell us what you know about Nat . . .'

So it went on, mile after mile. They reckoned they had found my weak spot and they were right. I felt so powerless and knew they had all the best cards in their pack when it came to Maya's status in the UK. But, if I was innocent, then she was whiter than white. British justice wouldn't stoop so low, I concluded. No way. They were just threatening me – trying to prise some info from me that I didn't have.

We stopped in Aviemore, just south of Inverness, pulling into a café. It used to be a train station and is right next to the railway line. They relented and took the handcuffs off my aching wrists to allow me to go to the toilet.

'Are you not going to check the toilets?' I asked. 'In case I slip

27

through a window and jump on a train.' I thought the sarcasm was ripe in the tone of my voice but obviously they weren't that observant. Fuck me but the cuffs were slammed on my wrists again while one of them went off to check the toilets.

'What a bunch of jokers,' I thought to myself. 'Some murder squad. More like Keystone Cops.'

As I was soon to find out, they weren't that funny and this was no joke. Maya was learning that too and fast.

THE APPEARING ACT

7 MAY 1998

Arlene's parents and sister had moved into her home in 2 Smith Street, Elgin. On that first day, they had done what any family would do and searched the house top to bottom for any signs that might lead them to Arlene. All that they found worried them.

Nothing but nothing had been removed. All her clothes, her passport, essential medicine for her Crohn's disease, her bankbook, money, make-up – they were all there. The more they searched the more they found and the greater they felt that the house was just as it would have been if Arlene had popped out quickly to visit a local shop, intending to be back in five minutes. There were dirty glasses lying on the work surfaces, make-up was left open and the front door hadn't been locked. All worrying, very worrying.

So, that first day, they had searched and searched, probably getting more frantic with worry as they found every sign that this was Arlene's house, just as it should be – if she was expected back.

Not only had the family searched the house, the police had a forensic team through it within a day of her disappearance. They had removed all sorts of objects, hoping for clues, and tested everywhere they thought they might find evidence of a struggle or rape or bloodshed. They found nothing. A police team also videoed the house, taking slow careful shots of every angle of every room. That first footage became corrupted so they had to repeat the process again but they found nothing of value in their search for Arlene.

Ten days after Arlene disappeared and after all these searches had been carried out, a find was made. On the 7th of May, Catherine McInnes, Arlene's father Hector's second wife, went to the bathroom in 2 Smith Street where she found three rings – wedding, engagement and eternity rings. As she later explained, 'The rings were under the mirror on the right-hand side, under the soap dish. There are two dowels and they were on the right-hand dowel.'

A quick check with her husband confirmed what she already knew – they were Arlene's rings.

How did those rings get there?

4

HOUSE GUESTS

JUNE 2001

Battering on the door woke Maya from a deep sleep. Trembling, frightened and half-awake, she snatched up a dressing gown and headed for the bedroom door.

'Get dressed,' ordered the stranger.

With trembling fingers and fear beating in her chest she pulled on the dressing gown, shoved her feet into her slippers and walked tentatively out of the bedroom.

'Good morning, Maya,' said one of the cops cheerfully in the living room as if they were old friends meeting. 'Sorry to disturb you but we'll need to explain a few things.' He was going to have to do a lot more than that.

The cops told Maya who they were, that I had been arrested and they would have to search the house. Maya understood well enough – at least she thought she did since there was a great deal of movement in the house and some of the police spoke with the strong guttural accent of the north-east of Scotland.

'Do you have any friends?' asked one cop.

'Yes, of course,' replied Maya. She had answered the question in its literal form, providing the cops with the specific answer, no more, no less. It was how she spoke in Russian – a polite approach – why should it be different when she was speaking in English?

'It's best if you go and stay with them,' he continued, 'while we're searching the house.'

'No,' Maya replied, setting a glimmer of annoyance in the cop's eyes. 'I'll be OK here.' She was already distressed by the raid so why would watching them search the house be any more distressing? Besides, with me away, she felt responsible for our home and wanted to make sure it was left in a good condition.

'No,' the cop insisted, 'I really do think you should stay with your friends.'

'But they live in London,' Maya explained, carefully and slowly, 'so far away.' She simply assumed that the police would just need a few hours to search the place and then she could have it to herself again. What was the point of travelling all the away south to London in that case, especially at five in the morning? She also wanted to be around the home in case I phoned. She had known me only a short period of time but she was convinced I was innocent of any of the charges to do with Arlene's disappearance. I was bound to be home again soon, she reasoned. The British police had a reputation for being fair – the best in the world. She believed in that and surely they would get to the truth soon. I would be back any time.

'Aye, a bit far, eh? Give us a minute.'

Maya was sent to the bedroom to await a decision. The cop wandered outside and was chatting to colleagues. A few minutes later he was back. 'What we'll do is take you to the local police station. They'll take good care of you there.'

'Thank you,' replied Maya, genuinely, 'but I'll be OK here. I don't want to give anyone trouble.'

'No trouble at all,' insisted the cop, 'so, if you could just get dressed properly . . .' He motioned with his head in the direction of the bedroom. 'Oh and bring your passport and papers – just in case you need them.'

'But I want to make sure the house is OK,' she persisted, motioning around the room with her hands.

'You'll be going to the police station.'

The police were no longer offering to shelter Maya for the day to avoid her distress – they were insisting on taking her out of the house and depositing her in the local nick. She dressed, grabbed her papers and headed to the door. She wouldn't need anything else, she reasoned, she'd only be gone a few hours.

By about 5.30 a.m., Maya was in the back of the cop car on her way to the police station. In spite of the very distressing events of the day, everyone had been overtly polite to her, courteous even. With her certainty that I was innocent, she believed she had little to fear. They were chasing some red herring and, as soon as they realised that, I would come home and her life would be back to normal. She knew all of that so why then did she feel such sickening dread?

When Maya arrived at the police station, she was shown into an interview room. She thought little of it as the officers were friendly and polite. Maybe it was the only private place they had and they were being kind to her, giving her some space away from the comings and goings in the station. Then an officer arrived and asked for her papers and passport.

'They already checked them at the house,' she replied politely, always wary of her papers being out of her possession. 'They are in order,' she insisted.

'To copy,' he explained. 'It's just routine.' When he arrived back in the interview room and returned Maya's passport to her, he sat and chatted. 'We need to ask you about a few things, Maya, since Glenn has got himself caught up in a very serious matter.'

The dread reared up in the pit of Maya's stomach. 'But I know nothing about this business,' she pled.

'Oh, we know. Don't worry about that. I mean you haven't known Glenn for long have you?'

'No, three months maybe four.' There was a stiffness to Maya's answer – a wariness – the cop spotted.

'Look, Maya, you're not being interviewed or anything. We know that business has nothing to do with you. So let's just chat like friends, eh? Please.' He smiled warmly, his face telling her to relax, to trust him. Maya did her best.

After talking about her time in England, her plans and ambitions for a while, he suddenly announced, 'We've been keeping a close

33

eye on Glenn for a while, you know – a very close watch indeed.' He nodded at her, asking if she followed his drift.

She did – loud and clear.

'Sometimes you find out things you're not looking for. Things you'd rather not know.' Again that nod.

Maya wondered and worried about why he was taking such pains over these statements after the easy talk so far.

'I'm sorry to tell you that Glenn is cheating on you.' He let the statement hang in the air, watching her face closely for signs of emotion. Eventually, 'He's a nasty bad bastard.'

Maya didn't believe a word. Though she'd only been with me for a few months, we'd hardly been out of each other's sight in that time. The way you do during the fresh, exciting early phase of a new relationship. So she didn't bite the bait and the conversation returned to calmer waters and ended after a few hours.

'You can go now, Maya,' a police officer told her around 9.30 in the morning. Maya felt as if it had been a long tiring day already and yet it was just breakfast time for many people. 'If you wait out front we'll get a car to pick you up and take you home.'

She strolled out of the police station relieved, chastising herself for worrying too much over the cops' intentions. Standing in the June sunshine with a strong but warm wind in her hair, Maya didn't mind the long wait. Probably the police were busy and giving her a lift home was close to the bottom of their priorities. She would have called for a taxi to save them the bother but she'd left home in such a hurry she hadn't taken any money with her plus the cops were insistent she only took the clothes she wore. She guessed that, strictly speaking, they had to search every item in the house – hers as well as those belonging to me. That made sense. She understood what they had to do.

Over an hour later, a familiar face emerged from the police station and tapped her on the arm. 'I'm sorry, Maya, we're having problems getting you a car. And we've got just a couple of other things to ask you. It won't take long. Do you mind coming back in?'

Of course she didn't. Why would she?

Back in the room, the cops ran over some routine points before hitting their stride. Two Scottish cops entered the room. Their manner was brisk, businesslike, and both wore serious, angry expressions.

'You do know that Glenn is going away to prison for a long time?' asked one. 'A very long time.'

'But he has done nothing,' complained Maya.

'Trust us, Maya, he's going down.'

'Going down?' She didn't understand the phrase.

'Going to prison,' he explained.

'What for?'

'You have teamed up with a very bad man. An evil man.'

'I'd say at least six years.'

'In prison for six years.'

'That's a long time.'

'You'd be better off without him.'

On and on and they went, bombarding Maya with a stream of statements about how nasty I was and how she was all alone in this country and would be for some time. She didn't know what they wanted from her. They never came out and asked for anything. All she knew was that they were frightening her.

'You've been up north, in Scotland, with Glenn haven't you?' a cop demanded to know.

'Yes.'

'When you were there, did you visit any sheds?'

Maya looked puzzled. She told them that we'd gone on social visits so that she could to be introduced to my friends. Why would they visit sheds? 'No,' she shook her head but her eyes beamed a lack of understanding.

'Work sheds,' the police officer explained. 'Are you sure?'

'Yes. Glenn didn't work when we were there. It was holiday.'

'Did you meet Nat Fraser while you were there?'

'Of course,' replied Maya, at least recognising a relevant question, one she understood the importance of. 'Glenn and Nat are friends.'

Both cops nodded in a self-satisfied way as if they had just confirmed something.

'He's Glenn's friend,' repeated Maya.

The cop changed tack. 'Did Glenn go off on his own at any time?'

Maya had to think carefully. Short as our relationship had been, she was already used to me breaking social trips to almost any part of the country to go and visit a fruit market or a local company. But not that time she reckoned. 'No. We were together all the time.'

'Are you sure?'

In truth, she wasn't. Who would be sure of all the details of a pleasant trip? But she couldn't remember me going off on my own so she insisted, 'Yes. Yes I'm sure.'

Just like earlier, they told her she could go home after a couple of hours – same offer of a lift and asking her nicely if she would wait outside the front of the police station. 'It shouldn't take long this time, Maya,' one cop reassured.

And, just like earlier, she waited and waited. This time the fresh air and prospect of going home held no optimism for her. This time she was unsettled and uncertain. She was right to be.

'I'm sorry, Maya.' It was that familiar cop's face again. 'Could you just come in again for a minute?'

They were the police and she always did what the police told her. As a good citizen, it was her way. With a heavy spirit, she walked in to the police station once again.

Back in the interview room, it was the same routine. 'Glenn is cheating on you.'

'He's a nasty bad bastard.'

'He's going away for a long time.'

'At least six years.'

Then the routine changed. Two Scottish cops entered the room and showed Maya a ring. 'Is this yours, Maya?' one asked.

Without hesitation she replied, 'No. I've never seen it before.' It was a dress ring, with cheap glass stones and tarnished metal. It looked like a ring that some child might be given as part of a dressing up game and it was clearly old and neglected. Maya didn't know any grown woman who would wear such jewellery.

'Are you certain?'

This time she had no doubts whatsoever. 'I'm certain.' She was puzzled again. What could a cheap, child's play ring have to do with a murder inquiry? She couldn't imagine. They suggested that maybe I would know about it and asked what she new about Arlene Fraser. I had talked to her about Arlene but not in any great depth. She just wished I could have been there with her to explain what was going on.

Then Maya was being interviewed by a female officer. By that time, she had become confused about who was who. The only cops she could identify were the Scottish cops. They were instantly recognisable because of their broad accents even to someone with little English like Maya. She knew she had spoken with someone from the Immigration Team from Boston and others from the Spalding station but couldn't remember which was which. The young uniformed cops from Spalding were nice and kind to her. The other plain-clothes officers all faded one into another. But this female officer was the cruellest.

'If we send you home to Russia, you'll never get back again,' she started. 'You can wave goodbye to Glenn and good riddance I'd say.'

By now, it was early evening. Maya was exhausted by her day of questioning and by her hopes of going home being dashed as she was brought back into the station.

'You will never return,' spat the female cop as a final emphasis.

Although not prone to showing her emotions, Maya was close to tears. Worse was to come.

'We're going to keep you here overnight, Maya,' announced another cop.

'But my papers are correct,' she pled. 'No?'

'Yes,' the cop conceded, 'but there are other things to consider.'

Without explanation or charge, Maya was led to a police cell. It was a standard cell – small, brick walls, a narrow bed with a thin mattress, a stainless steel toilet in the corner. The bleak chamber stank of urine and disinfectant. When the heavy metal door was slammed and locked behind her, finally Maya let go of the horrors of the day and sat down on the bunk and wept.

She didn't understand what was happening. She needed someone friendly to explain how she could wake up free and happy and go to bed that same day a captive of the state for no given reason. Some friendly face would have helped – preferably mine.

But hundreds of miles north, in a small country town, I was facing my own troubles.

CHOOSE

31 MAY 1998

Little Natalie Fraser couldn't believe her luck. She had visited a local sweetie shop, one she had been in loads of times before, with some pocket money to buy her favourite sweets, but this time it was different. A lady had given her a lollipop – for free. Natalie was happy. What child wouldn't be? Then the lady explained, 'Because your mummy is missing.'

Did she need to go and spoil it by reminding her? The little girl didn't need to be told excuses anymore. She had eyes and the whole of Elgin was plastered with big photographs of her mam. She thought her mam looked beautiful in them, all smiling and happy. Her mam always looked beautiful. Everyone thought so. But, at the bottom of these big photographs, there were words – too many and too strange for Natalie to read. But one she knew. One she had learned just in the past few weeks. It was in big letters and it read, 'MISSING'.

Jamie Fraser was a bright ten-year-old boy. He could read the posters and the newspapers and he understood what people were saying. But he didn't let it show. He was a bit like his mother, deep and quiet, keeping a lot of his feelings to himself. He preferred to do happy things, things that he liked, and to carry on as if nothing bad had happened. He would have been worried, upset, frantic about where his mam was. But to be distraught wouldn't have brought his mam back or changed a thing – except that he would have been distraught and that wasn't good. Jamie Fraser was wise for his years.

Down the road, Grampian Police were weighing up their options and were about to drop a bombshell. Detective Chief Inspector Peter Simpson said:

> People in the Elgin area think that Arlene has disappeared and will turn up sooner or later. We are dealing with a public misconception here. I cannot be 100 per cent certain that we are looking for a body but I do have real fears about that.

It was the first formal statement of doom to be made and it came some sixteen days after Arlene had vanished. They weren't searching the town or the great tracts of countryside around Elgin anymore. But the cops were on the streets, a team of forty of them was maintained at all times. They were not searching now but investigating and DCI Simpson made it plain what they were investigating when he announced, 'It is my personal belief that Arlene has been abducted or murdered.' That was blunt enough and, if the kids didn't hear it, the adults certainly did.

Isabelle and Hector, Arlene's mother and father, were trying their best. But imagine if it was your daughter who had disappeared and your son-in-law charged with trying to kill her and you had to try to explain these things to your two young grandchildren. Theirs was not an easy situation.

But the grandparents weren't alone. They had their other daughter, Carol, and Nat's sister, Lynn, and the kids' other set of grandparents – and they had Nat. Though banned from going near the family home, as a consequence of his bail order on the attempted murder charges, Nat took a liberal definition of the changed circumstances. His trouble had been with Arlene, the charges against him concerned her only and now Arlene wasn't there. Before she disappeared, he always saw his children regularly. Now that she had disappeared, he was going to see them regularly, except now he would be allowed to see them at the family home. In fact, Catherine McInnes, Hector's second wife, would later recall how Nat was in the home at 2 Smith Street on the day she found Arlene's rings in the bathroom. Not only in the home but he had also gone to the bathroom or so she remembered.

All the adults agreed that Natalie and Jamie had to be protected. After all, they still believed – hoped – that Arlene had gone away and would return. None of them wanted the children worrying or, worse, blaming themselves for their mother's disappearance. So they had to be told something, given a good reason why she was suddenly not there.

Granny Isabelle informed the press, 'We have just told them that their mother has gone away because she is not well.' It was a lie, of course, but it made sense. Both the kids knew that their mother had a long-term illness, Crohn's disease, and that she had to take medication for it every day and would have to for the rest of her life. If she didn't take her medicine, she could become unwell – it had happened before. So they agreed to tell Natalie and Jamie that Arlene had gone away because she was ill. They all told the kids that. Well, all the family did. The people in the community, the newspapers and the TV told them a different story entirely.

Isabelle and Hector, Arlene's mother and father, were trying their best. Hector sensed the messages, the chat and the buzz about Arlene around the town and decided to take Natalie and Jamie away from it for a while. A trip away to Blackpool Pleasure Beach and Chester Zoo would do the trick. At least for a wee while, they would be removed from a town that breathed and whispered in every corner with the latest developments in the Arlene Fraser case. The trouble was, Natalie and Jamie would still have to return to that cauldron. But Granny Isabelle had plans to deal with that.

Isabelle Thompson applied for custody of Jamie and Natalie. When she did so, she spoke to the press, something that was becoming almost part of her daily routine. She explained that she only wanted the best for her grandchildren and their father, Nat, had his work to get on with. She and her second husband could give them more. It all sounded amicable and calm – a family putting any differences they might have aside in order to put the interests of the children first. The custody application was submitted and an order issued that, if Arlene

Fraser wished to object, she should submit her grounds to Elgin Sheriff Court.

Arlene never showed – but her husband did. Nat Fraser was furious. He saw it as little more than child theft. Later he recalled, 'They never discussed it with me at all. I was grateful that they arrived to take care of Natalie and Jamie but then they just took over. They decided to take care of my kids for the rest of their lives. How bloody dare they?'

Nat Fraser went to a lawyer. A public bust-up was on the cards. But, unless the children's natural father consented, Isabelle Thompson would have no case. It was left to Arlene's sister, Carol, to explain again, as usual through the media:

> There was no need for it to come to this. We only wanted to give them a stable life. Unfortunately, solicitors were brought in and it got very dirty but it has been blown out of all proportion. We didn't want a battle with him in the papers. We thought we were doing what was best for the children. We wanted to take them away, give them a good time and try and distract them.

The custody application was withdrawn and the care of Natalie and Jamie was handed over to Nat's parents. The children would be staying in their own home, in the care of their own grandparents, going to their own school and still playing with their own friends.

In the meantime, their home town was still buzzing about where Arlene Fraser was. That was something they would have to live with. As Arlene's sister, Carol, said at that time, 'We didn't know if we were doing the right thing or not. Can anyone advise you on what to do in this situation?'

It was the best of questions.

5

HOME MOVIES
JUNE 2001

Eleven hours after leaving my home in Lincolnshire, the cop car pulled up at the back of Elgin Police Station. It had felt like the journey from hell, with every mile taking twice as long as it should have. I had been convinced that the cops were driving slowly, drawing out the tension, adding to my anxiety. In fact, they had made good time. Must have all been in my head – or maybe the company I was keeping.

Straight off, I was escorted to the front desk and booked in. The desk sergeant was the first kindly cop face I had met all day. He treated me with simple courtesy, the way you do with strangers you hold no grudge against. After what I'd been through, it felt like the greatest kindness.

Here I was, hundreds of miles from home, being booked in as a prisoner and who the hell else knew? I had to do something about that and pronto. 'Am I not permitted a phone call?' I asked the kindly cop.

'Not really,' he replied, 'but we can make a call for you if you want.'

'I thought I was allowed one phone call.'

'Not until you've been in custody for a while.'

'Since before five this morning! Is that not long enough?'

'Driving here doesn't count. The clock starts clicking when you walked through that door.' He shrugged his shoulders almost

43

apologetically but said nothing more. I had wondered why they hadn't taken me to a nearby airport and flown up. All that time being consumed by three detectives who must be well into overtime by now and weren't even finished for the day. Four flight tickets to Inverness or Aberdeen had to be less of a burden on the taxpayer. Yet it didn't count as custody even though they had held me captive and grilled and threatened me every mile of the way. So it was deliberate. The bastards were trying to spook me into saying something, anything, as long as it was against Nat Fraser. What else had they planned?

All day, I'd refused nothing but blows. Why change now? If they were willing to make a phone call, then so be it. I'd accept their offer. Who to have them call though? I didn't want them to phone Maya. She might not understand their accents. She should be made to feel reassured that I was OK and I couldn't trust the cops to convey that. I also wanted someone to phone round the family and let them know where I was – someone who wouldn't panic and would make sure that Maya was taken care of . . . my mother.

Strange as it may seem that I asked a seventy-eight-year-old woman to take that responsibility but she is a cool customer, calm in a crisis and strong – very strong. I could rely on her. I gave them the number and told them it was my mother. I'm sure I caught supercilious smirks on some of the cops' faces, as if to say something like, 'Involved in a murder and the big baby's phoning his mummy!' If only they knew my mother. She'd have wiped the smile off their faces yet she'd have done so politely and with impeccable manners.

Next, it was to the interview room. 'Right, Glenn, now we'll start the interview,' said one cop, going to switch on the tape recorder.

'Start the interview! What the fuck have we been doing all the way up here?' I asked angry and bewildered.

'That was just a friendly chat . . .'

'An interrogation more like!'

'. . . to pass the journey,' replied bad cop from the car.

'Before we start,' I butted in, 'I want a lawyer.'

'Do you have someone up here?'

'Not likely,' I replied. 'Why would I have a lawyer in Elgin?'

'We'll have to get you the duty solicitor then.'

'Fine. If you could, please.'

'We'll phone him for you.'

Handcuffed, not allowed to go for a pee alone, child-locked in the back of police car – it had felt to me as if I had been in custody all day. I hadn't exactly agreed to go for a wee drive in the country but the cops were the experts – the law. I was just the novice and suddenly I was aware of how inexperienced and unprepared I was for being arrested and 'processed' as they like to call it. It's not a bad word – you end up feeling like a lump of meat.

The cop reached out for the tape recorder again, 'Right, let's start.' Then they charged me with attempting to pervert the course of justice. It was the same charge that Nat's friend, Hector Dick, had been hit with in October 1998 and had actually admitted the previous June. In his case, he had lied about purchasing a beige Ford Fiesta and disposing of it. The cops clearly believed that car had been used for taking Arlene away or disposing of her body – or maybe both. Whether that was true or not, I couldn't guess but I wondered why Hector Dick had lied about it. Unless, of course, he knew more about Arlene than he was letting on.

My charge could have meant a range of things from withholding information, to hiding some vital clue, to telling lies, to protecting some guilty party – just as they had been accusing me of doing with regard to Nat all the way up the road from Spalding. Whatever the reason for the charge, they weren't about to give the game away right off. Instead, it seemed to me that they had run over my statement time and again, just covering all that old ground. But then the gloves were off. We were in their patch now and they tried to unnerve me, rattle me into breaking down.

Then they surprised me by ending the interview. I was knackered and thought they must be too. There were plenty of cases of people claiming unjust convictions that involved the suspects being interviewed for hours on end till, exhausted, they broke down and confessed to anything the cops wanted. The way the day had gone so far, I half-expected this mob to give me the same treatment. So, when they called an end to the interview, I sighed a sigh of relief and they went up in my estimation. It didn't last long.

A short while later, the second formal interview of the day kicked off. All in all, I'd been in the company of the police for well over twelve hours that day and hardly a minute had passed without some question, some threat, some comment being thrown at me. The record, of course, would read that eleven of those hours were transportation from Spalding to Elgin and no interview took place. My screaming mind knew better. This was a marathon and no doubt.

'You seem to have a bad memory, Glenn,' one of the policemen said.

'I don't think so,' I replied. 'I've a good memory.'

'But we've put around ten points to you and you don't seem to recall any of them.'

'That's because they're not true,' I answered.

The cops shook their heads and started off again. 'Did you visit Nat Fraser while he was serving time in Porterfield Prison, Inverness?'

'I've told you repeatedly I did.'

'What did you discuss?'

I had told them before. Women, gossip from the business, news about our families, football, women – a typical range of topics for Nat Fraser and I to talk about. I had always tried to make a point of not focussing in on Nat's troubles when I visited him in jail. A few weeks before Arlene had disappeared, he assaulted her and was later sentenced for it. My view was that being in prison itself served as a constant reminder to him that he was in deep trouble and his wife was missing. It wasn't a friend's role to open up those wounds but to try and divert him for a short while. That's what I was – Nat's friend – so we discussed women, football, music, gossip and women.

'We know different,' another cop butted in.

And that's when I realised exactly why I was in that cop shop.

The two cops declared they knew for a fact that Nat and I had discussed getting rid of a body, chopping it up and burning it. That was the instant I understood perfectly what the word 'dumbfounded' means. Once I found my voice, I told them plainly and bluntly that the conversation never happened. They insisted that they had video evidence. The night before, I would have found the revelation that the cops had taped a private conversation shocking but, that day, I'd discovered that they had been tapping my phone so why would they stop there?

Evidence on videotape is strong and they kept insisting that they knew for certain the details of the conversation. How the hell do you answer that? Confession? That was out since it simply didn't happen. Denial? For sure but there are only so many ways that you can say 'no'.

Again and again, the cops hammered home the point, waiting for me to break down and admit it all. It was like an endless game of ping-pong where the opposition fired exactly the same shots every time and the rallies went on forever. All I knew was that, with their claims of absolute proof, I was in serious trouble.

'If you have a video, then show me,' I demanded time after time. Mostly they just ignored me and went on pushing for some type of confession. But, eventually, one cop succumbed and hit the control button for the video player. There was Nat and me on the screen. It was a grainy, black and white picture but it was us all right. I was dumbstruck. All along, I thought they had been feigning, that there was no video. Now here we were.

'That's you and Nat Fraser, isn't it?' a cop asked.

'Yes, it's us all right,' I conceded with no other possible option available to me.

'That's you and Nat Fraser in the visiting room of Porterfield Prison, Inverness?' the cop was making statements but demanding a response.

'It certainly seems like it,' I replied quietly. On the screen, Nat and I were sitting at a table across from each other. He was dressed in his prison gear and I in my civvies. We were prattling on at each other. A wry smile here and a laugh there punctuated the long

47

serious minutes. We were talking nineteen to the dozen as we normally did. One problem – I couldn't hear a word.

'Turn up the sound,' I requested.

'You did visit Nat in Porterfield Prison,' the cop ignored my request.

'Please, I can't hear it,' I asked again. It wasn't the fact that I had visited Nat that was the issue – that was still legal as far as I knew. It was what we allegedly discussed that had landed me in cop custody. But I had thought they were bluffing about the video yet there it was. So maybe they had some recording of what had been said and I needed to listen to that to be convinced they had any right at all to have arrested and charged me. 'Please turn up the volume.' The cop hit the video controls and instantly the TV screen went blank with an electrical pop.

That was the closest I was to come to seeing the evidence against me. I saw it but I didn't hear it – yet I was supposed to accept that I deserved to be in trouble, that I had committed some crime. No chance.

Hours into the interview I asked again, 'Have you phoned that duty lawyer?' Right or wrong, I didn't want to be interviewed without a lawyer present but this was running out of control. I had spent practically the entire day in the company of cops who had done nothing but question me. Now here I was, late at night, in custody, charged with attempting to pervert the course of justice in one of the highest profile murder cases in Scotland for years and the bugger hadn't the courtesy to turn up.

'Aye, we've phoned him,' the cop replied. 'It's up to him how quickly he responds.'

'Who is it anyway?'

'A solicitor from Forres,' the cop answered, rolling his eyes.

'So chappie could be out on the piss or in bed with his wife?' I stated more than asked.

'Aye, well,' the cop shifted in his seat uneasily. 'Look, between you and me, I'd get another lawyer.'

'At this time on a Friday night?'

'As soon as you can. Get your family to fix you up. Just don't use this one.'

I realised that the tape had been switched off and the cop dishing out the advice was acting all friendly and conspiratorial. One of the cops who had more or less been calling me a liar for hours was now advising me about lawyers. Even though I was furious that the lawyer hadn't shown, I decided to make my own mind up about him.

Then they took my shoelaces and showed me to my 'room'. One look at my cell and I meekly pled, 'I want to talk to Jim Stephen', referring to the cop in charge of the investigation, 'there has to be some mistake.' It was how I felt. Someone somewhere among the squad had made some error that had landed me in this predicament. Maybe the soundtrack of someone discussing chopping up bodies had been mixed up with me and Nat chatting in Inverness Prison. Could that be possible? Ignoring my comments with a little shake of the head, the duty officer pushed open a door and motioned for me to go in.

Then the impossible happened. Things got worse.

CASE NOTE 6

ONE HUNDRED DAYS OF STRAWS

5 AUGUST 1998

The family had tried everything and were now close to exhaustion, worn down by lost hopes.

In June, they announced a reward of £20,000 for any information leading them to Arlene. To the public, it seemed a sweet, loving act – the type of thing where families got together, put their resources into a pot and willingly gave as much as they could afford. That's what the public saw.

Behind the scenes, there was griping and infighting. Relations between Nat Fraser and his in-laws had never been good since they fell out over the custody of his children. His own mother, Ibby, had moved in to the family home at 2 Smith Street to care for Jamie and Natalie. Arlene's parents and her sister, Carol, had offered to help Ibby but they lived down south, hundreds of miles away. Someone had gone to the authorities suggesting that sixty-seven-year-old Ibby was too old to care for the young ones. Nat Fraser wondered if that someone had been his in-laws. Of course Ibby Fraser could look after the two kids. Anyone who really knew the woman would know that.

When the issue of the reward money was first mooted, it felt like a competition rather than a loving effort to trace the lost Arlene. One side said they'd put up £10,000 so the other side felt obliged to do the same. It turned into a macabre see-saw game of anything-you-can-do-I-can-do-better with the highest of stakes – Arlene.

The £10,000 share of the reward money Nat Fraser put up was no minor commitment. The fruit and veg business generally is one where profit margins can be low and it depends on good purchasing power and high turnover of sales. Many of the smaller businesses make a living and no more. Taylor & Fraser, the company Nat ran with his good friend Ian Taylor, had had other difficulties to cope with recently.

Right at the start, the police had asked Nat where he had been on the 28th of April, the day Arlene disappeared, and kept asking him. All that day, he had been out in the van making deliveries in the company of a van boy. Nat could say exactly where he was and when he was there. The information was backed up by the people he made deliveries to, the order book, the van boy and, of course, his partner Ian Taylor.

Between 9 a.m. and 10 a.m., the crucial times when Arlene had last made contact with the school, he had stopped at a call box and phoned a woman. There was nothing new in that. Nat was always trying to get off with women. This one was Hazel Walker, the niece of one of Nat's fellow musicians in their band, The Minesweepers. He had phoned the attractive twenty-eight-year-old every day that week and had arranged to call that morning at the approximate time of between 9 a.m. and 10 a.m. – exactly the time Arlene disappeared. But it was all too neat for the cops.

The detectives on the case leaned harder and harder on Nat Fraser. They also pressurised Ian Taylor. To start with, they'd call him in to be interviewed at different times. Then they'd start arriving at the warehouse where Taylor & Fraser was based. It was all very disruptive. Some customers didn't want to be associated with the investigation at all and that meant not being associated with Taylor & Fraser. Inevitably, the friends and partners began to bicker and business dropped off.

This attracted the attention of another of Nat Fraser's pals, Hector Dick. Forty-two-year-old Dick was a most unlikely friend for smooth-talking, handsome Nat Fraser to have. A pig farmer and coal merchant, Dick would most often be in his work attire of boiler suit, long leather waistcoat and Wellington boots. While Nat Fraser was confident and successful in the company of women, Dick had met his wife, Irene, through a lonely-hearts column. Florist Irene had lived in Leeds and

Dick would go to visit her as they courted. After one such weekend together, he proudly confided in his pal Nat, 'We shagged fifteen times at the weekend.'

'Congratulations,' replied Nat Fraser turning away to smother his laugh.

It was a typical boast – almost adolescent – but Hector Dick felt that he had to impress the more sophisticated Nat. People wondered about their friendship and certainly saw Nat Fraser as the more powerful of the pair. In many ways, Hector and Irene Dick agreed. They had Nat down in their home phone book as H-Hung for Horse Hung, referring to the size of his penis. Yet they also had a cousin of Irene down as Mr Big since he was apparently equally well endowed. Sex seemed to be important to Hector Dick and sex was something everyone knew Nat Fraser was expert at.

Hector Dick knew Arlene well, often calling on her of an evening when Nat was away playing with his band. Other husbands might become a little suspicious of the awkward, scruffy Hector focussing his attentions on the young attractive woman. But the thought of Hector having designs on Arlene simply never entered Nat Fraser's head. To him, it was too ridiculous for words. Other people wondered though and people talk.

The cops had become regular visitors to Dick's farm at Mosstowie, near Elgin. It was a typical small, north-east Scotland farm – all out-buildings, machinery and livestock and a little bit messy and dis-organised to the unaccustomed eye. But the cops weren't much interested in the farm. Their main concern was where Nat had been on the night before Arlene disappeared. Nat couldn't quite remember but said that he always made a point of staying in on Mondays. So he said he'd suppose he would have been with Ian and Jane Taylor or at least at their house since that's where he was living. 'Suppose' isn't good enough for the cops when a young woman is missing, so they hammered on Hector Dick's door and asked about that Monday night time after time.

They also asked Dick about his movements on the day Arlene vanished. In double quick time, he produced a detailed diary account.

52

While it was all about feeding the animals, mending fences and that kind of activity, Dick gave specific times, stating who he had seen and when. It was just all too neat for the cops.

The family weren't faring any better. The £20,000 reward had produced only a few phone calls, none of which led to anything. What the family didn't know was that three people had gone to the cops, within a short time of Arlene vanishing, saying they had spotted her after the date she disappeared from her home. Three separate people, who didn't know each other and had nothing to gain from telling the cops, spotted her in Dufftown, Buckie and Elgin. This was long before the family put up the reward. Important information? You bet.

'How could you have seen her that night?'

'Are you sure it was the right date?'

'If you play bingo on the same night every week, how can you be sure it wasn't the week before Arlene disappeared? Or even the week before that?'

'You must get a lot of tourists coming through your shop. Must be easy to mix them up with someone in the newspapers?'

'You drink, don't you?'

That's the type of reception all would report getting from the police. Day after day, night after night, till most didn't know what to think. They would protest, of course.

'But I knew Arlene well.'

'I'd seen her lots of times before.'

'The shop was quiet and I'd just been reading about Arlene. Of course I didn't make a mistake.'

'Aye, I drink but I wasn't drinking that day.'

Eventually most of these good souls were completely baffled. Some were convinced they had been mistaken. Some would stick to their guns.

Why, in a case of a missing person, did the police treat these witnesses so poorly? Didn't they want a lead? Or had they already decided Arlene's fate? Decided that she had been murdered long before they admitted that to the public or even to Arlene's family?

Arlene's family had gathered together in Elgin to mark one hundred days since her disappearance. For some reason, her father, Hector, mother, Isabelle, and sister, Carol, thought that she might show up that day. However, they admitted that, deep down, they had come to believe that she was dead and it was the not knowing that was driving them to despair. Maybe, just maybe, if she was still out there, she would show herself to them that day. Maybe.

After all, it was also wee Natalie's sixth birthday. And, in a few days, Jamie would be eleven. And, in a couple of weeks, Arlene herself would be thirty-four. It was a significant month and a very significant day. Her family just knew that, if Arlene was out there, that would be the day she showed up.

Arlene Fraser didn't show or call that day.

6

BED AND BREAKFAST

JUNE 2001

The cell was disgusting. Clearly someone had had a copious and rancid shit in the open toilet in the not too distant past. The smell lingered, mixing with that distinctive acrid taste of stale urine and another stink that I decided was some kind of industrial disinfectant blended with the utter filth of the place.

Along one wall a concrete base formed a bed on top of which lay a thin, brown, plastic-coated mattress and greasy looking woollen blanket. I expected basic, Spartan but also clean. One look at my temporary accommodation and it was clear I was being punished. There I was, one of many thousands every year, an untried man being shoved into a hovel I wouldn't keep a dog in. I respect dogs. Whatever happened to innocent till proven guilty?

The system and its standards tell you that you are guilty, fit enough to be punished as soon as the cops put a grip of suspicion on your shoulder. And this was just the start – an easy introduction with the possibility of much worse to come. Here I was innocent and getting to be bloody furious. Is it so surprising that folk jailed unjustly for many years like T C Campbell, Robert Brown and Paddy Hill get very bitter and angry?

Confused, bewildered, I sat on the hard bunk and tried to unscramble my thoughts. Arlene had gone missing on the 28th of April 1998. That had been a shock to me and not just because I knew and liked her. You have to worry about someone who is suddenly not there. It's that not knowing that torments as every relative or friend of any missing person will tell you.

There was also Nat, of course. No matter how bad their relationship had been at the time, Nat, as I expected, gave every sign of worrying and fretting. Apart from him, there were two young kids suddenly without a mother. Natalie seemed to be so young as to be spared the nightmare thoughts about what had happened to her mum. But Jamie was old enough and he was the one who had returned from that school trip to find the house empty, his mother gone. I worried for him.

Grampian Police's decision to treat Arlene's disappearance immediately as sinister had percolated quickly through the public awareness. Guys in my business knew of my links to Nat and Arlene and were quick to take advantage.

'This is Inspector McTavish from Grampian Police,' the phone call at my office had gone, 'we want to question you about the murder of Arlene Fraser.'

Already on edge, I'd go for it. 'How can I help you, Inspector McTavish?' I'd reply calmly while my blood pressure dramatically rose a few points and I shifted uneasily in my seat.

'Well, can you confirm you were shagging Mrs Fraser on the very morning she disappeared?'

'You what?' Blustered into silence by the outrageousness of it all, I had left the door open for a quick follow up.

'Or was it the sheep you were more interested in?'

'Who the . . . ?'

'Or maybe you were just looking for a good deal on turnips?'

'. . . fuck is this?'

Of course, it was one of the boys from some fruit market or some business we had regular dealings with taking the piss. They are a crude bunch in my business and not slow to prod at any perceived vulnerability. If you show it's hurting, they just prod harder.

This game started within a week of Arlene's disappearance and didn't stop. Some were ingenious enough to choose the names of real cops like Detective Superintendent Jim Stephen who was in charge of the investigation. It was as if guys in companies the length and breadth of the UK had ganged up to torment me. In fact, they all got the same idea at the same time but thought they were the first to have a go and considered the teasing hilarious. I soon started telling them exactly where to get off.

On the 7th of May, not even a fortnight after Arlene had gone missing, another call came in.

'Mr Lucas, this is Inspector . . .'

'Fuck off, you twat,' I howled down the phone, not waiting for the man to finish his sentence, 'think you're fucking witty don't you, you cunt?'

'No, I am from Grampian Police and this is a murder investigation, Mr Lucas. This is a very serious matter.' Sure enough, that was my introduction to the Murder Squad. After I mumbled some apology, the cop brass continued, 'Two of my officers will travel to Spalding to interview you on Monday. Please attend . . .'

Two days later I was politely questioned by two Grampian detectives in Spalding Police Station. It was no surprise they wanted to know my precise movements on the day Arlene went missing.

On the Monday, I had moved on from Elgin and, on the Tuesday, I had driven to Applecross in the far north of Scotland to visit an old friend. They hammered on and on about the timings of departure, arrival and what I had done while I was there. All this I understood and accepted since I had been in the vicinity of Elgin at the time and could easily have doubled back into the town without being spotted. They were only doing their job and I was happy to assist them in any way I could.

Luckily, I have the type of mind that retains mundane details. Too often in my career I had been sent abroad to dodgy areas in Pakistan, Afghanistan or Iraq where everyone carried Kalashnikovs and would top you as soon as look at you. A great deal of fruit and veg comes from places like that and my employer, like every other, is always searching for better quality at lower prices. Often that's where you'll find the good deals. We're not talking about a few tons here but shiploads. The trade is worth a lot of money in other words.

When a new dealer pops up offering top grade at half price, they have to be checked out – quietly and undercover, usually. For some reason, I often got chosen to go on these trips. On one occasion, I had a camera confiscated and was given a hellish time by soldiers in Iran. It wasn't till long after I got back that I discovered I had been at an industrial complex at Bushehr, 1200km southwest of Tehran. This was where the Iranians were secretly making nuclear bombs with components shipped from Russia – or so the USA claimed. I felt lucky to get back at all. Maybe the bosses thought I was the most dispensable member of staff.

When you're the only obvious outsider in bandit territory in Morocco, Egypt, Iran, India or Israel, you learn to hold your bottle and to note routine details carefully. You can't take out a pen and notepad or the sods will suspect you're spying on them. In a sense, I was. Get in, get the evidence and get the hell out as fast as you can. That's the deal. And remember precisely what you found since your company stands to gain or lose a hell of a lot on your conclusions.

So I had remembered precisely what I was doing on Tuesday the 28th of April when Arlene went missing and I related the facts to the two cops. Then they asked again, of course. And again and again and again. Now that was getting on my tits and no mistake.

In between those questions, they would challenge my integrity, suggesting I'd forgotten something or wasn't telling the whole truth. They challenged my driving schedule claiming that it wasn't possible to cover certain distances in the times I claimed or then reversing it saying that I had taken much longer than was necessary. But my movements hadn't been exactly complicated. What would I forget? I had just visited my friends in familiar places so why would my times be wrong?

'You're adopting a defensive posture,' said one cop after what seemed hours of going round in circles. 'What is it you're hiding?'

What the hell did he mean by 'defensive posture'? I was leaning forward, weary with this futile exercise, occasionally looking down in exasperation at their repeated questions. I wasn't defensive – I was fed up.

Four hours later, I was told I could go. When I had reported at the police station earlier that evening, they had also taken my car for forensic tests. This was done at Spalding and, I presume, by local police. Thank God since they concluded what I already knew – there were no sinister forensic links with Arlene Fraser. But, three years later, sitting on that bunk in my stinking cell in the Elgin cop shop, I wondered if there would have been the same results if the car had been tested in Aberdeen or Elgin by Grampian cops.

Exactly six months to the day after that first contact from the cops, on the 7th of November 1998, Grampian Police came calling again – this time to my house. It was two different detectives but their manners weren't any better than that first pair. The cops' stated objective was to go over my statement from the first interview. Seemed a simple enough task since I'd been over it often enough previously but they clearly had underlying objectives.

As one cop spoke from the armchair across from me, the other strolled about the room, nosing around my books and videos. What did he expect to find there? A signed confession? A homemade video of some dastardly deed? A manual called *How To Commit Murder*? Instead, he found true-crime books, including one about the Kray Twins, a book about the IRA and some football books. I don't do fiction. Now those crime books interested the rozzers very much indeed. Did they really think those kind of books were only read by murderers? Or were they so stuck in the investigation they would clutch at any straw? It was the latter, I decided, and, when they left my home that night, I reckoned I wouldn't be seeing them again.

As I moved uneasily in the bed in Elgin Police Station, trying to keep the putrid-smelling blanket off my body, I looked round my dismal cell and realised how wrong I had been. In the early hours of the morning, as I finally nodded off to sleep, I reassured myself that at least Maya was OK. Or was she?

SEEKING ARLENE

NOVEMBER 1998

Sheep scattered in all directions over the hillside as the RAF helicopters swooped down low, just above tree level, looking for the landmarks that would lead them to their target. The pilots were familiar with the terrain, which was just as well. The rolling hills and farmland can be a rural maze of patchwork quilt to those who don't know it. A farm labourer mounted on a tractor pulled in on a narrow country road to look up and stare. Nearby, a fencer halted his sweaty work to wipe his brow, shield his eyes and wonder at the machines. At a nearby cottage, two old hands had abandoned their posts at the window of their cottage to stand in their yard and get a better look. This was some show. What is it about choppers that turn grown men into curious, marvelling young boys? Are they reminded of childhood dreams of adventures? Of games they would play with plastic toy airplanes? Maybe – but the crews of these helicopters weren't playing.

As they spotted their target of Wester Hillside Farm, Mosstowie, near Elgin, the pilots brought their crafts to a hover so they could get their bearings. Onboard heat-seeking equipment was turned on and the helicopters sidled down lower sideways to start their work. Up and down the land surrounding Hector Dick's farm they went, strip by strip, systematically covering each square inch of field, every burn, every gully, every building. Down on the ground, the noise was terrifying more than the beasts – the residents weren't too happy either. Hector Dick was under pressure.

The cops had been at Dick's door almost every day. They wanted to know about a car, an old Ford Fiesta. It was a beige car and well past its best days. They told Hector Dick that they knew it had been bought from a local dealer on the day before Arlene disappeared. He told them he knew nothing about it. The cops came back and told Dick they knew who had sold it and they knew who had bought it. He denied everything. Now they could tell Dick that it was registration number B231 PDY. He thought that was very interesting but he had never seen such a car, never owned it.

They asked his wife, Irene. She denied any knowledge of such a vehicle. But then a lot of old rusty vehicles moved through Mosstowie – it was just the way of her man, Hector. But he would know about any cars or so his wife said.

The cops asked the people who worked on his farm. One Willie Smith said, 'I don't remember seeing the car but there are always cars around here.' It was a scruffy farm, with vehicles and bits of trucks and old carts seemingly scattered with no plan. It was just that kind of a place.

So, the cops hit Hector Dick's farm team-handed. Bit by bit, they searched the outbuildings, the surrounding fields, the dump and the coal merchant yard. They didn't find the car.

Then they checked all the traders and the scrapyards and the official records and the Ford Fiesta didn't turn up. Someone had disposed of that car carefully, deliberately, or else they were hiding it and hiding it well. So they asked Hector Dick about the car again. Still he denied knowing anything about it. They reminded him that they knew the car had been delivered to his farm. Hector had told them he remembered nothing about any old beige Ford Fiesta.

Down in Fife, the cops visited some men – cousins of Hector Dick – who ran a large scrapyard but they said they knew nothing about any Ford Fiesta. But the police weren't taking that as an easy answer. Back they came again and again, checking the yard and threatening the brothers that they might just find something illegal. And, if they did, they'd get done. They would stop the brothers' cars on the road, checking them for faults, hanging around the gates to their yard, scaring away the customers – the police weren't giving in easily. The brothers told them to fuck off and complained of police harassment. The cops didn't fuck off but came back again and again.

They may have hit a brick wall with Hector Dick but now the cops had some good news to give to the public. And give it they did. One of Grampian Police's finest made a public statement. Detective Chief Superintendent Keith Wilkins said, 'I cannot stress enough the significance of this vehicle to our ongoing inquiries. It is a significant development, one of the few major breakthroughs we have had in the case.' And that was before they had even found the car. They launched a national appeal for information on beige Ford Fiesta registration number B231 PDY. This was special and they were willing to go to any lengths to get that car. Surely everyone could see how serious they were?

The cops never said what had caused them to become interested in that beige Ford Fiesta and nor did they reveal why they believed it was significant in Arlene's disappearance. Even to this day, they still haven't given the slightest clue as to what had triggered their desire to find the vehicle and interview anyone connected to it. But one thing was certain – the beige Fiesta was top of their list in their search for Arlene and how and why she'd disappeared.

But, whatever it was that had alerted them to it, Hector Dick was claiming he knew nothing about the car. Detective Chief Superintendent Keith Wilkins wasn't finished speculating about that car, 'To the best of my knowledge, it was not owned by Nat Fraser. I don't believe that Nat Fraser was involved in its purchase.' Now why did he say that?

The cops were as aware as anyone of the rumours that abounded in the Elgin area. Arlene had been missing for so long, everyone thought that she was dead – everyone except Nat Fraser and his two kids. He still said he believed she had gone away either with a man or to get her head straight. Was he just saying that to be positive in front of his kids? Then again, maybe he believed it. What other folk were whispering though was that she was dead all right and the most likely person to have murdered her was Nat Fraser, her husband. Wasn't he already facing charges of attempting to murder her? Isn't it always the partner?

So, when the cops came out and said the Ford Fiesta was the biggest breakthrough in the case so far but it had nothing to do with Nat Fraser, local people listened. Well, some of them did. Others always prefer to think the worst. They hadn't known that the cops had hounded Hector Dick over the car. They still hadn't been told. But now Dick had gone away for a while because he couldn't stand the police pressure and the RAF helicopters swooping over his property. Local people began to wonder what role Hector Dick played in Arlene's disappearance. The cops didn't say. They didn't need to.

The helicopters weren't looking just for the Ford Fiesta car. They were seeking Arlene.

7

THE FREE WORLD

JUNE 2001

Maya sat alone in her cell feeling lonelier than she had ever felt, her head filled with thoughts of me. I sat alone in my cell feeling equally lonely and thinking of Maya. Mirror images hundreds of miles apart.

The toilet in the corner summed up my changed circumstances and I thanked God I didn't need a crap. Maya wasn't so lucky – her period had started. Polite in her manner and fastidious in her hygiene, to Maya it was the ultimate humiliation. She felt vulnerable sitting on the exposed, stainless steel can, dreading that the door would spring open any minute and in would stroll a cop. It left her feeling dirty, unwashed. It was even worse was when she had to ask male officers for tampons. The indignity and powerlessness of it all was overwhelming for her.

Maya didn't know what was going to happen to her but now she feared the worst. When she was called back into the interview room, once again she asked if she needed a lawyer.

'No,' replied the officer, smiling, 'this is just a friendly chat.'

'But you have kept me in jail overnight,' she stated, believing the point to be self-evident, 'and you're thinking of sending me back to Russia.'

'Well, that'll be up to the Immigration people.'

'I don't want to go back,' Maya insisted. 'This is where my home is.'

'As I said, that will be up to the Immigration people.'

'I want a lawyer then.' It was Maya's final word.

On Saturday, after many hours of interviewing, a duty lawyer arrived at Spalding Police Station to represent Maya. More interviews followed where the police ran over the same ground from the day before.

'Your boyfriend is caught up in an evil business . . .'

'He'll be going away for a long time . . .'

'We have every right to send you back to Russia . . .'

'You'll never return. Never . . .'

And then a new question. 'Do you know anyone called Finnegan?' one asked.

'Who?'

'Tom Finnegan.'

'No.'

'Or Legg? Graham Legg?'

'No.'

'Are you sure? Glenn hasn't spoken about people with those names?'

'I don't think so,' Maya answered, aware that I mentioned a lot of people I met through work and my support of the Falkirk football team – just friends, colleagues or acquaintances. If I had mentioned somebody by either of those names, they wouldn't be so important. She had met all my closest people.

'Think, Maya,' said a police officer as if she hadn't been. 'Finnegan. F . . . I . . . N . . . N . . . E . . . G . . . A . . . N,' the cop spelled it out in a very loud voice, the way too many British tourists do abroad when trying to be understood in some foreign language. 'FINNEGAN.'

'No, I don't know anyone called Finnegan or Legg,' Maya was learning that the only way to deal with the interview techniques was to be firm, certain and brief. She knew that life was more complicated than that and, if they allowed her more thinking time, some space for discussion, she might recall either name from some trivial chitchat. But it was their game – their rules.

Maya wasn't to know and they didn't tell her, of course, but the cops were now in search of a hit man. 'That's Finnegan.

F . . . I . . . N . . . N . . . E . . . G . . . A . . . N. Or Legg. L . . . E . . . G . . . G.'
It wouldn't be the last time she heard those names.

By late Saturday afternoon, the lawyer advised Maya to return
to Russia voluntarily. It seemed that, if she cooperated, then she
stood some chance of being allowed back into the UK, albeit a very
slim chance indeed. She didn't want to go back to Russia – her papers
were in order and she had done no wrong. She also doubted that
someone who was returned – or even who returned voluntarily –
early to Russia would ever be allowed back into the UK. Still, she
was caught and couldn't win whatever she did. She would have to
decide and soon.

In Elgin, I hadn't slept well at all in my cold cell. Not only was
my mind in turmoil over my situation but the Friday-night drunks
had been rounded up and had been singing all night. But it was
morning and I had a routine to follow. I urinated in the toilet and
only then realised that it wouldn't flush. Banging on the metal door
I attracted the duty cop and explained my problem.

'I flush it from out here,' explained the police officer and yet again
I thanked God that my bowels had seized up.

'What about a shower?' I asked.

'You can have a wash,' replied the cop. 'Just give me a minute
and I'll take you along.'

The sink area was filthy and the facilities basic. Stripped to the
waist, I stood there in view of whoever happened by, trying to raise
a lather from the cheap soap and rinsing my face and under my
arms and soaking my hair. It was the best I could do in the
circumstances but I still felt sullied, unkempt. Not the best start to
the day, any day.

Back in my cell, I paced. After only one night, I already felt my
wits being dulled by the sheer boredom of the place despite still
being tormented by the charges and not knowing what was
happening to Maya. The only view from the cell was through a
barred window high up on the wall. If I stood on the bed, I could
get a narrow-angled glimpse of the outside world. It was just enough
to see some parked cop vans and cars and, very occasionally, a

human being passing by. It was next to no diversion at all. A big man, it took me only a few steps to stride the length of the cell. I felt like one of those lions who have spent all their lives in a cage in a zoo, pacing and pacing, backwards and forwards, and getting nowhere, slowly going demented, still pacing and pacing.

Food arrived – a beefburger, some bread and a cup of tea. The grub tasted of cardboard but I chopped it up with the plastic fork and forced it down, chewing hard on the rubbery meat. This was going to be a long haul and I had to keep my strength up. I looked at the plastic fork and laughed out loud to myself. What did they think? That I might kill myself if they gave me a metal fork? I could reassure them I wasn't suicidal but I was angry and hell-bent on getting out of that cell as soon as possible.

'Cunts,' I thought, remembering the two cops in the interview room the night before. The way they had badgered me and then threatened me with Maya being sent back to Russia . . . 'I'm twice as smart as you, you pricks,' I raged in my mind. 'And where the fuck is that duty lawyer? The bastard will be out shopping with his wife or having a round of golf, no doubt. Arsehole.' Even now, when left alone, the fury continued to build inside me. This wouldn't do at all. It would make me weak, sloppy, prone to outbursts when they came to interview me again. I had to calm down.

Calling for the duty officer, I asked for something to read. I was hoping at best for yesterday's newspaper or maybe an old trashy novel with a torn cover. It wouldn't matter as long as I could lose myself for a while. Instead, they gave me two mind-numbingly boring technical textbooks. It wasn't helping my state of mind.

At last, the door opened and the duty officer led me out into the corridor. A short walk later and I was being processed – fingerprints and mug shots. If asked two days before what I would think of the cops taking such records of me, I would have recoiled in horror. But, that day, I welcomed the distraction – at least I was doing something.

Back in my cell, lunch arrived – a fatty lamb cutlet with sticky gravy in a regulation plastic tray. The food smelled strong. Another time, another place, I would have eaten it without qualms or hesitation. I had eaten too much public school food to be put off by a bit of canteen-quality nosh. Yet there, in the police cell, it only served to remind me of the tacky blanket and slippery mattress. The filth of the place and the stench of the gravy made me feel queasy, nauseous. On a day when I should have felt strong with all my wits about me, the system was bringing me down. That was something I couldn't allow.

When the cops came to fetch me, I almost felt relieved. Getting out of the monotony of the cell had to be worth it – even if it was only to spend more time being grilled on the same questions over and over. But I was in for a surprise – we were going out for the afternoon.

'Did you visit any sheds with Nat?' one of the cops asked.

'Sheds?' I asked, wondering what the hell they were going on about.

'Aye, workshops, you know.'

I thought hard. Did he mean the industrial units based in the many developed sites around Elgin? If so, maybe I had visited some of those with Nat and Ian Taylor when they were setting up their own business. I couldn't remember doing so. But I could recall that none of that work had been going on at the time I'd visited my mates two days before Arlene disappeared.

'Why would I do that?' I asked, the way you would with an acquaintance or somebody who had stopped you in the street. But these were no ordinary folk. They didn't answer questions – they asked them. These were the cops.

'Do you remember Nat having any sheds? Maybe he mentioned them?'

'Sheds? What do you mean by sheds?' I was in the back of the police car as it drove through the familiar Elgin streets.

'Like these ones,' said a cop, as they pulled up.

'Lock-ups!' Now I understood. 'They're fucking lock-ups for cars.'

'Aye,' replied a cop simply, as if it had been obvious all along.

All Saturday afternoon we drove round Elgin, stopping and

68

getting out wherever they spotted lock-ups. The two cops persisted in calling them sheds – something that really annoyed me. Sheds were small wooden buildings usually found in gardens or large industrial units where they repaired trains or stored sizeable amounts of gear or stock like fruit and veg – nothing like a bloody lock-up. I considered the continual use of the term 'shed' to be sloppy, misleading and not the type of slip-up that you'd expect from a murder investigation squad.

'Where did you meet Hector Dick?' one cop asked.

I knew that the cops had gone after Dick. They had asked me about the pig farmer before and I'd told them that I hardly knew the bloke, met him maybe twice and, then, only briefly. I told them again.

'That can't be right, Glenn,' the interviewing cop insisted.

'It is fucking right.' Well, you knew somebody or you didn't. It's not like something you could debate.

'But you were a good pal of Nat Fraser's?' the cop was smiling, pleasant.

'Still am,' I said, insisting on accuracy.

'Good enough to visit him two days before his wife disappeared.'

'I visited him lots of times,' I said. 'But, yes, that's right.'

'And Hector Dick was a good pal of Nat's as well.'

'So?'

'And the two of you never got friendly?'

'No.'

'Close?'

'NO!'

Along with everyone else, I knew that the cops reckoned Hector Dick had some hand in Arlene Fraser's disappearance. Now that it had been declared a murder case, I knew that would be serious metal. But what had the cops in mind now? Linking me with Dick? Come hell or high water?

After I showed the cops where I'd met Hector Dick, they made a few notes and we continued on the tour of lock-ups. Hours later, we returned to the police station. I was almost relieved to be detained again in the tiny cell. There were only so many lock-ups you could see in a day – seen one, seen them all. I settled down on the bed and considered counting bloody lock-ups instead of sheep on sleepless nights. 'That would work,' I said out loud and proceeded to stay awake – wide awake and worried.

Hundreds of miles south, Maya was being driven through the streets of Spalding to the home she and I had shared for just a couple of short months. The visit would be brief – just a stop-off to pick up some of her belongings and some money. One holdall was to be all she would be allowed.

The usually impeccable house looked as though it had been ransacked. All the furniture had been shifted and an easy chair lay on its side. The TV and video had been gutted and wires, valves and connections could be seen glistening in the house lights. The books had been scattered from the shelves. Nearby, lay a pile of videocassettes with some cases cracked and others were lying open with the tapes spread over the floor. The piano looked ruined – as if someone had broken its beautiful spine. The kitchen had suffered similar disruption. Food had been removed from the cupboards and the fridge door had been left open. Something had been spilled on the kitchen floor and just left there, trodden in by the search party's feet. The hatch to the attic had been pushed aside and the trap left gaping. The bedroom was in chaos with the mattress lying lopsided like some marooned boat. The cupboard and wardrobe doors were open and clothes were scattered everywhere.

The house appeared to have been burgled and vandalised yet it had been the police who had inflicted the damage, not some villains. The devastation brought home to Maya how our lives had changed in just a short twenty-four-hour period. If she had been given a quiet moment, just a second or two's reflection on her own, she might well have burst into tears. The police had abandoned her to her own lonely thoughts in the cold cell but, there in our home, they bustled her and urged her to get a move on.

Five minutes later, they slammed the door of the house behind them. As the police officer turned the key, Maya automatically moved to make sure the door was locked – force of habit. Peering out through the car window as it drove away, Maya doubted she would ever see the house again.

At about 4.30 a.m., the police car pulled in to a detention centre for asylum seekers near Gatwick Airport. It was the middle of the night and the place was ghostly and sad. Maya wondered if it was any different in daylight hours.

'What do you mean Maya is in Russia?' I demanded of my estranged wife, Anne, and our grown-up daughter, Rachael. It was Sunday afternoon. My mother had rallied and informed the family, just as I knew she would, and Anne and Rachael had travelled north to make sure I got a visit and some essential items.

'The police told us,' Anne shrugged, almost apologetically as if it had been her fault.

'When?'

'What?' asked Anne unsure of what I meant.

'When was she bloody sent to Russia, of course?' I rumbled, my anxiety making me brusque and in severe danger of appearing to shoot the messenger.

But Anne and Rachael were used to my ways. 'Today – earlier today, they said.'

'So some copper made that phone call,' I said.

'What phone call?' asked Rachael.

'The call that got Maya sent back to Russia.'

The two women looked perplexed, struggling to understand.

'It's a long story,' I continued. 'Let's just say they threatened to do it.' I was calmer now, letting the information sink in. Sadness cooled my anger. Now I must figure out not only how I could secure my release but also how to end Maya's enforced exile.

Early on Sunday, Maya had been driven to the airport in a marked police car. Cops had stayed with her till the rest of the passengers had boarded the flight to Moscow. Then they escorted her on to the plane and made sure she was seated and belted in. She could feel the eyes of the other passengers on her and knew what they were thinking – 'What has she done?' 'She must have tried to sneak into

England?' 'I'll bet she's one of those young prostitutes.' 'Maybe worse . . .' 'Maybe she's with the gangsters, the Moscow Mafia . . .'

Maya was only too aware of the lengths young women would go to to escape the former Soviet countries and live in the UK. Too many were hoodwinked into paying for being smuggled in through years of selling their bodies in the saunas and brothels of the bigger British cities. They weren't working girls but slaves trying to repay a debt that could never be paid off. It was a life of doing what the men told them till the same men thought their good looks or health had gone, at which time they were thrown out on to the street. That's what some of the passengers would think she was – a sex slave who'd been caught out and was being sent packing.

Maya tried to ignore the smirking looks around her and settled down. Although she was exhausted, she couldn't get comfortable in her seat. Nor could she read or distract herself in any way. She stared out of the window as the airplane raced down the runway, the fields rushing past faster and faster. Maya wasn't a quitter. But she couldn't believe she would ever see those fields – or me – again.

I'd been so grateful for Anne and Rachael's friendly familiar faces. In spite of the bad tidings they brought, they were a welcome relief in that hostile place. The following morning I was to appear in court. The cops would try to convince the judge to lock me up while I awaited trial – that much I knew. But what I didn't know was how the proceedings would go – who would say what to whom and when. I didn't know when I could speak up for myself or what I could say apart from repeating that I was innocent. And still that duty lawyer hadn't appeared. I wished I'd arranged my own brief.

'Bastard,' I fumed, 'what's the point of paying taxes and supporting the state when wankers like that can just ignore you even if you're up to your arse in alligators. Bastard.'

That was when I was told there was a lawyer to see me. I cut my visit from Anne and Rachael short and went to see him pronto.

'You took your time,' I said, getting straight to the point.

'What do you mean?' the lawyer replied, looking perplexed but calm.

'I've been in here since Friday night.'

'When did you get them to call me?'

'Friday evening. Early.'

'I can assure you that I only got the call at seven o'clock tonight. That's what?' the lawyer asked, looking at his watch, 'Half an hour ago and almost precisely the time it takes to drive here from my home. I left as soon as they had called.'

I eyed him up and down. Was he lying or were the coppers? As far as I was concerned, I had every reason to believe the lawyer. The police were accusing me of all sorts of evil deeds and claiming to have a tape and proof that I knew couldn't exist. They had grilled me in the car all the way up from Lincolnshire – then and only then, did they start the formal interviews and kept them going late into the night. I still couldn't work out why they had called me back in late on that Friday night when I was dead on my feet and they must have been knackered too. All they seemed to want me to do was to try to identify some women's rings and some keys – lots of keys. It wasn't till the next day that I realised that they had handed me every item and, like a fool, I had taken them, turned them around in my hands, lifted them up with my fingers before finally saying I didn't recognise any of them. What a fool. Now my prints would be all over those objects, whatever the significance of them might be.

They had grilled me twice on Saturday, stopping off in the car park to threaten me that they'd make sure I was put away for a long time. Then there was the tour of all those bloody lock-ups. And, on Sunday, it was back in again. Who was Tom Finnegan? Who was Graham Legg? And they weren't taking no for an answer. The cops had more or less admitted they had tapped my phone. For no reason I knew of, they had made sure that Maya was sent back to Russia on a one-way ticket with little chance of ever getting back. So why should I trust the cops when they had handed me keys and had told me they had phoned the lawyer on Friday night?

But, if they had lied to me, they had lied repeatedly every time I'd asked if the solicitor had been called. Then why had the cops tried to persuade me not to use that particular lawyer? Why had they even tried to talk my estranged wife, Anne, and daughter, Rachael, into hiring another brief, any brief? That was just after they had lain it on thick to Anne and Rachael about what terrible trouble I was in.

Maybe I was right in thinking they didn't like that lawyer because he didn't play their games. I eyed the brief up and down. He looked quirky – different somehow – though I couldn't quite put my finger on why. But then I spotted colourful beaded African bangles round one wrist – hardly the style you'd normally expect from a lawyer.

'My name is Andrew McCartan,' said the lawyer, holding out his hand.

I grasped his mitt firmly and shook. 'Glenn Lucas,' I replied. 'I'd say it was a pleasure but under the circumstance . . .'

Andrew McCartan smiled a little twisted ironic grin.

'He'll do me nicely,' I decided to myself. 'Someone a little different from the run-of-the-mill – that's just what I need.'

As I proceeded to tell Andrew McCartan what had happened with the cops, I wasn't aware that I'd just made one of my best decisions ever.

In the early hours of the morning, I was struggling to sleep. There were no drunks that night but the town hall clock chimed on the hour, mocking my insomnia. The cell light was left on at all times. What was that for? In case I topped myself? To make it easier for them to look in and check on the prisoner and screw my need for sleep?

Some preparation. I was going to go into court the next morning scruffily dressed, half-washed and sleepwalking because of sheer exhaustion. Did the cops deliberately set me up that way so that, in the dock, I'd look like I didn't care, couldn't be bothered, like some low-level scruff? Like the type of people we all tend to assume are up to no good? Wrongly assume in some cases.

Standing up, I paced the cell, rubbing my hands together to keep warm, and thought of the morning that lay ahead of me. It was the most threatening day of my life so far but at least I wouldn't have to face it alone.

DANGEROUS DRIVING

OCTOBER 1999

The cars and vans rumbled steadily down the country road. Most folk travelling that way were going about their business at the local farms or the distillery. At all times of the year, the odd tourist's car would drive slowly and cautiously along, admiring the lush green pastures. But this convoy wasn't admiring the view. They were out to make an arrest.

The cars carrying the cops arrived at Wester Hillside, Mosstowie first. 'Hector Dick, you are charged with attempting to pervert the course of justice . . .' the lead officer rhymed off.

Hector Dick said nothing as he was handcuffed and led away into the back of a police car to be formally interviewed at the local station.

But the cops weren't finished. Officers in black boiler suits disembarked from the cars and vans. Some entered the farmhouse and began a rigorous check. Others entered the outbuildings with plastic bags and tools. A group carefully edged their way across an expanse of recently tilled ground. Inch by inch, they prodded deep and cautiously. What were they looking for? A car? Or a body? Both?

Its back doors open, a van reversed up close to the farmhouse door – so close no passer-by could see what was going on. But there were no passers-by – the cops guarding and blocking the roads saw to that. It was the 1st of October 1999 and Hector Dick was in big trouble.

The police attention hadn't wavered for a day since Arlene disappeared. The biggest investigation squad ever mustered in the north-east was permanently based in Elgin. There had been some turnover in the officers. Some local men transferred out and some outsiders moved in – Detective Superintendent Jim Stephen, orchestrating the investigation from his base in Aberdeen, was determined to get the best team. At least that's how it seemed.

As far as pressure from the cops was concerned, over the past year and a half, it had moved off Nat Fraser and they seemed much more interested in other people. Early in 1999, they had traipsed off to the Canaries, raising hopes all around Elgin that they had managed to find Arlene's trail.

No such luck. They had been interested in an Irish bodybuilder, by the name of Brendan Surgenor, who had lived in Elgin for a good number of years and had been close friends with Nat and his business partner, Ian Taylor. He was an important witness, according to the cops, and one they had wanted to interview since the beginning. Now, with the help of Interpol, they had tracked him down to the holiday resort of Puerto del Carmen on the island of Lanzarote where he managed a nightclub. Elgin folk held their breath, thinking this could be the big breakthrough.

It was a red herring. Apart from soliciting Surgenor's opinion – well everyone who had paid any interest in the case had an opinion – that he didn't know Arlene but thought she was dead, the trip produced no great leap forward. Eyes were now off the Canaries and Brendan Surgenor and it was the turn of Nat's pal and business partner, Ian Taylor, to land in hot water.

Ian's roving eye had caused him and his wife Jane to have many rocky times in their marriage. When the media exposed him as having visited Surgenor that same year, he had some explaining to do at home. Apparently, he had told Jane that he was going on a skiing holiday to Canada but instead headed for the sunny island. Either way, he was thrown out of the house. He moved in with Nat who was now staying at 2 Smith Street again and there was talk of divorce between the Taylors.

Ian Taylor's life had already been turned upside down over his friendship with Nat. He would frequently be interviewed by cops and reporters or be stopped while driving his car. His delivery lorries were often pulled up and checked mechanically when they were only a hundred yards from the warehouse and filled to the brim with fruit and veg to be delivered. It was as if Nat Fraser was damned and all who associated with him were too. At least those close to him were no longer allowed to lead a normal life and had to assume their every move was being watched. And that was the situation when guns entered the scene.

Following a tip-off, local cops made a dramatic raid on Nat Fraser's home. For once, it wasn't to do with Arlene but with alleged illegal guns. Nat had a high-powered rifle and enjoyed hunting or just target practice, very often on land owned by Hector Dick. But the cops found nothing of great import at Nat's so they raided Ian Taylor's family home at nearby Lhanbryde. There they found a cache of illegal arms, including four shotguns and ammunition designed to expand on impact – dum-dums, in other words.

However, city dwellers should put this into context. The area was rural and guns abound in rural areas. Gun licences are readily dispensed to farmers for pest control and to a wide range of the population for hunting deer, rabbits or grouse. In many ways, the north-east of Scotland is redneck territory, filled with conservative-thinking folks who are used to dangerous weaponry, almost seeing it as their God-given right to lug a gun about with them. The temptation to own a few illegal shotguns and decidedly dangerous ammo is just too great for some. It was for Ian Taylor.

If the police didn't bother much with Nat Fraser during that time, local gossip and the media were very interested in him. At around 9.40 a.m. on the 28th of April 1999, the precise anniversary of Arlene's disappearance, a posse of journalists and photographers hung around his business, Taylor & Fraser, hoping for a picture of the grieving husband. They were out of luck because Nat was on his rounds delivering goods. But they had spotted him earlier that morning, smiling and relaxed. Surely that was not the countenance of a grieving husband that the local people and much of the media expected to see.

Another public appeal was planned and delivered by Arlene's family but Nat Fraser was not involved. Where was he? Arlene's mother and sister had already gone public, claiming that they had been banned by Nat from seeing young Jamie and Natalie. Relations between Nat and his in-laws had never been the same since the dispute over custody of the kids. Now it got worse.

As far as the public were concerned, Nat Fraser was a cold, calculating man who not only didn't care that his wife was missing but went on to deny his own kids comforting contact with their grieving grandparents. Cruel. That's not how Nat Fraser saw it.

Nat Fraser had become increasingly concerned over the emotional pressure being placed on Jamie and Natalie by Arlene's parents in particular. He thought both of the youngsters should lead as normal a life as possible. They didn't need to be constantly reminded that their mum was missing. They certainly didn't need to be told that she was dead, especially since he still believed she was alive and had probably gone off with some man. As he would later recall of that time:

Natalie and Jamie were just young bairns. Bad enough that their mother wasn't there but they didn't need reminding of it all the time. I'm their dad but certain people were trying to take over with the kids. I just wanted them to have as ordinary a life as possible.

His own mother, Ibby, lived in the family home and took good care of the kids. A quiet, dignified and respectful woman, she just continued as usual and what's more normal than a granny looking after her grandchildren, being interested in their school lives, their pals and their hobbies and making sure they were well fed, had clean clothes and were safe? That was Ibby Fraser's approach and that was what Nat wanted.

Ibby had had to put up with a lot. Not only was her daughter-in-law missing, she was also being harassed by the cops. Ibby held down a job as well as caring for Natalie and Jamie. The cops knew that and knew where to find her. One night, she came home to find the back door of 2 Smith Street busted in so badly that even the adjoining

78

brickwork was damaged. The cops denied it was them. This wasn't to be the last time the house would be broken into in her absence. And every time it happened, the cops denied responsibility.

Whenever the house was broken into, something always went missing but it was never anything valuable, like in a burglary. One time, Jamie's library books and tickets disappeared from the spot he usually left them. Ibby asked the cops to give them back. Surely the boy's library books had no value to them? Of course, the police denied they had even been in the house, let alone taken the books. A long while later, some items that had been removed from the house during the official search were returned. In the pile, were numerous items that had disappeared at the various times when the house had been broken into – including Jamie's library books.

But Ibby was taking it all in her stride. She had to be mam and granny to young Jamie and Natalie so there was no point in doing anything other than just getting on with it. And Ibby was actually happier with her lot than some others.

After many heated rows, particularly between Nat and Arlene's father, Hector McInnes, Nat Fraser decided that contact between the kids and their maternal grandparents was destructive during what was already a destructive time. But, in the unknowing eyes of the public, breaking off contact between young children and their grand-parents was a bit like shooting Bambi. People at large could only see the outward signs and all they were told by Arlene's parents was what a bad man Nat Fraser was. It was a family row being conducted in the public eye. The only folk talking to media were Arlene's parents and sister. So many people were now seeing Nat as cruel and, of course, as guilty.

By the first anniversary of her disappearance, Arlene's family were convinced she was dead. Who could blame them? For the first time, the man in charge of the investigation, Detective Superintendent Jim Stephen, publicly announced that the cops were now looking for a dead Arlene. A year after she had gone, everyone thought that. Everyone except Nat Fraser, that is. Jim Stephen made another state-ment at the time, one that not many people noticed. He revealed that

Nat Fraser hadn't been invited to attend the public appeal. Wasn't that strange, given that he was Arlene's husband and one of the few people who believed she was still alive?

But Nat had other problems to deal with. Local people and the media were watching him very carefully indeed. Some didn't like how he continued to play with his band, The Minesweepers, in pubs and clubs in the area. Others thought it disgraceful that he had moved back into the family home, the very place he was banned from after being charged with attempting to murder Arlene within those walls.

Then there were the women like local barmaid Jacqui Milton who got to know the kids well. There was Vera Mair, a blast from the past, who was dubbed an Arlene lookalike. And there were others. Many people and most of the media saw these relationships as inappropriate for a man whose wife was missing. But Nat had always chased women, even during his happy years with Arlene. She'd almost called their wedding off because of his philandering. A fortnight into their marriage again there was a mighty blow out. And again and again. At one point, she left him and went to live in a women's refuge for two weeks.

Women, other women, had always been Nat's problem. That might be a fault some would criticise him for but he certainly couldn't be accused of changing his ways. Also, Nat and Arlene were separated before she had gone missing. For many months prior to her disappearance, the couple had been leading their own lives – their marriage was dying on its feet and they were inevitably heading towards divorce.

Rumours were circulating Elgin that Arlene had already seen a lawyer about ending her marriage. Also, it was rumoured that she had instructed her solicitor to pursue a settlement of £250,000, a sum that would have broken Nat Fraser for sure. It was all merely gossip of course but the gossip this time was true. Arlene's solicitor would later confirm that £250,000 was the divorce settlement she was seeking. Everyone knew that, on the day she vanished, she had an appointment with her lawyer – an appointment about the divorce, an appointment she never kept.

While the cops were letting it be known that they weren't that interested in Nat Fraser they were quietly beavering away on a plan. In Scotland there's a rule that, if charged with an offence, an accused person has to go to trial within a limited period. Serious charges have been known to be kicked out of court if the time limit is breached. They were running out of time with Nat's attempted murder charge.

After an application to Elgin Sheriff Court, an extension was granted because of the unusual complexity of the case. Why did they do this? Were they hoping that Arlene, as the injured party, would turn up and give evidence against the man? But some of the cops publicly admitted that they believed Arlene to be dead. Yet, even if the judge turned out to accept that there was no proof that she was dead, how difficult would it be to convince the court that poor Arlene had run off after terrible treatment by her man?

With each passing month without Arlene, the earlier case against Nat Fraser for attempted murder would look worse and worse. He was going to go to jail for sure.

If life was heating up for Nat it was nothing compared to what was happening to one of his pals. The year of 1999 had been a bad year for Hector Dick.

The cops had been busy. They had brought in profilers and other experts. In December 1998, they had engaged search expert Peter Simkins and his company Oceanfix. All around the countryside bordering Elgin – including Hector Dick's farm at Mosstowie – Simkins deployed hi-tech equipment that could scan the ground down to a depth of sixty feet. It could find bodies, buried objects – anything you want. The same gear had cracked other difficult cases such as the buried cache of £140,000 ransom money paid to murdering kidnapper Michael Sams and, further north, it had been instrumental in finding the body of sex-slaying victim Helen Torbet back in 1993. This equipment was the business and cops let it be known informally that they thought they were close to finding Arlene's body. They weren't but they did find somebody else.

Kevin Ritchie was a young, dope-smoking, hard-living mechanic and, some would say, heavy who happened to deal in second-hand cars. After a great deal of pressure from the cops, Kevin coughed up what they wanted to know – he had sold Hector Dick that beige Ford Fiesta.

Hector Dick had approached Ritchie, saying he needed a car in a hurry. He didn't care what type of car it was but it must, absolutely must, have an enclosed boot. It was obvious Dick wanted to transport something that he didn't want anyone to see. Ritchie found a car fitting the requirements, the beige Fiesta and delivered it to Hector Dick's farm at Mosstowie. According to his pig-farmer customer, it was perfect. Dick gave the young man an extra £50 for his troubles. Unusual, thought Ritchie, for someone known to be fond of keeping his cash.

But Hector Dick was very pleased with the motor. Especially since Ritchie had delivered it just on time. The date of delivery? The 27th of April 1998 – the night before Arlene went missing.

The car was going to do for Hector Dick. Or would it?

8

WATCH YOUR BACK

4 JUNE 2001

It was the Monday morning to end all Monday mornings. Up from my half-awake slumbering before dawn, toilet, a wash-down and some breakfast I couldn't taste or eat – in just a couple of days it had become an unchanging routine. How easy it must be to get stuck in the ways of an institution. But this morning was going to be different.

I paced up and down, edgier than ever. By the time the cops came for me and chained my wrists together, I was numb, unfeeling – just somehow glad that, at last, I was on my way to court. All I can remember was being in the back of a police van that rolled up to the back door of the court. My folks used to call that the tradesmen's entrance in a house. Here, at court, it was the villains' entrance – guilty before you've even been tried. And I thought justice was meant to be seen. I would have preferred to use the front door and I wouldn't have cared who was watching.

The night's worrying and the morning's pacing had left me feeling physically weak. The world seemed unreal. People sounded as if they were talking in an echo chamber. There I was in the court, my liberty at stake and completely clueless as to what was going on. Thank God the lawyer, Andrew McCartan, would be there to represent me. You only realise how little you really know about the justice procedure when you're in the hot seat. Too many courtroom dramas have conned us into believing it's all *Perry*

Mason or *Rumpole of the Bailey.*

'Were you in Inverness on . . .?' It was the beak, in the small wood-panelled courtroom, asking me some questions about a day I had visited Nat when he was in jail for the assault on Arlene. The cops had asked me about that day time after time. For hours, they had asked me what we had been chatting about so I told them – women, football, gossip from the fruit and veg industry, women – just the usual. It had struck me as a particularly strange question but they had asked me about loads of weird things. About a bloke called Finnegan, rings at my house, a book about the IRA, visits I made to Cuba for my work and, of course, there were those bloody lock-ups. But now I knew that this was the day they reckoned Nat and I had discussed disposing of bodies and, to support this accusation, they showed us apparently speaking about it on a videotape of one of my visits to him at Porterfield Prison, Inverness, where he was serving eighteen months for the serious assault on Arlene. But even that was weird since they showed me the images but no sound. I'd always thought this crime-investigation palaver was a lot more straightforward – that evidence had to be a lot more clear-cut and concrete.

'Attempting to pervert the course of justice,' I heard someone say. That'll be me then. All I had done was cooperate with the fuckers but I'd probably annoyed them greatly by remembering precise details from three years before. Every date they had asked me about I could link to work, football, a visit to friends or whatever. Slowly I had pieced together a full picture. I thought that's what they wanted. But did it make them suspect me? Like I had made it all up as a cover, knowing that the dates they mentioned were key? So what? There was nothing I could do about those suspicions. The truth was the truth – whether they liked it or not.

The prosecution side were making out that I was a dangerous, untrustworthy man who should be locked up for three months. Andrew was arguing the toss, saying that I was a decent, reliable citizen who was a risk to no one and wouldn't run away. At that time and place, I guess both sides were wrong to some extent. Being caught up in this mess did make me feel like fleeing and no question. After a bit of toing and froing, the beak announced, 'Seven days.' That was that – end of debate. I was heading to Craiginches Prison, Aberdeen on remand.

Two young cops led me out of the court. They locked me into the back of the car, climbed in the front and started off on a journey I didn't want to take. Thankfully they were silent, leaving me alone with my depressed thoughts as the car sped along the A96 road from Elgin to Aberdeen and prison.

Preying on my mind were the comments the two arresting officers had made the day before. After one of our trips round the lock-ups of Elgin, they had pulled in to a car park.

'You're going to have to keep your back to the wall, Glenn,' one cop had said, adding, 'you've no idea what you might get put into you when you're not looking.'

'What the fuck are you on about?' I'd asked.

'This is going to be your first time in the jail, right?'

'I've no intention of going to prison,' I'd protested, honestly.

'Well, look at you,' another cop had said, ignoring my comment.

'And listen to you,' the other had added.

'What?'

'You look like a Bobby,' he'd continued, using the favoured local term for police officers.

'I'm not going to jail,' I'd protested again but it fell on deaf ears.

'Aye, CID – and you sound like a fucking lawyer,' the other had chipped in.

'Not good, Glenn. Not good at all.'

'Spell it out then, you bastards.' I'd known they were winding me up but, then, what did I know about prison except what I had gleaned from the media like everyone else?

'Some of them will want to try it on – sexually. And you don't mess with these boys. They're not pansies if you catch my drift.' The cop had been smiling.

'Others will just give you a smack to make sure you know your place in the order. You're a big guy, Glenn, and they'll see you as a potential threat.' The two cops had really been enjoying playing tig-tag with me, like a couple of cats tormenting some mouse they had cornered.

'I'm not a threat to anyone,' I'd protested again while getting increasingly worried.

'Aye, you're a big man, all right,' one of the cops had continued, ignoring my comments entirely, 'but have you ever had to deal with a knife attack?' He hadn't waited for my answer which would have been in the negative anyway. 'That's why I'm telling you not to turn your back. Particularly in the showers.'

'Or in the common area.'

'Round the pool table.'

'The jail is crawling with homemade knives. Believe you me.'

They had been trying to unnerve me but they were wasting their breath. I was already on edge and I'd been getting more and more frightened with each passing hour that day. I'd known then that the following day I had to appear at court in Elgin where the prosecution were going to ask for me to be held in prison on remand. Given all that had happened since the cops had turned up at my door forty-eight hours before, I realised prison was a likely option. And I was scared shitless.

What had been the cops' point in trying to scare me further? As far as I was concerned, they had already followed through on their threat to have Maya sent back to Russia – something they'd been willing to trade on if I gave them information on Nat. So, did they think I didn't really care about Maya? That maybe the thought of being buggered and stabbed by hairy-arsed prisoners was more of a threat than losing my beautiful young Maya? They were wrong. All of this was hell. Pure hell. There was only one problem – I had no information to trade, no confession to make.

I suppose most of the public would think their approach was all right, given they were investigating a murder. Any type of game might be acceptable to nab a dangerous bloke and get him off the street. But what if the bloke was innocent? And what if the crime they were investigating had no evidence, no forensics, no corroboration and no body? That's how I saw their position but, then, they were only telling me what they wanted to tell me. So were they trying to shake some kind of case out of Nat and his friends? Or, then again, were they simply enjoying tormenting me?

'And watch your feet,' I remembered one of them suddenly declaring as if he had just remembered something on a list.

'My fucking feet? What are you on about?' I'd wondered what they were going to give me next – a lecture on the horrors of verrucas and how infectious they are?

'Needles,' he'd replied. 'Syringes. Dirty needles. And blood splattered razor blades. Half the prisoners are junkies and not too careful where they dump their gear.'

'One jab from a dirty needle and you're in serious trouble,' the other had butted in. 'Hepatitis for sure. Or worse – AIDS.'

'It's best that you know this, Glenn,' the other one had added. 'You're in for a long stretch.'

'I heard you earlier, you bastards, like you knew I could. I know you're going to try and convince the judge to hold me over for three months. What's that about? Like who am I a danger to?' I'd asked, grateful for the chance to have a dig at them.

'This is a complicated case, Glenn,' he'd said, almost with a note of pride, 'but that's not what I mean. Though you're spot on – we will try to persuade the court you should be remanded for three months.'

'Thanks a bunch,' I'd snapped back at them and then I'd realised that my comments had been as weak as a five-year-old kid's retort.

'But that's nothing,' he'd gone on. 'What I mean is the sentence you'll get when this goes to trial. I reckon at least six years.'

'Maybe ten,' his mate had added.

'As much as twelve, depending on the judge.'

'I know what you two are at,' I'd growled at them. 'You're just trying to put the wind up me.'

'No, no,' one cop had said with a smile, adding, 'Tsk, tsk –' as if I was some kind of misunderstanding child, 'just educating you. Forewarned is forearmed and all that.'

'Yes, yes,' I'd replied, 'but let me tell you, if I go down for this, for something I didn't do, no matter how long I get sent away for, I'm coming after you two. One way or another, I'll get you bastards.'

'Don't think so, Glenn,' one had sniggered. 'We'll be retired by the time you get out.'

More, much more, along the same lines had been said to me that afternoon but suddenly I ran out of thinking time – we had arrived at the jail.

There isn't one gate – you have to pass through a series of them. You pass through the first one, then it's locked again behind you, the next is unlocked and you pass through it and then it's locked and so on and so forth.

It's a slow, frightening process but one that was actually familiar to me. Back in my days working in Inverness, we had won the contract to provide fruit and veg to Porterfield Prison in Inverness. Porterfield was infamous as the place where they built cages to keep the wild men that ordinary prisons couldn't handle. Guys like Jimmy Boyle, Larry Winters and Hugh Collins ended up there and they didn't take it lightly. That was where they carried out the first dirty protests of covering themselves in their shit, rioting and assaulting the prison staff whenever they could. So the governor of Porterfield was understandably a wee bit cautious about who he allowed through the gates and that included delivery men. In the entire company, I was one of the few employees the prison service deemed acceptable and not a security risk. Now here I was a prisoner, bound over in jail, because the cops wouldn't trust me on the street. Ironic or what?

The staff of Porterfield and I got on well. At the time, a guy we'll call Horace – not his real name – was serving time. He was a kind of local celebrity but his claim to fame was the kind no one wanted. Some years before, near his Highland home, he had been caught and convicted for having full-blown nooky with a donkey. You'd have thought that first public humiliation would have been his last. But, no – he got caught again and was sentenced to more time. Needless to say, he was the butt of much humour. One day, one of the wardens asked me if I could bring a bale of hay the next time I delivered goods.

'Sure,' I answered, 'but why?'

'It's for Horace. We're going to say, if it's good enough for his girlfriend, it's good enough for him.'

Inside Aberdeen Prison, there was a formal handing-over ceremony. A big prison officer behind a counter at reception was passed some papers by the cops. He marked down my name and details and took my money, making a great show of counting it in front of me. Then I had to sign and that was it – I was now officially in the care of HM Prison Aberdeen.

The reception staff handed me some clothes, a few essential items like bedding, soap and a shaving brush that looked just like the one my old man used. Then it was off to what I took to be the medical wing. I assumed this for two reasons – the screws were wearing white jackets over their uniforms and I was told to strip. They looked in my hair with a torch – I suppose this was in case I was crawling with lice. Then I had to open my mouth wide and ordered to move my tongue up and down. After that came the classic, that everyone who knows anything about prisons dreads – I was told to bend over. They don't just look at your arse but get you to pull your cheeks apart while they train the torch on your hole. Degrading and humiliating? You bet. But then I suppose, with drugs being so rife in our jails, it is an essential check. I almost felt sorry for the staff as I thought of all the cracks they had to examine. Well, if it isn't your thing . . .

With each step of the process, I was getting fidgety and bloody terrified. All those warnings the cops had given me in the car . . . OK, I suspected they were winding me up but I also knew they might well be telling the truth.

One big, obvious concern was how I reckoned I was going to be perceived in that jail. Tall, well-built, a middle-class English accent that's straight from the public school and an obvious ignorance of what the hell happened in prison, I was going to have to ask questions every step of the way. That would confirm everything I feared they were going to suspect about me.

When a nurse with manners straight from Waffen-SS started checking me for needle tracks and suggesting I really should have the hepatitis jag, my bottle began to go. I've been to countries we all tend to think of primitive, disease-ridden backwaters and didn't need that jag. Now, here I was in a jail in my own homeland and the nurse was going on and on, shifting gear from suggesting to telling me that I needed that protection. In spite or maybe because of her insistence I refused. It's through such small victories you maintain your dignity. I preferred to take my chances with the virus than concede to bullying.

But it was a wake up call. I was seconds away from entering a real jail with all the drug addiction, violence and mental illness that most of these establishments are home to these days – and I shouldn't have been there. I asked to see the officer in charge immediately. Well, I had to tell somebody. Much to my surprise it was promptly agreed. The helpfulness, cooperation and pleasant manner of the prison staff already stood in stark contrast to my treatment by the police. On that day, at that time, I was just too bloody scared to notice.

The officer in charge was sympathetic and patient. He sat and allowed me to explain that there had been a big mistake – that, whatever evidence the cops claimed to have, it had surely nothing to do with me.

'I'm alone here,' I twittered, 'and I don't know how prisons work. I don't know anybody in here. No pals to show me the ropes, keep me right.' He nodded and listened as I ranted on. 'And I'm bloody terrified.' Tears welled up in my eyes. All the man I was ever going to be and I was petrified. 'I mean, who'll look out for me?' I went on. 'Look at me. Do I look like a con to you? A cop, more like. God knows what the other prisoners will make of me.'

The prison officer must have heard every sob story plus some in his career but that didn't show. He seemed genuinely concerned by my predicament although, even as I bemoaned my situation, we both knew that there was little he could do to help. I was held at

Her Majesty's pleasure and that was that. 'Will you and your staff look out for me?' I asked finally.

'Of course we will, Glenn,' he reassured. 'We always watch out for men new to the system.'

Terrified as I was, I believed him. It was like a doctor telling you that some treatment wasn't going to hurt much, meaning it would hurt, of course, but it had to be done and he'd be as gentle as possible.

In a calmer state, I was led away to the cells. With every step, my heart was beating stronger and stronger in my chest. What the hell was I walking into?

HANDS UP
22 JUNE 2000

It was that bloody car. At least that's what people first thought when the police went south again to Fife and pulled five men off the streets. Some were involved in the scrap business and owned a huge yard. One was a cousin of Hector Dick and, by now, everyone knew the cops believed Dick had possession of the old beige Ford Fiesta that they reckoned was important in Arlene's disappearance. But there was another reason to go south – booze.

One of the biggest cartels in the UK to be involved in the distribution of smuggled booze is based north of Edinburgh. The operation spans the border between Lothian and Fife. But this isn't bootleg booze. Bootleg implies that the alcohol has been made in an illegal still somewhere. This was your bona fide, labelled, high quality falling-down liquid with just one catch – no tax had been paid on it.

By constantly increasing the tax on alcohol, successive Chancellors of the Exchequer have made smuggling booze a highly profitable business – one that's worth billions of pounds a year in Scotland alone. It's of little use to anyone on the small scale apart from those who want a few cheap bottles for the New Year or for their friends. They aren't part of the business – they are its customers.

There are many ways of introducing duty-free booze into Britain but most involve diverting an articulated lorry full of the goodies to some European site where a bogus company will give them duly stamped papers, indicating that the appropriate tax has been paid.

Armed with these documents, the drivers then cross back to the UK and deliver the large load at a knockdown price but still making a whacking profit for the moneymen behind the lark.

Though Elgin has a population of only 20,000, two articulated lorry-loads of smuggled booze were sold in the town every week in 1998. Depending on the make-up of the load, that could be as much as £300,000 profit every week – big business, in other words.

The cops knew the goods were coming in. The steadiest, most regular small-order customers the smugglers had were the local rozzers. They just didn't realise the scale of what was coming in. Or maybe they didn't care. Smuggling booze had a long tradition in that part of the country where most of Scotland's whisky distilleries are based. Many of today's most world-renowned brands were originally made in illegal stills on sites in the area. Now there are massive duty bonded warehouses guarded by the Customs and Excise. Someone once calculated that, if all the tax had been collected on all the whisky stored in the tiny village of Dufftown alone, it would have been enough to wipe out the national debt.

All that alcohol lying around, albeit guarded, is, from to time, too much of a temptation for locals. To get their mitts on the goods, some have gone to considerable lengths, coming up with ingenious ploys like secretly sawing a hidden trapdoor in the roof. So the tradition of smuggling still goes on, even under the nose of Customs and Excise.

But at least the cops knew the local faces of the business. Who were they? Hector Dick, for one. And that's who the cops bought their own illicit supplies from.

After Arlene had gone missing, Dick boasted to his pal Nat Fraser that the cops wouldn't touch him because he had something over them. It was the booze he meant.

But now the cops decided to put the squeeze on Hector Dick – they wanted to find out the southern connection behind the smuggling trade. That and hassle his cousin who ran the big scrapyard in Fife. One way or another, they'd rattle Dick. As far as the police were concerned, his time was running out fast.

In February 2000, Nat Fraser's lawyer negotiated a reduction on his attempted murder conviction. The charge was commuted to assault to the danger of life and it was a concession by the Crown that depended on Nat Fraser pleading guilty – which he promptly did. They say there is no plea-bargaining in the UK – that our legal system is superior to the American equivalent because a guilty party can't negotiate their sentence. It's a fallacy. Every day, in every court, in every town in the UK, deals are struck which inevitably affect the sentences that are doled out. Nat Fraser didn't receive special treatment. His was a very ordinary, everyday situation.

On the 3rd of March 2000, Nat Fraser was sentenced to eighteen months in jail and sent off to Porterfield Prison in Inverness. Some will say he got off lightly for a serious assault on a woman, a woman who had mysteriously disappeared within weeks of him committing the crime. No doubt his lawyer did a great job in representing him and getting a much lesser sentence than he could have expected if he'd been found guilty of attempted murder. Other people also thought he had got off lightly. After the trial, Arlene's sister, talking to the press, demanded, 'Come on, be a man and tell us where she is buried.'

But, if Nat Fraser was feeling that luck was turning in his favour and his troubles were nearing an end, he had a pal that was a very worried man and whose troubles seemed just to be starting.

On the 22nd of June 2000, Hector Dick was charged with attempting to pervert the course of justice in particular relation to the beige Ford Fiesta. After all his denials about the car, the cops reckoned they had him now. Kevin Ritchie, who had sold him the car and delivered it to him on the night before Arlene went missing, had gone to meet him again, this time carrying a police wire. Ritchie wasn't easily persuaded. For a young bloke who was reputedly handy with his fists and boots, Ritchie was frightened of Hector Dick. Since Arlene had disappeared, more and more Elgin folk would admit privately that they were terrified of Dick. Was this because of Arlene's disappearance? Or had they always been scared of the man?

A farmer who specialised in pigs, ran a coal merchant's yard and would hire himself and digging equipment out when there was a decent wage, Hector Dick led a very ordinary life for that part of Scotland.

He dressed in his working gear of boiler suit and long leather jerkin most of the time, even when socialising. In conversations that weren't about his work, he was slow to respond. He lacked the quick wits and easy turn of phrase that are normally the trademarks of gangsters and street fighters, making him the opposite of those who engender a cautious reception from the public. But, in private, Elgin people would say he was 'unscrupulous', 'greedy', 'sneaky' and 'determined', especially where money was concerned. Whether he had earned such reactions or not, Hector Dick was already a much-feared and reviled man in his community.

Kevin Ritchie was in all sort of trouble with the cops – trouble that could have made his life very difficult indeed. So he went against Hector Dick and handed the police the evidence they needed.

Dick had repeatedly denied any knowledge of the beige Ford Fiesta. His wife, Irene, had denied any knowledge of it. The men who worked on his farm had denied any knowledge. Dick had even instructed his lawyer, Ian Cruickshank, to make the public statement saying, 'Neither Mr Dick nor anyone connected with his business has any knowledge of the car.' That had been in December 1998. The denials from Dick ran on through all of 1999. Now, at last, he had been charged – at least in relation to the beige Ford Fiesta. People assumed there was no smoke without fire and were asking why Hector Dick had openly and blatantly lied about that car. Why should he lie if the vehicle hadn't been involved in Arlene's disappearance? And, if he could lie about a motor, what else was he lying about?

Hector Dick was in big trouble. But first they would leave him to sweat.

9

NEW BOY AND OLD LAGS
MAY 2001

Nasty stinks and constant noise – that's what hits you first about a prison. With two prison officers marching behind me, I looked around trying to size up just what sort of company I had joined. There were few people about. Some stared, others ignored me – just another con being locked up.

'This one,' indicated one screw, halting me in my tracks at a cell door. One officer pulled up a huge bunch of keys at the end of a chain attached to his belt and unlocked the cell door. As he did so, a whiff of body odour and stale air came out and filled my nose. The inside of the cell was almost in darkness, the strong light of summer blocked out by some material draped across the small window. On the bunk bed against one wall, there was what appeared to be a mess of blankets crumpled on the mattress. It wasn't. It was my cellmate.

My new room-mate was from Ghana and his skin was that deep, true black. No wonder I hadn't noticed him till he stood up.

'You're on the top bunk,' said one prison officer.

'A very astute observation,' I thought, laying down my carrier bag holding my worldly goods on the bed and proceeding to spread out my sheet. It had a tear in it and I cursed under my breath knowing the hole would get bigger and more uncomfortable every night.

The cell had a TV in it, a luxury I didn't expect, a kettle and that bloody open toilet in the corner, just sheltered from the room by a partition, for all the good it did. That was going to be a problem since this time I shared the small room. Handing me some coffee, sugar and a few tea bags one screw told me, 'You have to make your own fucking drinks.' Like what did he think I expected? Room service? 'And recreation is in thirty minutes, Lucas,' he finished off.

By the time I had rigged up my sparse bedding and hung a few of my clothes on the end of the bed to stop them getting totally creased in that plastic bag, it was time for recreation. Out in the corridor, I had my first sight of the other inmates. Now I was really starting to shit myself.

Young blokes, barely adults, walked past with glazed eyes and pinhead pupils. Clearly out of their boxes on some type of dope. A few older guys, ancient scars creasing their faces, trailed thin blue fumes of smoke from their roll-ups sticking to their lips. A clutch of black blokes, none of whom seemed to be with each other or talking to anyone. Three diminutive Chinese yapped away amongst themselves twenty to the dozen. I hadn't anticipated such a mixed bunch. I was hoping to get some signs as to which might be the most dangerous cons, the ones to avoid at all costs, but they all looked dodgy to me.

While on remand, prisoners can choose to wear their own clothes. Some were in expensive tracksuits, others in jeans and T-shirts but a higher percentage than I'd have thought were dressed from head to toe in prison-issue gear. I mean, who would opt to wear such crappy-looking clothes that had been worn by God knows how many others? Instinctively, I decided that the last group couldn't have much money so were unlikely to be the nastiest gangsters. Then I thought of me and of how I'd been brought to that jail with only the clothes I was wearing – if I wanted a change of clothes, I'd be forced to don the prison kit unless someone from home made a wardrobe delivery and soon. So the gear was no guide really. The mixtures of colours and styles made it look like nobody fitted in together or belonged in that place. That kind of sums up what being on remand means. It's a place where anyone and everyone can find themselves in, where nobody really seems to belong – apart from the uniformed staff, that is.

No sooner had I arrived at the recreation area when a minor squabble broke out between two men. The halls were immediately cleared and we were all ordered back to our cells. Shortly after that, my cell door was banged shut and locked from the outside. It was going to be a long night.

The television was on and my cellmate huddled in bed under his blanket and what looked like a mess of rags but which must have been his clothes. He was constantly drawing on a cigarette and filling the small cell up with a rank fug of stale smoke. I'd soon learn that would be how I would see him most of the time – sprawled back, a blanket covering his head, apart from his eyes, which were constantly watching the flickering set. We were going to be stuck in the same confined space for at least a week. So I decided to try to get to know him.

'How are the staff in here then?'

Nothing.

After a while I tried again. 'Is the food any good or is it the usual canteen shit?'

Nothing.

I wasn't going to give up that easily. 'So, do you know anyone else in here?'

Nothing.

Sod that. Maybe he couldn't speak English. Maybe he was deaf. Maybe he was a racist. Whatever, I was just going to lie in my bunk and watch the TV. What else do you do in a barren cell with no paper, no books, no other option?

The news came on Grampian, the independent TV channel covering the north-east of Scotland, and, sure enough, there was coverage of my arrest and appearance in court in connection with the alleged murder of Arlene Fraser.

'Fuck's sake,' came the voice from boyo in the bottom bunk, 'you look like that big cunt on the telly.' So he could speak, hear and had a sound grasp of English.

'That's because I am that big cunt, you prat,' I replied.

I thought that was the ice broken between us but my cellmate had other ideas, quickly returning to silently watching the TV. Worse that that, the bugger had his mitts on the remote control and wasn't for relinquishing it. As soon as I was getting interested in some programme the bastard would change the channel. What was this? Some type of added torment? Like the prison staff had put me in with this git, knowing what he was like? What was I supposed to do? Challenge him? I didn't know if he was in for murder, rape, torture or what. And, until I did know, I was going to leave him well alone and let him play with the bloody telly.

I had no option but to crawl into bed and try to sleep but, immediately, my brain flooded with thoughts and worries. And anger. 'What the fuck am I doing here, stuck in a stinking box with some dysfunctional character for company? Who knows what that saddo in the bottom bunk is up to? What the fuck might he do if I nod off to sleep? And I'm innocent. Yet I'm here. Some bastard is going to pay for this big time.'

It wasn't as restful as counting sheep. Or even lock-ups. The more I blanked off and tried to sleep, the more fear and fury filled me. 'What's the point of trying hard? My family have done nothing but graft and try their best. My old man was forty years in the services, worked his way up the ranks to be a major in the Royal Marines. Fought in Italy and North Africa during World War Two and God knows where else after that. Then, when he retired, he did his bit in local government as a councillor – a Tory councillor, of course. He was even given the MBE. I'm the black sheep of the family but what I mean by that is that I didn't go to university, can't stand fools and used to shag around a bit. That's as bad as our family ever get yet I'm here because some bloody cops have decided that I'll be here.'

I moved my foot to get more comfortable and the tear in the sheet ripped wider. 'Bastard!' I spat out loud and continued with my inner ranting and raving. All the while I smelled the bedding and it smelled rank. The stench made me imagine all the men who had been here before picking their arses and masturbating in their lonely cribs. All night I held the sheet off my body till sleep caught me unawares and I nodded off and my arms would drop. Then I'd waken with a disgusted, frightened start and lift the sheet away from me again. It was how I slept that night and every night in prison.

The next morning they allowed us to lie in late – well, it was late for me. I'm more used to pre-dawn wake-ups. Breakfast – a bowl of cereal, some toast and tea – had to be collected from a central point on the gantry and then eaten back in the manky cells.

Allowed to organise and pay for a morning newspaper, I promptly did so and I got an extra one for my cellmate. It was a small act, the kind I'd respond to with gratitude. Another effort to reach across the divide. All I got from him was more silence. I never felt more lonely in my life.

It was dread time – I was allowed a shower. By then, I'd looked around me with a clearer head. There were some real evil-looking men in that wing. The cops' threats and warnings came flooding back to me. 'Watch out in the showers,' they'd said, 'especially the showers.' This was the place I was most likely to get raped or stabbed apparently. The other problem was my eyesight. Without my glasses I was almost blind, vulnerable as hell. What should I do? Not wash? No chance. I hadn't showered since I was arrested four days before. I was feeling dirty and greasy and it made me feel like crap. A good wash would lift my spirits and make me feel more like myself again.

A short queue had already formed at the shower room. What the hell do I do? Stand around and become some sitting target. That was how I felt. Exposed. Only one thing to do. 'Mind if I nip in?' I said in my most pleasant tone.

'No problem,' said the guy at the head of the queue pleasantly enough but God knows what his expression was like since, glasses-less, I couldn't see his face. I thanked him and went for it. Sure enough, all I could see were shadowy outlines shrouded by steam. No matter, the hot stream of water was delicious. Mind you, it was the quickest shower on record and I was dried and out of there in a jiffy. I had survived without a buggering or a knifing. Maybe those cops were totally winding me up after all.

Unlike convicted prisoners, you don't have to work when you're on remand. It's something to do with you still being innocent till proven guilty. It was the only part of my experience so far that seemed to be about that ancient legal principle. Instead, you are either confined to your cell or in association – that is, with the other prisoners.

Milling about among the other men, speaking only when spoken to, I spent a quiet, though nervous, first day at the jail. It gave me a chance to look about and take in what and who were around me. I was amazed at the range of tattoos from very elaborate, expensive dragons or spirits spread across a man's entire back to rough hewn, painful looking homemade jobs declaring LOVE and HATE on knuckles, MUM on forearms or, more often, CELTIC or RANGERS. There was even a natty red one declaring THE SHEEPSHAGGERS, the colour and nickname of the local football team, Aberdeen FC.

Soon I worked out that, as with the quality of clothes, an expensive tattoo was no indication of status, wealth or potential threat. The guys who were the real players didn't show off and wore standard denims with T-shirt or polo-shirt tops. Nor were they loud like some of the blokes. They just watched what was going on and made sure they and theirs were OK. When they needed to intervene or pull someone up, they did so with a quiet word, sometimes just a look, and it was sorted. And, as far as I was concerned, they were welcoming guys.

'Want to play pool, big man?' one con asked me. What was going on here? In serious danger of looking a twat because I couldn't play the game well, I weighed up the protocol of agreeing or declining. Not being able to work it out, I went for it. 'So what you in for, big man?' the same inmate asked.

I worried that they might take that line of treating me as a woman murderer. Along with child abusers, sods who have done that get hell from the other men in jail and quite right. I just didn't want to be mistaken for one of the evil bastards so I held my breath and started to explain. But there was no grief coming my way – perhaps because I was charged with attempting to pervert the course of justice rather than murder. Then again, some declared they weren't convinced that Arlene was actually dead.

'How can they be so sure she's snuffed it,' said one, 'with no body and no forensics?'

I couldn't have put it better myself.

They all knew about Arlene being missing, of course. The whole case had been big news in the north-east of Scotland since that fateful day in 1998. Maybe that helped since everyone had their own theory about what happened to Arlene or what Arlene did. Soon there was a big discussion going on around the pool table. The ice was broken and I was in.

It was right for me to worry about jail but I needn't have. Prison was like any other gathering of men with good and bad, strong and weak, addicts and keep-fit enthusiasts and every other shade of humanity. When one of the officers came along and asked me to fill in a form for what I'd want to eat the next day, that sealed it. Every day of my childhood at public school, I had done exactly the same thing. Even the food tasted much the same. Already I was beginning to feel at home.

They were a mixed bunch. This greasy fucker kept going on and on, complaining about being inside. He had a sandwich shop that was selling cannabis and he got done when someone informed on him. Seemed straightforward to everyone but him. 'Grassed for selling grass,' laughed one young con when sandwich man was bemoaning his predicament for the umpteenth time. Another young bloke was in for managing to defraud some big oil company of £550,000. Now that was impressive.

There was a handful of tall, strong-looking black guys who kept themselves to themselves. They would all carry these little notebooks and spend hours on the phone – setting up deals, I reckoned. Later, I'd find out they were involved in trafficking crack cocaine into Aberdeen from Birmingham.

Nobody seemed interested in the Chinese men but I was. After a bit of strained social chit-chat, it was obvious their English wasn't great. They faced being deported and had to write to people and agencies to fight the action against them. It was obvious that their written English was even worse than their spoken English so I became their official letter writer.

Other blokes told me that my cellmate was in for something minor and that his main hassle was the efforts being made to return him to Ghana. Just an antisocial sod then who was constantly bumming biscuits, paper, stamps off me – a bit of a pain but nothing to worry about.

One bloke they did warn me about was Willie Johnston. Even the prison wardens told me not to go near him. He was a big-time player in Aberdeen and was in for offences to do with violence. Actually no one ever told me precisely what he was being charged with. It was as if they didn't need to. Everyone should have known about Willie Johnston apparently. He looked like a serious player. Handsome in his day, some old war wounds on his face made his demeanour as rough as fuck and a serious, confident manner told me this was a man who had earned the right to be scared of nobody.

After a few days, I was sitting at a table in the recreation area when Willie Johnston sat beside me and said hello. What do you do? Ignore him? I reckoned that would be inviting his wrath more than anything else so I responded and the next I knew we were chatting. Johnston had heard about the case, of course, and knew what I was charged with. He had his views on the whole saga, including what had happened to Arlene and what he thought Nat was or wasn't up to. We spoke for ages and, the next day, found ourselves together again. He relaxed with me and talked about his own case. He reckoned he was going to get off by blaming his partner. Then we were talking about our families and he shared my anger at what had happened to Maya. He talked a lot about his own family, constantly reassuring himself out loud that they would be OK. They seemed to be his biggest concern – his family. At the time, I couldn't tie this in with the fierce gangster he was meant to be. Now I know better – most of his ilk put their families first.

Willie Johnston was a bright man with an extensive knowledge of current affairs, sport and so on. An articulate voice emanated from that rough, forbidding face. It seemed to me that here was a waste of a man who could have made something of himself rather than living a life of crime. Then he went and spoiled it all by talking about how to stab, disembowel, burn and kill people – tricks of his trade, I suppose. At least I was being educated in topics the public-school system didn't touch.

I was to go on to learn that Johnston, along with his friend, David Kennedy, had been charged with killing a bloke called George Simpson by punching, kicking and stabbing him repeatedly. Worse, the attack was said to have had no motive. It's the dread crime. We all fear that, some dark night as we leave the pub or somewhere, someone is going to jump us and end our lives in a bloody fashion.

Later on, in March 2002, Willie Johnston constantly delayed his trial at the High Court in Forfar by sacking his lawyers time after time before eventually deciding to represent himself. His approach had caused there to be a retrial and added an extra £1 million to the costs of the proceedings. It had such an impact that the Lord Advocate Colin Boyd QC made a formal statement after the trial, blaming Johnston for all the procedural difficulties.

From the outside, it must look as if Willie Johnston was disrupting the trial out of pure badness. Knowing him as I do now, I reckon he had good reasons for every move. He felt he was not being represented properly. At one point, the prosecution made a letter available indicating that he had been in jail before – strictly against the rules as such information could be deemed prejudicial. If Willie Johnston thought he wasn't getting a fair trial, he wouldn't stand for it – plain and simple.

Whatever the impact of his shenanigans, Johnston didn't falter from his not guilty plea. He had been friends with Simpson, the victim, and claimed, as he had revealed to me in jail, that he had heard his co-accused and Simpson argue and then saw the latter slump to the ground. But it was all to no avail – Willie Johnston was sent down for a minimum of fifteen years.

My friendship with Willie Johnston had unexpected social consequences for me. To put it bluntly, no one in the prison dared cross me. There was a greater social distance around me but it was polite. Those cons who had been friendly remained friendly but the ones who would yelp on about being set up or the others who constantly tried to welch on deals they'd made with other prisoners backed off. Though I had only started out by being sociable, the fact that Johnston and I clicked at some level now made me feel as safe as safe could be in that jail. Thank you very much, Willie Johnston.

Apart from my loss of liberty and the charges hanging over my head, there was only one part of jail I struggled with – having a private shit. The only toilet available to me was in my cell. With my cellmate a constant feature on that bottom bunk, I could not and would not sit there in open view and have a crap. So I had to devise a plan.

There was no point politely asking him to leave the cell. He maintained this habit of ignoring anything I said to him, only speaking when he had something to say which usually involved asking for something. I'd sit and wait for him to leave the cell but he'd just flop down on his bunk, cover himself up and flick on the TV.

Then I thought I had hit on the solution. Even if he hurried his shower, as I had that first day, it takes a good ten minutes to get showered and back. But I soon discovered the trouble with this plan – he didn't take a shower, a fact that was emphasised by his increasingly strong body smell, a bit like a wet dog or even a horse lathered with sweat.

The whole bloody business was getting me down – not to say screwing up my guts. Then I clocked the only time he ever left the cell. It was at the beginning of recreation or the exercise in the yard. Next time recreation was called, I waited till we were all in the designated area and then told the nearest screw I needed a piss. They just let me go back to the cell. With each movement on that solitary pot, the relief grew – talk about having a weight lifted from you. Shitting on schedule – that's how it had to be every time.

Within a few days, I realised that prison was no threat to me.

105

Perhaps I had been too well trained in the regimes of the public schools. Perhaps I landed lucky in terms of the other inmates. Perhaps it was the help of the prison staff who were genuinely supportive. Whatever it was, I could take as much of jail as they wanted to throw at me but I really didn't want to spend a second longer than necessary there. Maya was abandoned in deepest Russia, my house had been pulled apart by the cops and I was facing serious charges in a major murder investigation.

I had to get out. And quick.

TRAPPED AND TAPPED

FEBRUARY 2001

By Christmas 2000, Nat Fraser was home from jail. As he strolled around the Elgin shops with his sister, Lynn, local folk thought he looked pale, drawn and worried. Most Elgin people have had no experience of prison and wrote off his sombre mood to the effects of that place. True, he didn't like jail – in fact, he hated it, as most people do – but he had buckled down, behaved and got maximum remission. Although he served only nine months, that was long enough in anyone's book. But Nat Fraser was worried about something else – going back to prison soon.

Nat Fraser had been caught out – not for murdering his wife, Arlene, but for cheating. And, this time, he hadn't been caught cheating on her with other women – it was that other weakness of his, money, that had proved his downfall.

If you asked the people of Elgin, most of them would seem to think that Nat was one of the richest businessmen in the town. When the rumours of Arlene seeking a divorce settlement of £250,000 were running through the houses, no one was surprised. It was far too large a sum of money for the majority of them to be able to scratch together but most believed that Nat Fraser had that and a lot more. But, actually, Fraser was close to being broke.

Arlene's family let it be known that she wasn't good with money. What they meant wasn't that she was bad at budgeting but that she didn't really understand how it worked. So Arlene put up with accepting

£60 per week housekeeping money on the promise that Nat would pay the mortgage – a non-existent mortgage, so they said. From that same source came the rumours that Nat was dealing in stocks and shares and, at one time, he had advised Arlene's family to invest in diamonds. But those close to Fraser knew differently.

While Nat was in prison, Glenn Lucas had helped relaunch Taylor & Fraser, the fruit and veg company. The company had suffered badly due to adverse publicity from the Arlene investigation and, to get away from the tarnish of being associated with it, Taylor & Fraser needed a new identity. Ian Taylor and Glenn Lucas came up with the name Speyfruit. Those who only picked up that snippet were curious to know who the 'Mr Big' behind Speyfruit could be. There was talk that, whoever he was, he might be taking over the company and that Nat's partner, Ian Taylor, having been unhappy with the impact of the Arlene investigation on the business, might be trying to edge Nat out. In truth, Glenn Lucas was a much more common figure around Elgin than the mysterious 'Mr Big' tag suggested. But it was also true that it was the beginning of the end of the business partnership between Ian Taylor and Nat Fraser.

From the time Arlene disappeared in April 1998, Glenn Lucas had done as much as he could to support Nat and Ian. When Nat hit the skids and ended up in jail, Glenn Lucas tried his best to help the Fraser family as well as the business. He was a friend and believed that was what friends did.

Taylor & Fraser had had their troubles in all sorts of ways. Rumours buzzed round the town about a room at their warehouse being kept as a shagging pad. Then one of their workers was exposed as a convicted rapist. Alan 'Sheepie' Johnstone was only twenty-eight years old but he had already served five years in jail for his part in the gang rape of a young woman in an Elgin car park in 1995. It was a horror assault that nearly ruined the young woman's life. Now Johnstone was delivering fruit and veg for Taylor & Fraser. The work often entailed visiting shops and some homes where he'd meet women on their own. He'd only been taken on to cover for Nat Fraser while he was in prison.

The media and local people were outraged and somehow tied the young man's criminal record into Nat Fraser's reputation as a womaniser. As soon as the news broke, Ian Taylor phoned Glenn Lucas in a panic seeking urgent advice. Lucas penned a letter reassuring staff and the public that the company would take every step to ensure their safety and advising them that Alan Johnstone had been sacked – as indeed he had. The prospect of a business calamity had been averted but, once again, the public's perspective of Nat Fraser had been spiced up.

Nat Fraser was barely scratching a living with Taylor & Fraser, his fruit and veg company. Compared to his partner, Ian Taylor, Nat wasn't that interested in money. Ian owned some property, including flats in Aberdeen which he rented out. He had a pleasure boat down on the coast and was forever exploring other ways of making his fortune. Ian Taylor worked hard at making cash but Nat was content to work at the one business and play his guitar. He was so laid back that he and Ian quarrelled on numerous occasions about the lack of effort he was putting into the business. However, when Nat was inside, Ian made sure that his wages went to Nat's mother, Ibby, to care for his youngsters, Jamie and Natalie. Despite this, Ian was getting the impression that Nat expected more and there was trouble brewing in their partnership.

When Nat needed legal representation to fight the attempted murder charge, he pled poverty – literally. His lawyer filled in the requisite forms and applied for Legal Aid on his behalf. Nat got Legal Aid and the case went smoothly. But he had lied about his income and now he had been caught out. Nat Fraser was in trouble again.

Fraser wasn't alone. In January 2001, his pal, Hector Dick, was going to court to face a charge of attempting to pervert the course of justice over possessing and keeping the beige Ford Fiesta that the cops reckoned had been used in connection with Arlene's disappearance. Dick pled not guilty and was set to go for trial at Dingwall Sheriff Court. It was a court beyond the jurisdiction of Grampian Police and many miles further north of Elgin. It was an effort to make sure the jury wasn't biased. There was no one in Elgin, where the trial should have happened, who didn't have an opinion about Arlene Fraser and Dick's part in her disappearance.

The car had never been found and no one around the farm at Mosstowie had admitted ever to having seen it. At the trial, Hector Dick's wife, Irene, used her legal right as his spouse not to give evidence against him. Why did she do that if she had been telling the truth all along and knew nothing that would incriminate her husband? But another party didn't have that legal luxury – Kevin Ritchie.

Ritchie revealed that, at the time, he worked in a scrapyard, Williamson & Co. He was known in the area as someone who bought and sold second-hand cars. Dick had phoned him from a call box on the 27th of April 1998, saying that he needed a car and fast. The car must have a boot but just an ordinary, cheap, everyday car would do, as long as it was legal and reliable.

Ritchie knew of a couple of cars available for a few hundred quid but didn't think he would be able to get them on time. That night he went over to see Dick and, while he was there, Nat Fraser came in. Dick motioned to the young man not to mention the car in front of Fraser. 'I need it for going down the road,' Dick said – as if that explained anything.

Later that night, Kevin Ritchie had a choice of two cars – a Volvo or a Ford Fiesta. 'Just buy whatever is handiest,' the farmer had replied when asked which he preferred. Ritchie bought the beige Ford Fiesta, B231 PDY, from Elgin man William Cabrera then drove the car over to Dick's farm at Mosstowie. The pig farmer seemed pleased with the car and, along with Ritchie, he drove it to a shed where they parked it, leaving the keys in the ignition. When back at the farmhouse and Dick was paying Ritchie the £400 they'd agreed for it, he gave Ritchie an extra £50 – an unusual gesture for a man renowned to be tight with his money.

'Don't mention the car to anyone,' Dick said as he handed over the extra £50. Then he added, 'Don't tell Nat.'

The next day, the 28th of April 1998, Arlene Fraser went missing.

A couple of weeks later, Hector Dick started visiting Kevin Ritchie at his workplace, Williamson's scrapyard. Many weeks after Arlene disappeared, Dick visited with one of his Fife cousins and told Ritchie that the car had been done away with though didn't explain how, where or when. Young Ritchie didn't ask, didn't want to know. Somehow the double-headed visit spooked Kevin Ritchie and he told his wife he wouldn't be doing any more deals with Hector Dick or, to be precise, he said, 'He's no fucking chance.'

Two weeks later the cops raided Ritchie's house and arrested him in connection with the abduction and murder of Arlene Fraser. He was terrified. They kept him in police cells for three days and constantly interviewed him haranguing him about,

'Nat Fraser . . .'

'Ford Fiesta . . .'

'Arlene . . .'

And, especially, 'Hector Dick . . .'

Suddenly Hector Dick's trial had to be stopped. The prosecution had vital evidence that needed a debate between both legal teams and the sheriff. The jury was sent home. When they returned, they were told they would see and hear some filmed and taped evidence. The cops had filmed Dick talking to another man about the beige Ford Fiesta. They had also convinced Kevin Ritchie to have his van wired for sound when he was going to meet Hector Dick.

Hector Dick's game was finally up. He changed his plea to guilty.

Afterwards, Grampian Police didn't gloat or beat their chests – they complained. Detective Inspector Alan Smith said:

The car has always been our biggest clue and the hindrance we have suffered has, so far, prevented us from solving it. Officers from the inquiry team have carried out exhaustive inquiries throughout the UK, looking for this car. The cost to the public is a major issue but, to us, the real issue is the damage that has been caused to the investigation which cannot be measured.

They had begun looking for the beige Ford Fiesta very soon after Arlene disappeared. For almost all of that time, Hector Dick, his wife and his workers had solidly denied any knowledge of the car. Now he had finally admitted it. Dick's lies had cost the murder team three years.

Arlene's family didn't complain – they begged. Her sister, Carol, said:

Dick could have confessed two years ago but he didn't and must have something to hide. I'm convinced he could tell me where my sister is buried. He knew all about the car yet said nothing. What does he know about Arlene?

It was the question on everyone's mind and a question the cops intended to answer. Outside the court Detective Inspector Smith added, 'There is absolutely no way that this is the end of the Arlene Fraser inquiry.'

In February 2001, Hector Dick was close to being a broken man. His few weeks on remand when first charged with attempting to pervert the course of justice had taught him something new – he was terrified of jail. Given the significance of the car in a major murder investigation, the sheriff wasn't too harsh when he sent him down for only one year. But it would be a year of hell for Hector Dick.

10

FLUFFY WALLPAPER

JUNE 2001

Andrew McCartan, the lawyer the cops had tried to put me off, was spot on. He visited me on my first night in jail. 'You'll have to sit down and record everything you have done on any day possible since Arlene disappeared, Glenn,' he said calmly, in the interview room at Aberdeen Prison.

'That's over three years ago,' I gasped at the enormity of the task.

'I know and it's a huge undertaking but they'll come at you with dates for sure. It's just we don't know which ones yet.'

'I'm in serious trouble,' I said, more of a question than a statement.

'The most serious,' he replied. 'So we have to prepare ourselves for whatever questions that may arise.'

If Andrew meant to put the wind up me, it worked. But he was an experienced man as I was finding out. On the Moray Firth coast at a town called Lossiemouth, a few miles from Elgin, there's a major RAF station. It's been there for years and many of the staff live in the area with their families. As is always the way, the top RAF brass were highly influential figures in the locale. As important people, in charge of a massive unit that brings wealth into the economy, of course they were influential. Most of the staff who got into trouble and faced court-martial tribunals would choose Andrew McCartan as their lawyer for a very simple but important reason. They wanted to ensure impartial representation. In short, he was an outsider. Not being part of the social set, Freemason Lodges or golf clubs that abound in the area, he was free from any influence of the RAF hierarchy. That's how the troops in trouble saw it anyway.

For one woman at least, Andrew was also a great lawyer. She was in the RAF and they sacked her after she became pregnant. Andrew challenged them in court and won her a massive payout in what was to prove to be a landmark case for women serving in the Forces. He probably helped a little to drag the RAF into the modern times as well.

Andrew's reputation as one of Scotland's foremost military lawyers had spread. When I engaged him to represent me, he was also representing a Rwandan accused of genocide during that country's civil war. The accused was an arrogant bastard who kept sacking Andrew and claiming the court wasn't fit to judge him. He was also clearly guilty of some atrocities. It had to be a most uncomfortable, complex position to be in but Andrew stuck it out. He'd laugh and say, 'The guy was charged with killing 300,000 souls and his defence is self-defence. Not easy.' Not half. It seems he believed in that old principle that everyone has a right to legal representation. Something he backed up when he took on the case of a Serbian accused of war atrocities. And, for Andrew, everyone really did have the right to legal representation – regardless of what they were accused of. Andrew McCartan would do for me.

The court had remanded me for seven days. That meant I'd be back in court in a week's time with another opportunity for Andrew to plead my case for release. He didn't see why I shouldn't be released. So far, I had cooperated with the cops in every way. I'd never been in trouble before and he assumed I had a clean record. That was when I shared the story about the cop's death with him.

Years before, when I'd been living and working in Inverness, my personal life was a mess and I had been torn between two women, Anne and Linda. I was living in a caravan with no heating, no water and an outside toilet. Linda lived with her folks, making it extremely difficult to get time alone for a bit of how's your father. When I discovered that Anne was the live-in receptionist at the Muirton Motel in Inverness and her chalet came with central heating, showers

114

and hot running water, there was no competition – selfish young bugger that I was.

One night, we had been out at some dinner dance in Inverness with my uncle from Beauly and his wife. Like the good responsible citizen that I was, I held back on the alcohol and gave them a lift home. Around one in the morning, as I was driving back into Inverness and nearing the Muirton Motel, I spotted a man on the side of the road clearly the worse of wear for drink. On that stretch of the road there were no pavements so I decided to be careful, reduced my speed and gave him a wide berth. Next I know he staggers right in front of me, hits the bonnet and comes smashing through the windscreen. The man was an off-duty cop and he died.

After the ambulance sped away with the poor bloke, the police gave me hell. Where the accident had happened meant that the car was in the middle of the road, on a corner and at night. Thinking of the safety issues, I moved the vehicle into the side of the road. Apparently I disrupted a possible crime scene and they set about threatening to charge me with culpable homicide.

Of course, the cops came after me again and interviewed me time after time. They berated me for 'calmly' going to my work hours after the accident and working as 'normal'. Calmly? Normal? How the hell would they know what I felt?

The whole affair made my life very difficult as it hung over my head for months. The cops wouldn't give me my car back and then, when they did, no insurance company would cover me. Being without a motor in an area like Inverness is a serious handicap.

The police reminded me that, a few years earlier, I had been in police custody. I was up in Beauly at that time and I ran a company called Mother Tucker's Promotions. The idea was to set up dances and discos and make a few quid while I was at it. The most common location was the Phipps Hall in Beauly but we also did Buckie and Inverness. Because of the rural nature of the area and the need to draw people from a wide circle, I used to lay on free buses. For a few weeks running, some drunken rowdies had caused problems on one of the buses so, one night,

I decided to travel on this bus on its return journey from the dance.

When the bus stopped in Dingwall, the inevitable happened and a bit of a fracas broke out. I was stuck right in the middle, trying to calm the whole thing down, when someone slapped me on the shoulder. Instinctively, I turned round and smacked him one on the chops. It was a great punch that sat him square on his arse on the pavement. Big mistake – I had just walloped a cop.

That was me, thrown into police cells for the weekend, charged with police assault. I ended up getting a small fine and thought nothing more of it – that was until I ended up in Aberdeen's Craiginches Prison charged with attempting to pervert the course of justice.

'Though I wasn't charged over the car incident, the Grampian cops are likely to know about both of those escapades, aren't they?' I asked Andrew in the interview room at Craiginches. The two incidents had happened in a region covered by the Grampian Police's neighbours, Highland Police.

'As you know, this is a large geographic area but it has a very small, tight-knit population. I think it is highly likely they'll know all about your past exploits,' he replied.

'Cops have long memories, eh?'

'That's for sure.'

'Think they bear a grudge?'

'Seems to be handed out with the uniform,' Andrew replied.

'Enough to make them charge me with trumped up charges in a murder case?' I was getting very worried again. How the hell do you fight a large police force if their motivation against you is personal?

'Enough to consider you a bad man,' he replied. 'Worthy of suspicion, at least. But, for these charges, they will have more. They must have more about this conversation between you and Nat where you allegedly discussed disposing of bodies.'

'I've told you that didn't happen,' I butted in.

'I know and I believe you,' he replied, ever calm. 'But they'll need

Arlene Fraser. This soft-focus studio picture of Arlene was taken c. 1990.

Arlene with Jamie. Nat and Arlene's son was born in late 1987.

Nat Fraser playing guitar with his band The Minesweepers c. 1991.

A young Glenn Lucas clay pigeon shooting c. 1990.

Nat and Arlene on their wedding day in May 1987 with Nat's business partner, Ian Taylor, as their best man.

Paul McBride QC. Paul was part of Nat's legal team at the trial at the High Court in Edinburgh in January 2003.

Alan Turnbull QC. Alan led the prosecution at the trial at the High Court in Edinburgh in January 2003.

Detective Superintendent Jim Stephen. Jim was in charge of the investigation into Arlene's disappearance.

Glenn Lucas arriving at the High Court in Edinburgh. His well-groomed appearance certainly wasn't typical of most of those standing trial there and the circumstances that led to him being there were pretty unusual too.

Photograph courtesy of PA/EMPICS

Photograph courtesy of Peter Jolly

Nat Fraser. Here Nat is being led hand-cuffed from court to a waiting police van in 2002.

Nat Fraser. The police again lead Nat handcuffed from court. Just seven months after the earlier photo, his hair has turned white, he has lost a lot of weight and he has the look of a very worried man.

Photograph courtesy of Mirrorpix

Arlene's family after Nat's guilty verdict was pronounced. Her sister, Carol Gillies, her mother, Isabelle Thompson, and her father, Hector McInnes, express their relief to the press that Nat has been convicted of Arlene's murder.

Photograph courtesy of Mirropix

Hector Dick with his wife, Irene. Hector's decision to turn Queen's evidence was crucial to Nat's conviction and Glenn's acquittal.

Photograph courtesy of Mirropix

Hector Dick's farm. The farm was the site of several extensive police searches for Arlene's body and clues to her disappearance and the cops brought in all the latest hi-tech equipment to help in the hunt.

Photograph courtesy of Mirropix

Willie Lauder (right). The Dicks offered to look after the old man when his health failed. Hector Dick was a main beneficiary of his estate.

Photograph courtesy of Perthshire Picture Agency

Andrew McCartan's wrecked car. Andrew was Glenn's solicitor. He died following a crash on a lonely country road in circumstances that have never really been explained.

Photograph courtesy of News of the World/NI Syndication

Photograph courtesy of The Northern Scot

Glenn Lucas taking a lie-detector test. Although the results of lie-detector tests have never been admissible in Scottish courts, Glenn felt a lie-detector reading that showed he was telling the truth about not being involved in Arlene's disappearance could only be helpful.

Ex-policeman David Alexander. David claimed that his complaint to his superiors about the way the investigation into Arlene's disappearance was being conducted led to him being taken off the case. He later resigned and spoke publicly about evidence tampering and other dubious aspects of police procedure.

Glenn Lucas in Moscow. Following Glenn's arrest, his partner, Maya, was deported to her native Russia. Glenn went to the British Embassy in Moscow to try to obtain the necessary permission for her to return to Britain.

Maya and her mother. Having been deported from Britain, Maya took the opportunity to visit her home village in the remote Russian region of Stavropol.

Glenn and Maya on their wedding day. After overcoming many obstacles, Glenn and Maya were eventually free to marry and a civil ceremony was held at the Spalding Registry Office on the 8th of October 2002.

Maya Lucas. Looking happy and relaxed, at last Maya was able to settle into her life in Britain with Glenn.

Glenn, Maya and Baby Andrew. Glenn and Maya's first child was born in October 2004. They named him after Andrew McCartan, the solicitor who fought so hard for Glenn and who died so tragically.

to present the evidence in court so they must have something more than a grudge.'

'But what evidence?' I was really frustrated and in despair. Still clinging on to the belief that, if they just let us hear the alleged statements on that videotape, I could clear up the mistake in no time.

'I'm sure we'll get that in due course,' he replied.

Andrew McCartan visited me almost every day while I was in prison. While that's bloody good service in anyone's book, it had an added dimension in that part of the country – distance. Andrew lived near Aviemore and had an office in Forres. That was over an hour's drive away, one-way – and not an easy drive at that. So, every time he managed to spare me an hour, it cost him four hours really. I knew all of that and warmed to him. As a result, I opened up more and earlier than I would have with most other men. So I started sharing little snippets from the wider case, things to do with Arlene, Nat and Hector Dick.

I had met Hector twice and then only briefly. According to Nat, I had met him one other time when we had gone clay pigeon shooting with some of the lads from work. We had formed a gentleman's club called the Barnton and District in 1990 and had been on trips to Ireland and Paris and had been on a diving trip up in the north of Scotland. Ian Taylor had organised the clay pigeon shooting and it was only years later that we realised it had been on Hector's land. Whatever, the man hadn't made a big impact on me. When the cops started hammering on Hector's door about that beige Ford Fiesta, I realised that he was more important in this whole saga than I had thought. So I sought him out, making efforts to speak with him.

'This is a really bad situation, Hector,' I had said to him one time on the phone.

'Aye, it is but I'll be all right,' he replied.

'Nobody's safe in this investigation, Hector,' I continued. 'The cops seem determined to convict somebody – anybody – and it looks like we're their targets.'

'Aye, I know but I'll still be all right.' He spoke calmly but insistently. 'I've got something up my sleeve.'

'How's that?'

'Eh, I've got something that'll keep me safe. A right ace card, you might say.'

My curiosity was well fired up now. 'What?' there was no point in being anything other than direct.

'Och, let's just say some papers – that type of thing.' He wasn't for spelling it out and sounded almost coy but very pleased with himself.

'Mmm, that's handy,' I replied. 'But hasn't your place been searched?' I knew the answer.

'Aye.'

'They might come again, you know. It seems they're at Nat's place all the time.'

'Aye, I know.'

'Do you want me to hang on to your papers for you. Find a safe place for them down here?' It was a genuine offer and one made with the best intentions.

'No, no that's all right. Thanks. There's more to worry about up here though. Very bloody worrying.'

'What do you mean?' And I held my breath thinking maybe, just maybe, he knew something about Arlene's disappearance.

'Somebody tried to shoot me.' His unexpected response almost poleaxed me.

'Shoot you!'

'Aye, when I was driving my lorry.'

'No.' I didn't mean no – I meant that I couldn't quite believe this was happening.

'Aye,' he insisted. 'I know fucking guns – been around them all my life.'

'I didn't mean . . .'

'Bullet just whizzed at the cab. Missed me by a couple of feet.'

'For fuck's sake. Who'd want to shoot you, Hector?'

'I think it was that Kevin Ritchie.'

'Who?'

Hector Dick explained that Kevin Ritchie worked in a local

scrapyard and had a sideline of buying and selling second-hand cars.

'Why the fuck would he want to do that?'

'I think the bastard's mixed up with that Ford Fiesta the cops are hunting.'

At the time, I had to give it a great deal of quiet thought. Was this man just fantasising? I didn't know him well enough to make a judgement. But, by that time, everyone knew the cops kept questioning Dick, his wife and his workers about that car. What if the motor did have something to do with Arlene's disappearance and Kevin Ritchie was involved? If Dick was killed, wouldn't the cops decide that their only link to the car had died and call off the search?

It sounded more like a plot from some crime novel. But it wasn't. It was real. Now Hector Dick had been charged with attempting to pervert the course of justice over that beige Ford Fiesta, it was all too real and my lawyer needed to know.

Every time Andrew visited me, I felt more and more that a competent lawyer was handling my case. Whatever was going to happen here, at least I would be represented well. But I had made contact with him simply because he was the duty lawyer the night I was arrested. Imagine if, instead of Andrew that night, some duff solicitor was on duty? What a bloody mess I would have been in.

Confident that Andrew was covering my defence well, I had to find out what was happening with Maya. With the help of my mother on the phone and Rachael, who had decided to stay at her father-in-law's at nearby Nairn so she could visit me regularly, I had a strategy. Well, at least a plan to speak with Maya on the phone.

Maya was staying with her mother, Vera, in a remote, rural community in south Russia near the border with Georgia and Chechnya about eight hundred miles from Moscow. The place was a typical Russian village with hardly any modern facilities. The nearest phone was in a gas station a few miles up the road from Maya's mother's house. That's gas as in what we use for cooking and heating as opposed to what the Americans call petrol and it mainly involved a little old lady sitting watching pressure dials, on the lookout for any hitting the danger marks.

Eventually, after a process that resembled a military operation in its complexity and coordination, I stuck a full credit phone card into the prison call box one night and dialled. I had Maya on the line. At least she was alive and well and still talking to me after all the grief I had put her through. The relief of simply hearing her buckled my knees. Though people told me she had been sent back to Russia, how it happened left me wanting to know for sure. Not having been allowed to see her after my arrest, speak to her before she was deported or know anything at all about her from any official source made me feel that she was missing. She was missing to me. When a person leaves to some unknown place and there's an end to it – they are missing. And it's a horror.

Precisely one minute after saying hello, the card ran out and the phone went dead. A mere sixty seconds was all that we could have. But it would do me for the time being. At least I knew she was alive and where she was. Now I knew where to go to fetch her home.

In jail, it's the emptiness and down time that can be the most destructive. When you're used to an active, varied life like I am, you fill in that void and that's when you can start turning your plans in on themselves. I mulled over whether Andrew McCartan was a good enough lawyer for me. That I liked the man, right from the start, there was no doubt. That he had experience wasn't in question. But should I have hired one of the big names? The guys you read about in the papers all the time like Joe Beltrami, Donald Findlay and so on? What about Glasgow? That place was the murder capital of Europe with the busiest courts in Europe – there had to be red-hot lawyers there who'd be more accustomed to guys caught up in what was clearly a murder investigation. That was the trouble – I didn't know enough about criminal law, I'd never had to. As a result, I didn't know enough about good criminal lawyers.

Another lawyer was playing on my mind, Lord Derry Irvine, my second cousin. Derry wasn't just any old lawyer but the Lord Chancellor, the primary politically appointed legal post in the

120

Westminster government and a close adviser to Prime Minister Tony Blair. In other words, he was the top man. It was my mother's idea to contact Derry. In truth, I had forgotten all about him. He was my mother's cousin and my second cousin – and we were not really that close. But families are families and, when my mother suggested we contact him for advice, I grasped at the idea with enthusiasm. But then I was grasping at any passing piece of flotsam.

Lord Derry Irvine of Lairg – even I have trouble calling him plain Derry now – was steeped in controversy. But this was nothing new to him. As a young lawyer in 1971, he had stolen his best friend's wife, Allison. It happens all the time, of course, but this had complications – his best friend was a bloke called Donald Dewar. Along with Derry, he was a lawyer and a leading activist in the Labour Party in Scotland. Two prominent people in one of the most respected professions in the most powerful political party in a country that is small enough to be half goldfish bowl, half village. It was a very public affair, in other words, but Derry didn't seem to mind that at all.

Donald Dewar was deeply hurt apparently and never married again. Of course, he too prospered politically and became the very first First Minister in the newly devolved Scottish Parliament in Holyrood, Edinburgh. Then the poor sod went and died all of a sudden of a brain haemorrhage. At least they erected a statue in memory of Donald Dewar. I can't see them ever doing that for Derry Irvine.

Love is love and we all pay a price in some way. But wallpaper is mere decoration and Derry even managed to make that controversial. When appointed to the post of Lord Chancellor, Derry was also given a tied house though there the resemblance to a farm labourer's cottage ends. This place was in the Palace of Westminster, right in the heart of London, the most expensive street in the country. Top digs and quite right, some would say, for someone in such an important position.

If he had left it there, the controversy would never have happened. But Derry decided that the place needed renovated and kicked off

with 200 rolls of wallpaper at a cost of £60,000. That's £300 per roll and it was too much for the media at a time when the government were making students pay for tuition, NHS waiting lists were going up, schools were running out of books and Derry himself had publicly slated lawyers for their 'fat-cat' greed.

The wallpaper became a standing joke that wasn't very funny and an open sore for every opposition politician and journalist to poke. They poked it mercilessly. I was on their side. And Derry didn't stop at wallpaper – he bought beds at £8,000 each, £9,640 for a table, brass fittings at a whopping £56,000 and curtains a mere snip at £200 a metre. Never mind the brass fittings, Lord Derry Irvine had a brass neck and survived the almost daily whippings he was getting in the media. Now that might well be a measure of the ability of the man or it could be an indication of just how much he was valued by the Prime Minister.

What did I expect from Lord Derry Irvine, my cousin? Everything and nothing. The notion wasn't to pull strings. Obviously the Lord Chancellor couldn't be seen to be doing that – not even a Lord Chancellor who had courted controversy as he had. However, I must admit that, if I had been offered some kind of dodgy Get-Out-of-Jail-Free card, I would have grabbed it without a second thought. After all, I was innocent and convinced I faced made-up charges in order that the cops could be seen to be doing something in the Arlene case. If they wanted to play that game, then so would I.

There clearly couldn't be any overt pulling of strings but maybe he could offer me or even to my mother some advice just to make sure I was handling the situation in the best possible way. Perhaps he could put me in touch with someone else who would be willing to help on a formal basis – someone who was knowledgeable about the shit hole I had fallen into and the mess poor Maya had been dumped in.

Maybe it's me but, if I heard of a relative, no matter how distant, in trouble, I would make contact to give some moral support, if nothing else, to the family – even if it was only to explain that I couldn't help directly for whatever reason. That kind of reaching

out is part of my world. Is it part of yours? I just think that's how decent folk behave and I had no reason – wallpaper farce and all – to think that Derry Irvine was anything if not decent. Then again, how would I know?

But time for thinking had run out. The following Tuesday, I was to return to the court at Elgin, this time resplendent in one of my smartest suits. My good friend, David Hilton, had gone to my home in Spalding, looked out a full set of clothes and a few items for day-to-day wear and had them couriered to me in Craiginches Prison. At least this time I would look as if I cared.

By the eve of my court appearance, there was still no word from Derry Irvine. I would have to make decisions on my own and with the help of Andrew McCartan who had visited me almost every single day. He obviously believed in my innocence and had worked hard to secure my release. That much I could see. Stuff your Lord Derry Irvine. Andrew McCartan would do for me.

But would he get me out of jail?

GOTCHA

JUNE 2001

Most prisoners, even short-term ones, crave for a day beyond the jail walls. Not Nat Fraser. While he had been serving the eighteen months for the serious assault on Arlene, Grampian cops had come for him.

The police drove him through a busy, buzzing Inverness to the HQ of the Northern Constabulary. Several hours later, he was returned to the jail, having been charged with cheating on his application for Legal Aid. In February 2001, Fraser knew fine well he was going back to prison, even as his pal Hector Dick was being jailed for attempting to pervert the course of justice. Since the investigation into Arlene's disappearance had kicked in, his life had been hell. He couldn't go about his normal life without it ending up in the news. Arlene's parents and her sister were openly accusing him of murdering Arlene and were still fighting for access to Jamie and Natalie. His enthusiasm for work had melted, relations with his partner were at rock bottom and it looked like their business was going to be dissolved. His two young kids had had to be told that he been jailed for strangling their mother. Now he was set to go back to court and return to jail again. No wonder he wasn't happy.

At one point, early in 2001, Nat Fraser realised he had to change how the world saw him or his life would continue to get worse. Almost everyone thought he was a wife murderer. That was the main point but what could he do to prove otherwise?

'I want to take a lie-detector test,' he had said to his lawyer one day.

'But lie-detector tests have no standing in Scots law,' replied his lawyer.

'But they do have in America and elsewhere, right?' asked Nat Fraser.

'Yes, but . . .'

'And people in Scotland believe that they're valid, believe that they work?'

'It still won't help you,' reasoned the lawyer. 'Besides, what if you fail the test?'

'I won't fail the test.' The fact that his lawyer had even raised this as a possibility made Nat Fraser angry. Did no one believe in his innocence?

'It's a test, Nat, and you don't know how it works. It's carried out by someone you don't know.'

'But I'll pass . . .'

'And,' the lawyer interrupted, 'there are very good reasons why they're not accepted in this country's legal system.'

'But . . .'

'I strongly advise you against pursuing a lie-detector test.'

Like all wise citizens, Nat Fraser took his lawyer's advice. But, even as he did so, he wondered if he had made a mistake and if he would ever regret his decision.

In April 2001, Nat Fraser was jailed for one year for cheating on his Legal Aid application. It was the same sentence his friend Hector Dick had received for attempting to pervert the course of justice over that beige Ford Fiesta. That same Ford Fiesta the police had been vigorously seeking for three years. That same car the cops described as the first and crucial clue in the investigation into the murder of Arlene Fraser. The car Hector Dick denied any knowledge of and, by doing so, lost the cops crucial months and years in their hunt for Arlene. Or should that be their hunt for Arlene's body and her killers? Yet Dick's conviction was seen by the court as worthy of the same punishment as Nat Fraser whose crime was defrauding the state of some money.

As he was driven away from Elgin towards Porterfield Prison in Inverness, Nat Fraser sat and pondered over his pal, Hector. They would be reunited soon anyway at the jail but that wasn't what was bothering Nat Fraser. He remembered something that Hector Dick had said many months before. What was it? 'I've got no worries about the cops,' he'd claimed to Nat when the two were alone. 'I've got something over them – something that will embarrass them.' Nat had been sure Dick meant the sale of smuggled booze to a number of them. Dick had claimed that, even while they were putting the heat on him and Nat over Arlene's disappearance, some cops were still coming to his place to buy a few bottles. Nat had been positive that was what he meant but he'd thought he should make sure. 'What's that then, Hector?' he'd asked.

'Show you.'

Dick disappeared through to another room of his home. 'One of them left this,' he said on his return, holding a briefcase up in one hand.

'That's theirs?' Nat had asked.

'Aye. One of their forensic boys left it when they were searching the house.'

'Anything interesting in it?' Nat had asked the obvious question.

'Oh, aye,' Hector Dick had replied. 'Very interesting.'

At that, he had walked out of the room and that had been the last time Nat Fraser had seen the briefcase.

Nat had dismissed the briefcase as Hector Dick acting the big man. He had been aware that his less sophisticated pal had always tried to show off, as if he felt he needed to appear bigger and better in Nat's eyes. He recalled how, when Hector and Irene had first met, he'd give Nat a running tally of how many times they'd managed to have sex. That type of childish thing was typical of what Nat saw as Hector's desire to impress him. So, at the time, Nat had dismissed Hector telling him there was something interesting in the cops' briefcase as just another of his big-man routines – but now he was beginning to wonder.

So, by early June 2001, Nat Fraser, Hector Dick and Glenn Lucas were all in prison. And that suited the cops perfectly – they were about to pounce.

11

SICK AT HEART

JUNE 2001

Court day dawned. This time I didn't have the same optimism of freedom.

I'd now been banged up for eleven days, counting from the day of my arrest. Even after such a relatively short time in the nick, I was beginning to get numbed to expectation and hope. I found that was the best way to approach my circumstances – never expect a result and always assume the worst despite all the while working bloody hard to succeed. Eleven days in jail – OK, that's just the way it goes sometimes. If you didn't get what you had applied for, fine – that's what you expected. If you hit the jackpot, then BINGO. It beats the shit out of moral outrage and retaining the naive assumption that justice always prevails – which would have been my way of looking at things just two weeks before. Now I know that my new approach is exactly what experienced cons do and it worried me about how quickly I cottoned on in that system, how soon I adapted. Did everyone adjust so quickly?

Back in that small wood-panelled court in Elgin, I listened to the cops argue that I should be remanded in jail for three months. Say what you like about Grampian Police, they keep their threats. Andrew argued that I was no threat to anyone, that I wasn't charged with hurting anyone, that I had always cooperated fully with the police and that I was of good reputation. If it hadn't been so bloody serious, I would have interrupted him and told him I wasn't that good.

But we got a result. I was freed on bail to await trial and I was out that door like a shot. A warm smile from Rachael and a firm hand-shake from Andrew and we were on our way.

For two weeks, I'd been writing a statement for just this day. It was a tirade on what a waste of money and lives this all was. I knew I was innocent but, for nefarious reasons, a bunch of plodding coppers had decided to dump me in jail. What had that cost the taxpayer? How many real crooks were going on undetected because these arseholes were wasting their time on me? Wasting my time for what?

In the event, Andrew did a decent though polite job of making my sentiments known. 'The police have forty officers on the case. In the last seven days alone, that equates to about 2240 man hours at an average eight hours a day.' That was the sort of thing he said and the cost of the investigation he referred to wasn't an exaggeration. It was the most expensive operation in the history of Grampian Police. It was so damned expensive that many of the cops had to wait months and months to get their fat overtime payments. But the public would have no problem with the cost if they could see that the police were actually making progress.

Following the post-release statements, some newspapers accused me of going off on a rant. But, they can take it from me, I was biting my lip – being very well behaved. If I had allowed myself to say what I wanted to say, the air in Elgin would still be blue. Of course the real meat of what Andrew and I said wasn't reported anywhere. That didn't bother me much. The cops were the ones who I wanted to hear it. After his longer spiel, Andrew had added, 'Glenn Lucas has been charged by the police in order to cover up the inadequacies of this investigation.'

The cops heard that all right.

The journey from Elgin to Nairn on the Moray coast was lovely. I'd always enjoyed that road but, that day, it was especially sweet. Rachael, my daughter, had made arrangements to stay with her in-laws in that beautiful seaside town so she could visit me regularly when I was in the pokey. It really is when you end up in the shit that you appreciate the people who love you. All my family, even Anne my estranged wife, had been so bloody helpful and caring. Well, not quite *all* my family – since my cousin, Lord Derry Bloody Irvine, still hadn't responded to my mother's messages. But my people had made those eleven days behind bars more bearable in every way. What must it be like for those in jail with no family or whose relatives and lovers desert them?

From Nairn, we drove on to Inverness Airport to get a flight to Luton. Three of us were travelling down and I had to do the honours. But there are no cheap flights when you travel on the day. It's one of the impacts that the so-called criminal justice system is blind and deaf to. They arrest you at your home in the south, drag you all the way up north and then, when you're legally released, you're on your own. It's like dumping you hundreds of miles from home. Thank God for credit cards.

My good pal David Hilton picked us up at Luton Airport. He had really proven himself to be what I knew he was – loyal and ever ready to help. In fact, David probably knows me better than anyone – even better than I know myself in many ways. Yet, to this day, the cops have never gone near him. Dropping Rachael off at her place at Wendover, we headed to Spalding but it was going to be late before we got there.

Approaching the house, I felt spooked, shaken. It was as if I was in a waking nightmare and I was returning to that last time I stood outside my home handcuffed, being led away by two burly cops as, around me, car loads of rozzers prepared to hit my home. At least then, Maya was asleep in our bed still blissfully unaware that her life was about to change dramatically for the worse. A bloody nightmare. If I was the tearful type, I reckon I would have wept my eyes out standing there in front of my home.

The house was neat, tidy and the fridge was stocked with milk and some grub courtesy of my mate David Hilton. Early doors, I met with him to thank him. He didn't want gratitude, of course – he was a friend. But he did tell me what a state he'd found. 'The place was ransacked, Glenn,' he said. 'In every room, everything was disturbed with big items of furniture turned over and abandoned as if raiders had to leave in a hurry. Food was poured out of packets and jars and left scattered over surfaces and trodden into the floor. Fuck knows what they've taken but I'm afraid they've broken a few things.'

The cops had taken quite a list as it happened:

Diaries
Mobile phone
Phone books
Anything with writing on it – Post-It notes, scraps of
paper, instruction books, envelopes
House keys
More keys
Pay slips
P60
Cameras

The list went on and on, from the expensive and essential to the trivial and irritating. They had hassled the poor woman who did my tax returns for me, taken all my bank statements, chequebooks, credit cards and the like. That made getting money an awkward bugger. The bank also made me pay for replacements.

'Do the cops think I hired some hit man,' I grumbled to David, 'and paid them by fucking cheque? How many O levels do you need to become a policeman again?' We laughed at that. As it turned out, I was going to learn it wasn't that funny.

My employers had been great. A couple of years earlier, I'd moved down from Elgin to work in Lincolnshire for a company called Fesa, big nobs in the fruit and veg wholesale game. Fesa stood by me one hundred per cent. While I was away, they didn't dock my wages by one hour. In jail, I received a letter from them with a sheet with handwritten notes of support from all the staff. I knew I'd have to repay it with some new nickname and a hell of a lot of slagging about being a 'murderer' but it was all worth it. That would be their way of saying that they cared. Yet they hadn't had it easy.

Even before my arrest, they had been hounded repeatedly by the newspapers and the cops. The journalists were just doing their job but, when it was revealed I was helping relaunch Taylor & Fraser, they had come on the bell again to my office hoping that they would dish out the dirt. Well, that would have made it a better story. The boss just brazened it out and said that he knew I was friendly with Nat and Ian and said I was perfectly at liberty to help them as long as it didn't interfere with my work.

Fesa got a worse time when I was arrested. That same Friday, the cops swooped on their offices and took over. They searched the place and then removed my computer and the hard drives from several others PCs. Even in 1998, a business like Fesa's was increasingly dependent on information technology. But it was the law, right. I'd brought that down on them yet they didn't blame me at all – they just stuck in there with me, loyal through and through. From most companies, I would have got the sack.

The people at my work weren't the only folk in Lincolnshire to get harassed the day I was arrested. The cops also tracked down and interviewed the woman who had been my cleaner in April 1998. She had been a serving policeman's wife. Talk about nothing to hide. Believe you me, cleaners earn their wages in my place. I just let them get on with it, poke in any corner, and am seldom around when they are. Yet, at the time I was meant to have been somehow implicated in Arlene's disappearance, a copper's wife had the free run of my home.

The cleaner in 1998 was called Anne Gardner and her man was a dog handler. They were very nice people. By 2000, I had a different cleaner and, two days after my arrest, the Scottish press found her and made her life hell for a long while. I've no problem with the media pursuing stories – that's their job, after all – but how did they get this family's details? It could only be from the cops I'd guess – unofficially, of course. We don't pay their wages to pass on juicy titbits that then screw up decent, ordinary people's lives. Or do we?

132

SICK AT HEART

Within a day of returning home, I got on with the task Andrew McCartan, my lawyer, had urged me to fulfil. I was going to try and identify accurately what I was doing, where I was and who I was with for almost every day since the 28th of April 1998. Difficult enough as that sounds, the cops had also tied one of my hands behind my back by removing every phone book and every scrap of paper with every number, as well as my mobile phone. These days you are dramatically cut off when you lose all your phone numbers. Crucially, in this exercise, they had also removed all my diaries.

I didn't keep a diary as such but I was good at using the pages to make a note of appointments, social as well as work-related. That would have made the job a lot easier. The search party hadn't removed other things like my football programmes.

Where football's concerned, I'm a fanatic. I can recall off the top of my head results Falkirk FC had against some run-of-the-mill team in a meaningless end-of-season league fixture from years before. For most of my adult life, people have ribbed me about my support of Falkirk. My fascination with the game and willingness to travel north many hundreds of miles at least every second Saturday had some folk calling me a saddo, geek or anorak – as if supporting that team was the equivalent of trainspotting or stamp collecting. Believe you me, it's a lot more nerve-racking than that.

But my undying support of the bold Falkirk was to come to my rescue. Saturday away to Stranraer – oh yes, I remember that game. Alloa at home – easy meat, we should have scored more goals. Raith Rovers away – I had a couple of pints at that pub at the bottom of the hill I sometimes stopped at. My work schedule, backed up by contracts and sales order slips at work, augmented by my memory and helped by my mother – don't they always? – meant I was getting there. Mum was the type who used to note in a diary when I had phoned, when she phoned me, visits between us and that kind of thing and I'm so glad she did as it really helped and I managed to plot a chart for every day for over three years. It was hard, time-consuming work but I was filling in the days great style. I think the bastards thought they had me but sorry, boys.

133

At least back at home it was easier to phone Maya in Russia though it still had to be orchestrated and planned like some military operation. I also decided to get a pay-as-you-go phone and only call her from that. The cops had more or less admitted that they had been tapping my house line. No way did I want them listening in on our conversations particularly when we were going to be plotting her return and I was certain that the cops would do all in their power to stop us. Pay-as-you-go mobiles are the safest phones if privacy is your concern.

My house telephone line would still be bugged, I reckoned, unless the cops had removed whatever device they had used while they were searching the place. After some inquiries, I was able to get hold of a piece of equipment designed to test for phone taps. The way this worked was that you plugged it in, switched it on and, if a surveillance device was present, one red light would go on. If there were two devices, two lights would shine and so on. I plugged the machine in and the whole bloody thing lit up like a Christmas tree. So no way was I going to be speaking to Maya, Andrew or anybody on that home line.

A couple of weeks after I had been released from prison, I returned home from work one night and noticed my door had been opened. Cautiously I edged into the house. I might be a big man but God knows what or who I'd find inside. Room by room, I checked and found . . . well, nothing. Nothing had been disturbed. Nothing had been taken. The whole place looked exactly as it had when I'd left that morning. It was a puzzle.

I lifted my house phone and called the local cops to report a suspected break in. They were very professional and sympathetic, saying they would visit the next day to interview me and check for fingerprints on the breached door.

Later that night, I couldn't stop thinking about the door. The thought that someone's been in your home when you're out is quite disturbing. Then I got thinking. Andrew McCartan, my lawyer, had warned me that strange things were happening to his mail – but only the mail to do with my case. A number of important packages hadn't arrived, others had obviously been opened and one or two had been delivered to the wrong address. His office was in Forres, a sleepy little town where everyone knew everyone and certainly the postmen would have been certain of the whereabouts of his office.

Andrew was quite clear that he believed the powers that be were up to sinister tricks. He suspected our calls were being intercepted and took to linking up with me from a series of call boxes. He warned me to take great care – that there could be a big price to pay for being caught up in this case . . . the ultimate price.

'And they bugged my fucking phones,' I grumbled out loud to my home empty of anyone save myself. 'Yeah, they did. They bugged my phones.' The penny had dropped. I had the bug tracer out in a jiffy and plugged in. Where there had been a row of bright red lights only the day before, now there were none.

The next day when the cops didn't appear as promised to take fingerprints, I called them and asked what was happening.

'Sorry, Mr Lucas,' said the policeman, 'but we've been run off our feet.' Fair enough and they made another arrangement to come out.

When they didn't keep that arrangement, I called them again. Same type of answer. Another broken arrangement, another call. Same explanation. Even to this day, years later, I'm still waiting for the police to come and investigate that break-in at my house. I guess they are not coming now. I guess they were never coming.

But all that was to come. Initially, I had a bugged landline and I needed to use a mobile phone to call Maya in Russia. Yet the mobile phone lark wasn't as straightforward as it sounded. A standard phone and card cost a bloody fortune. Not that I resented it one iota but I was aware that this trouble had already cost me a fortune and there were going to be hefty bills to come for travel to Russia, lawyers and so on. I just needed to be a bit careful so I could afford any eventuality. I chatted to a couple of my customers who regularly phone their families in India and Pakistan and they were able to suggest the right phone card for making frequent long-distance calls.

So, eventually, I got one that made calling Russia less expensive but it still cost an arm and a leg. Again I was mindful of those who might find themselves in my shoes without a bit of dosh – they'd have been beaten before they started.

In prison, I'd only managed to connect with Maya twice and for exactly one minute on both occasions. Now we could relax more and chat and she told me the whole nasty saga of how she had been deported. Since her return, the stress of the whole affair had made her hair fall out in big handfuls and the weight drop off her by the kilo. I'd been angry a few times over the past weeks but what they had done to Maya pissed me off big time. I was going to get even somehow and the best way to start out was to get my woman back.

In double quick time, I arranged an appointment with a solicitor. As I gave him the whole story, his face visibly blanched and his mouth fell open.

'So,' the lawyer said, well into the meeting, 'let me see if I have this right, Mr Lucas.'

'Fire ahead.'

'You are on bail on serious charges in connection with a . . . what shall we say . . . somewhat controversial murder investigation.'

I nodded my head in agreement.

'And you had known this lady for some . . . two months?'

'We've known each other for four months and we've lived to-gether for two,' I corrected him, at the same realising that even four months didn't exactly constitute a long-term relationship.

The lawyer paused. Rattling his pen against his pad, he seemed to be concentrating hard. Then he resumed, 'This lady, who is Russian, has no right to permanent residency in the UK and has been deported back to her country of origin by the Department of Immigration?'

He paused again while I nodded. Seemed like a fair summation to me so far.

'And you wish to instruct me to ensure her return?'

Yep, laddio had cottoned on. He fiddled with papers on his desk, fanning some yellowish A4 sheets out and then replacing them exactly where they had been before he had picked them up.

'And as soon as possible,' I added. 'I know it will cost but that doesn't matter.' I'd just been reading something in the media about how some lawyers were struggling because of some changes to do with Legal Aid. I wanted to reassure him that he had a paying client here who was perfectly aware that the bill would be substantial and was willing to pay more to hasten Maya's return.

'Quite,' he eventually replied. He didn't look comfortable. 'I'll need to give it some consideration, Mr Lucas. It's a complex matter and the terms are defined by legislation we don't have to visit often.'

I reckoned he was telling me that he'd have to read up on it. Fair enough.

'I'll be in touch,' he said as he stood up and held out his hand to shake, signifying the end of the meeting, 'let's say in a couple of days.'

Next morning I received a letter from the lawyer saying that he wasn't willing to take on the work and thought my chances of success highly remote. The day after that I received his bill for £141.00. So he charged me for saying no – nice work if you can get it.

Over the next couple of weeks two other lawyers more or less gave me the same short shrift as well as similar bills. At least I had the cash to be told to piss off. What does someone in this country in similar circumstances do if they're penniless? Weep with a broken heart, I suppose.

Maya had started to open up more about her worries over the phone. In her lovely broken English, she explained that she held no grudge against me and didn't blame me at all for what had happened. But she had to reconsider whether she still wanted to live in England after being strong-armed out of the country.

This was an enormous turnaround. Maya's father had always loved all things British. He had even given some of his kids English names and taught them how great our political system, our writers, poets and our footballers were – he even followed the cricket scores.

He never wanted to move to England – just for his native Russia to be more like England.

The old man had left his daughter, Maya, with that same enthusiasm and an ambition to live in Britain. Now she had a man here, a home here, a future here but she wasn't sure she wanted to come here. Why? Because our cops and government officials treated her brutally. Remember she was from a state that had suffered generations of pogroms and brutality. Under the old Soviet regime, it was nothing more than a police state – now a lot of it was bandit territory. Yet, sick at heart, she was considering staying there because the UK authorities were too hard.

As I struggled to find a lawyer to do the business and bring my woman home, I was also fighting on another level by trying to convince her that Britain would be a good place to live. With every refusal from every lawyer, I still had to stay ultra-positive with Maya – do my best to reassure her that I could and would make things better for her. She would be safe here – that was my personal guarantee. And, even as I repeated that promise, I knew I wasn't sure if I could deliver. Lately in my life, all the certainties had disappeared – apart from one. I'm a stubborn customer and strong willed. I'd keep going till the bastards took my legs from me and then I'd shout. The one thing I had going for me was strength, of that there is no doubt.

But just then, someone unexpected had run out of strength. Or had they?

A BAD DAY

20 JUNE 2001

It had been the worst of days. Hector Dick was already suffering in prison. Other cons watched him as he moved slowly around the jail, silent, pale, withdrawn. They knew the signs. He was a troubled man. He would jump at the smallest noise. He might well have been troubled but he was also terrified.

One con described a practical joke that went wrong. 'A particular prisoner was well known to be a lazy bastard. He'd always be in the queue for the morning clinic, pretending he had migraines, getting a couple of paracetamol from the quack and spending the rest of his day in bed in his cell.' Jails for long-term prisoners are well known for having more than their fair share of hypochondriacs, especially among the most intelligent and brutal of men. Guys who have carried out daring crimes against all the odds, putting up with huge personal risk and pain to get the loot, are the most susceptible to believing they have a series of major health problems. But jails like Porterfield Prison in Inverness, with its abundance of short-term prisoners, are well known for those who malinger – the ones who knowingly pretend to be ill.

'I was working in the kitchens,' the former prisoner explained, 'along with Nat Fraser, as it happens. He was fine. Not happy, of course – who the fuck is in prison? But his pal Hector was a mess. In fact, though they were pals they didn't really chat much. Part of my job was to take these trays from the kitchen. One day I took a wee diversion past the cell where that guy with the bogus migraine was snoring his head off. Just as I got to his open cell door, I lifted the trays as high as I could and let them drop. What a fucking clatter. I hadn't noticed that Hector Dick was walking towards me, maybe ten yards away. Wouldn't have made any difference to me anyway. But, when the trays hit the deck, I thought Hector Dick was going to hit the roof – never seen a man jump so high before – and he gave out this little yelp like some dog that just had his paw stood on. Funny thing was the noise didn't even waken the lazy bastard lying in his kip. It wasn't that loud.'

Of the basic rules of survival in any prison, not showing fear is high up on the list. Prisons are stuffed full of men who can sense weakness a mile off and will step right up to take advantage. In a jail, there's no hiding place.

'I said to him, "Fuck's sakes, Hector, you all right?" He just stuck his head down and walked past me. But he had tears in his eyes and was mumbling to himself. Things like that were always happening with Hector Dick. In truth, I felt sorry for him back then but now I'm not so sure.'

Hector Dick had been in prison for four months and, by all accounts, they were four months of hell. But, on the 18th of June 2001, life started to get worse.

To the world at large, it seemed that the police action came out of the blue. The current comprehensive reporting of murder investigations con the public into thinking that they know exactly what is going on. But the cops only release what they want to release – officially and unofficially. For the most part, they keep their own counsel.

At Elgin Police Station very early in the morning, the full murder investigation squad of forty bodies were in attendance. All the cops knew what they had to do and where they had to go but it was important that this operation was coordinated properly. This was to be a double-headed raid.

Almost simultaneously, half the squad hit Nat Fraser's house at 2 Smith Street and the other half showed up at Hector Dick's farm at Mosstowie. Both places had been searched several times since Arlene disappeared. But the cops were doing it again and were being as thorough this time as they had been at any time. Something was afoot.

Nat Fraser and Hector Dick heard about the raids on the phone to their families. Then it hit the news. Other inmates would report that Fraser just smiled and shook his head. Later he would reflect, 'They had been in and out of my house for three years. In that time, Jamie and Natalie, Arlene's mother and her man, Arlene's father and his second wife and my mother had all been living there for various periods of time – as well as me, for a while. What did they possibly expect to find? And, if they found something they thought important, who had brought it in? I just wrote that house search off as show – the cops needing to let the world see they were doing something.'

In Nat Fraser's house, the cops ripped up floorboards and sent in dog teams specially trained in finding human remains. The same rigmarole was repeated in Hector Dick's place – except, there, they concentrated on the outbuildings and barns. But why carry out those types of searches now, three years after Arlene disappeared? Weren't they too late? Or had they received new information?

Journalists were just as curious about this new outbreak of action and they put that question to the cops. Head of the investigation, Detective Superintendent Jim Stephen, normally talkative and helpful to the media, was in a different mood. All he said was, 'We will take as much time as we need.' And that was supposed to be that. Except it wasn't.

The day after the searches on the two sets of premises, a police posse arrived at Porterfield Prison, Inverness. Nat Fraser and Hector Dick were escorted, handcuffed, from the jail, locked in the back of police vehicles and driven all the way to the police station at Elgin. That was an hour away – driving to the Northern Constabulary HQ in Inverness would have taken them ten minutes. This was serious business and Grampian Police didn't want to get anything wrong.

Formal indictments, laying charges against the accused, can be long documents. And they are often written in language that makes their meaning completely obscure to those who have no legal training. But, that day, in the police station, the language was simple – they stood accused of murdering Arlene. And there was more – conspiracy to murder, abduction, chopping up her body, removing her teeth and disposing of her. It was a gruesome set of charges and no doubt.

After being charged, as the two men were driven back in separate cop cars to Porterfield Prison, both were deep in thought. Nat Fraser was determined to prepare for what he knew was a challenge that could have him sent away for the rest of his days. He needed a good lawyer.

Joe Beltrami was famous for winning many complex cases against the odds. He had been the lawyer for the Godfather of organised crime in Scotland, the infamous Arthur Thompson, who had a reputation of rarely going to jail. That was all down to Joe Beltrami. The lawyer had also secured a unique royal pardon for Paddy Meehan who had been wrongly convicted of murdering elderly Rachael Ross in Ayr. The lawyer's heritage and class go on and on and merit several other volumes to do justice to him. Let's just say that, from the 1970s into the 1990s, if you asked a streetwise career criminal what they would do if caught bang to rights, they would simply reply, 'Get me Beltrami!'

Nat Fraser got Beltrami.

Hector Dick was silent and morose. He knew then the cops must have clear evidence. People don't get charged with such heinous crimes when the cops don't have evidence, do they? He knew he wouldn't be getting out of jail soon. The pair of them would be kept locked up at least until the trial he reckoned. That was likely to stretch on and on as everything had in the Arlene case. Hector Dick knew little about criminal law and even less about the time limits between being charged and going to trial. Then there was the trial. What did Hector Dick expect to happen at that trial? Did he have the same kind of naive optimism that Glenn Lucas had displayed, thinking that he wasn't guilty and, therefore, he would walk free? Or did he expect to be convicted and sent down for twenty-five years or more? That night, he took his private thoughts to bed.

Early the next morning during a routine check, they found Hector Dick in his cell, slumped on the floor a makeshift noose around his neck. He was rushed to the local Raigmore Hospital and survived.

Had he lain awake all night and, only a short time before being discovered, tried to top himself – or did he know that the routine check on cells was about to take place and chose that time? If so, why? Curiously, the pig farmer hadn't made a very good noose. Those who knew him were surprised. This was a strong man used to working with his hands – he tied knots every day of his life. And he couldn't make a noose?

Almost immediately there was talk around Elgin about why Hector Dick had attempted suicide. A few said it was because he hated jail so much. Others said he was terrified of Nat Fraser. Most said he had a guilty conscience.

But Hector Dick wasn't for telling . . . yet.

12

BEATING THE SYSTEM

JUNE 2001 – OCTOBER 2002

Murder – well, that got the old bottom twitching and no mistake.

It wasn't a surprise as such since, for the past two years, the newspapers had been full of speculation that Arlene had been abducted and killed. Even the cops had come right out and said several times that they now believed Arlene was dead. My little sojourn in the jail, the charges I faced and snippets from the interviews where the cops had mentioned hit men and all sorts of stuff. No surprise but there's a difference between all that brouhaha and a friend and a mate of his actually being charged with murder. Then for Hector Dick to try and do away with himself. That was a wake up call, I'll tell you.

Confession time. The first thing I did was devise Plan B. In almost everything I do, I always have an alternative option since life seems to have a way of not quite working out how you hoped first time around. I can't stand people in business who moan and wail if some deal doesn't come off. Like they had put all their eggs in that one basket and now they were stuffed. Silly buggers.

I'd always held our police in highest esteem but now I was learning fast how incompetent they could be. Opening the drawer where I always kept my passport, there it was – exactly where I had left it. Yet, according to Maya and my pal David Hilton, the cops had turned the house over good style. In fact, they had been so thorough they broke several things including my piano. Did they not want my passport? Or had they merely forgotten it? Either way, I intended to use it.

Do not be in any doubt – if this case looked like it was coming down against me and I was facing years in jail, I would have been off. I would have slung some gear in a case, lifted all my cash and been in the Republic of Ireland within hours. It wasn't a case of right and wrong – it was about survival.

On hearing the news of the murder charges and Hector's failed suicide attempt, I belled my lawyer Andrew McCartan right off. There was nothing new in this since Andrew had been in touch with me regularly. On this occasion, the advice I was seeking was obvious – HELP!

My lawyer was his usual calm, cool self. 'Just because Nat and Hector Dick have been charged doesn't mean that the police have a strong case against them.'

'But surely they would never be charged with murder, for fuck's sake, unless the cops had evidence – concrete evidence.'

'No? And what about you? How you were charged?' Yet another reason Andrew McCartan was growing on me more and more was that he obviously accepted and believed I was innocent.

'True enough but I'm not charged with murder.'

'Glenn, you have been charged with a very serious offence and it's now clearly tied in to a murder case.'

He was telling me what I already knew. I suppose, like most folk, I was just trying to adopt the stance that other folk – in this case, Nat and Hector – were in bigger shit holes than I was. Why is it that we find this so comforting?

'What about that so-called evidence against me? That video of Nat and me talking?'

'I haven't got it yet but I'm doing my best. One more thing though, Glenn, I don't think you should speak to Nat Fraser while this is going on.'

'Why? He's my pal.'

'I know but the two of you are too closely implicated in this case. Besides, you don't know what he might say. You might be . . .'

'Compromised?' I finished off his sentence for him

'Yes, compromised.'

Much as it pained me, I didn't talk with my friend, Nat Fraser, over that long period and nor did I have contact with his family or any mutual friends. I'd heard the message loud and clear from my lawyer that I was in serious trouble. As far as I was concerned, I would follow his instructions right down the line. Anyway, I had other business to attend to – getting Maya home.

There was a little extra complication in bringing Maya back into the UK – well, two complications really. She and I were both separated from, but still legally married to, other people. We had both been separated from our former spouses for years but just hadn't got round to getting divorced. So, when I had quickly ascertained that the easiest way to get her back would be under a fiancée visa, this presented a bit of a problem.

My first call to the British Embassy in Moscow opened my eyes. It wasn't just that they were polite and helpful but they could tell me more about my criminal case than my own lawyer had been told back here. Clearly the powers that be were communicating with each other. That meant only one thing to me – they were ganging up to ensure that Maya would stay where she was. I was going to have to beat the Home Office, the Foreign Office, Grampian Police and God knows who else.

Certain papers would need to be delivered to the British Embassy in Moscow. The quickest and safest way to do that would be to have the package delivered to her in Georgia then for her to set off on the 1,600-mile round trip to Moscow. Sitting working in my lounge one night with the TV on for background noise, I spotted the advert for DHL. It emphasised how they delivered, fast, guaranteed and door-to-door, all over the world. That would do me nicely.

Next day I handed over my parcel and paid my forty quid, checking again that they could deliver to that part of Russia. No problem apparently. One week later they returned the package saying they didn't deliver to the Stavropol region where Maya lived

– nobody did, they said. Buggers didn't even refund my dosh but much more important was that I had just lost one week.

In spite of the fact that I was on bail, no one challenged my plans to leave the country – then again, I hadn't exactly asked anyone for permission. So, by the end of July, I was out in Moscow and reunited with Maya. Wonderful. She had lost a stack of weight and her hair looked thin and lacked its usual lustre. The poor woman had paid a hell of a price for all these shenanigans and it wasn't over yet.

My first impressions of Russia were that it was a romantic place. Childhood stories floated through my head of the great battles of the Second World War, the huge losses of population and the people coming together to chase the militarily superior Germans out of their patch all the way to Berlin – of the Stalinist era, the KGB, the Cold War and espionage. Knowing my lack of enthusiasm for learning, my understanding of Russian history was probably gleaned from adventure books. I'll bet I came across as a typical bloody tourist!

Maya's home village opened my eyes. It looked lovely and rustic but some folk lived in what looked like little more than substantial wooden shacks. Many didn't have running water and most had outside toilets – and that was in a part of the world where temperatures plummeted to well below zero for several months in the winter. No family seemed particularly poor but the whole community lacked the sort of facilities that we took for granted long ago.

We'd been to a couple of meetings at the British Embassy in Moscow and we returned there early in August 2001 to be interviewed both jointly and separately. We looked upon just getting to that stage as a success. At every opportunity, some civil servant had questioned our papers – this form wasn't right, that date couldn't be correct and so on and so forth. But we'd persevered and waded through all that nonsense and got to the interviews where the decisions would be made. However, I'd learned enough in jail not to be optimistic. Those interviews were like fighting your way through to a cup final where you stood a chance in equal measures of winning or losing. Except in this final, maybe, just maybe, the referee had been nobbled.

The day after our interviews, I flew home alone to England and, a few days after that, my divorce came through. I had to lie a little to achieve that. I phoned up the relevant department, sweet-talked the female member of staff dealing with my query and then told her the divorce application had been submitted a long time before it actually had been. Just a little white lie to oil the mechanism and it worked a treat.

Maya had already obtained her divorce so now there were no obstacles standing in our way – apart from the bureaucrats and cops, that is.

We'd been told that the decision would be made soon so I gave the British Embassy in Moscow a week before I started phoning and faxing every morning. I was determined to catch them at the start of their working day, reasoning that, at that time, they'd be sitting at their desks. With the time difference between the UK and Russia, this meant phoning at 5.30 a.m. It made no difference to me since that was when I was up and ready for work anyway.

After a month of daily phone calls and faxes, the decision came through – refused. I could almost hear the sniggers from those who told me that I couldn't beat the Home Office and I could just about see the smirks of satisfaction on the faces of certain Grampian cops. Was I angry? You bet. Was I finished? No way.

Telephones are wonderful when you need to rattle people up and my line was burning hot. Eventually, I discovered that the most significant interview in the whole process had been the final one with a certain woman. I also managed to get her reasons for refusal and I wasn't going to accept them. So I promptly phoned the Embassy and spoke to the British Consul himself. 'I'm told that old bat had the final say,' I started after introductions. It wasn't just my anger talking – it was observation. The woman was a fucking horror, straight-laced, prudish and as dried up as a prune.

'Eh, the final interview is the most important one,' he blustered, a little surprised by my manner.

'And she concluded that Maya and I had no real feelings for each other?'

'Emmm, yes.'

'That Maya just wanted to use me to get into Britain and I was infatuated with her like some soft touch? Does that about sum it up?'

'Reasonably.'

'Do you think that she's well placed to make those kind of assessments?'

There was silence.

'Let's face it, my guess is that she's never been fucked in her life and she probably knows sod all about relationships.'

I swear I heard a soft snigger and his hand being placed over the mouthpiece. Then he said, 'Come now,' in a serious, mirthless voice, 'that's being too harsh you know.'

'I know you guys have done your homework on me,' I continued, 'and, in case you haven't, let me admit, loud and clear, that I've been a shagger all my life. That's not a boast – it's just the reality. But, tell me this, does that sound like a man who would be infatuated with a woman?'

'I do see your point,' he conceded.

'Isn't it more likely that, given the number of women I've been with and I'm going to all this bother over Maya, I know I have the right one? After my loose background, isn't that more likely?'

'Perhaps,' he conceded again.

'As for Maya,' I was going to get this point in, even if it ruined the whole application, 'she isn't even sure she wants to live in England after the way she was treated. All she knows is that she wants to live with me.'

When I hung up the phone, I wasn't sure if my rant had simply blown it for me. Admitting that Maya still harboured strong reservations about living in a country when the process we were going through was her application to come and live in that very same country. I cursed myself and went to my work.

We appealed against the refusal, of course, and set about hassling them to change their collective mind. That took me back to Moscow again and more meetings at the British Embassy. This time Maya and I took time off. Well, this appeal had drawn on so long it was becoming a way of life. So we relaxed in Moscow, visiting the ballet, the circus, Red Square, that sort of thing. Then I came back to Britain for New Year's Eve – Hogmanay, the bells and me on my own. Usually, it would be no big deal but, that year, I felt lonely for the first time ever.

I had written to my local MP, John Hayes, who worked hard on our behalf. The Immigration folk based at Boston kept calling me and grilling me over the phone. Sometimes they were actually very helpful but still this didn't seem to be going anywhere. As this was going on, cops from Grampian would turn up at my work unexpectedly and demand that I sign some papers or whatever. Why did they do that? All they had to do was phone and arrange for me to be wherever, whenever. But their approach caused maximum disruption for me and my work. Now that wouldn't be the reason would it?

The cops were interviewing various people I knew – work associates and people I had done business with. The blue suits didn't tell me that, of course, but my friends did. It seemed a common theme was two blokes called Finnegan and Legg. When I shared this with Maya, she told me that, when she had been asked about Finnegan and Legg just after I had been first arrested, of Finnegan she had answered in all sweet naivety, 'Isn't he something to do with Mark Twain?' Meaning the author, of course. It wouldn't surprise me if they had added Mark Twain to their list of folk they wanted to interview.

From the feedback from my friends who had been interviewed by CID, it seemed plain that Finnegan and Legg were names of possible hit men – professional killers, adept at chopping up corpses, burning bodies . . . the whole thing seemed like a bad plot. But the really worrying thing was that it was my people they were asking about possible hit men. Did they think that trail led to me?

In February 2002, when my mind was firmly focussed on the

fight with Immigration, Andrew McCartan, my lawyer, sent me a package out of the blue. In it was a videotape – the videotape of Nat and me chatting in the visiting room of Porterfield Prison, Inverness. At last, I had the evidence they said they had used to charge me with attempting to pervert the course of justice. The film made for very interesting – yet very boring – viewing. There was no sound. What had they done? Sent one where they had blanked out the voices? This tape lark was beginning to feel like some game of cat and mouse.

A short while later, we were advised that the tapes had been interpreted by one Jessica Rees, the only forensic lip-reader in Britain. What did they need to lip-read for? Throughout the visit, a warden was never more than four feet away. Jessica had given evidence in several high-profile trials in England and it had helped the prosecution to secure convictions. Then we were shown a copy of her interpretation of Nat and me chatting in that prison visiting room.

'Dispose of her body . . .'

'Get rid of it . . .'

'Chop up . . .'

Jesus H Christ! If those words were accepted as an accurate reflection of the conversation, I was a dead man. Well, jailed for a long time at least. But she had it wrong. I knew she had it wrong and would have to prove she had. Suddenly those tapes became enormously important but they'd have to wait. I had my woman to bring back home.

Local lawyers had refused to represent me in our appeal against the Immigration people's decision and I needed to have the best guidance I could. At last, I applied my slow brain and came up with the solution. Where I lived, there were very few asylum seekers or refugees. In Leeds and Bradford, on the other hand, there was an influx of them. The first lawyer I was recommended, Richard Collins of Fox Hayes, promptly agreed to take on the case. Yet again, money struck me as an issue. The final appeal was coming up and Collins was to accompany me and present our case. But his letter confirming this insisted that the fee of £1,468.75 was payable before the hearing with the word 'before' in deep, black bold. This country was becoming like America with the only people who got justice being the ones who can afford it.

The Home Office had made great play of telling me that they were sure that Maya knew the exact gravity of the offences I was charged with and the charges faced by Nat and Hector. Knowing this, they said, she may not want to come back to Britain, may not want to live with me.

'We know that she knows,' the official kept emphasising. The bastards had been listening in to the phone calls I had made from the landline at my house, including a good few I'd made to the British Embassy in Moscow. I thought the bugs had been lifted and started using the home phone again. Obviously I was wrong. I could just about understand why the cops might need to tap phones as part of a murder investigation but what right had anyone else to that information? What had our application to allow Maya into the country got to do with Arlene's disappearance? However much that lawyer cost, I needed his services badly.

At first, we were promised the result of the appeal four weeks after the hearing, which would have been in June 2002. Then it was July and then it was August. By that time, we knew they couldn't delay it any further so Maya moved to Moscow and I made sure she had an open flight ticket from there to London.

She was told to phone the British Embassy on the 7th of August. When she did, she was told that the decision had not yet been made. Then the next day – still no outcome. And so on, all week, till the Friday when she called me. Result. We had won.

It had been such a long bloody battle the sense of achievement and euphoria we both expected was dulled, still, calm. It was more a sigh of relief that, at long last, we wouldn't have to fight the buggers. At long last, we could just settle down and get on with the rest of our lives.

'I'll be there tomorrow, Glenn,' Maya said on the phone from Moscow.

'Tomorrow? Are you sure that's not rushing it? You must be exhausted.'

'No, I'm fine and I have the ticket so I'm coming.'

'Marvellous. It will be great to be together at last.'

Confession time. Falkirk had an important game against St Mirren that Saturday afternoon up north in Paisley and I wanted to go. Maya's flight was due to land in the evening but too early for me to drive from Scotland to England and be there on time. Now, if she travelled on the Sunday, no problem. Selfish bastard? Maybe, but daft Falkirk fanatic definitely. Maya knows this only too well. But that day, of course, I forgot about the game and was there bright and early to greet my woman.

As I watched her walking out into the concourse at Heathrow, pushing her laden trolley, looking weary but beautiful, there wasn't one thought about football in my brain. All I was concerned about was Maya and me.

A few weeks later on the 8th of October 2002, we were married at Spalding Registry Office. Even then, they tried to stop us by questioning our papers, her divorce settlement and so on. But we'd come through too much for too long to allow local officials to get in our way. No longer did I care for their rules. We were just two people who wanted to spend our lives together. Why should there be rules to make that difficult? At last, they didn't even upset me that day. I was just too happy.

However, I did give a little nod northwards in my thoughts – to Grampian Police and to Detective Superintendent Jim Stephen, in charge of the Arlene Fraser case, the mob who still stood in the way of my freedom for no reason at all. But here I was married to the lady they tried to take away from me. The cops would know all about it, of course.

'Maybe now you'll realise you've picked on someone who's not a pushover, Mr Stephen,' I thought as happy friends clinked glasses around us. 'I have the rest of my life here, right here by my side. You're not going to take that away from me again.'

Friends were good. Maya was lovely. We would have done it

differently if the circumstances had been different – if they hadn't interfered. But I was so happy to be married and nothing was going to change that.

'Maybe,' I thought, 'you've picked on the wrong people this time, you arseholes.'

In the north of Scotland, the cops were working on a plan. Ours wasn't going to be a long honeymoon.

TRUST

OCTOBER 2001

Nat Fraser and Hector Dick were lucky men – or so some people thought.

In July 2001, a few weeks after word broke that they had been charged with Arlene's murder, they appeared in court. The formal charges were laid out on an indictment from hell, in two senses. They were accused of abducting, murdering, chopping up and destroying the woman who was Arlene Fraser. That meant pulling out her teeth, disfiguring her, burning off her fingerprints and other uniquely identifying features then somehow making all the bits disappear by intense heat, crushing or whatever other means. Hell. But the indictment was also a legal hell. As Nat Fraser's lawyer, Joe Beltrami, said outside the court after the hearing, 'Both men have been charged with conspiracy to commit murder and murder – two separate charges and an unusual combination.'

It was the legal equivalent of throwing everything at them to see what would stick and suggested that the prosecution's case wasn't that clear in their own minds yet. Or was it a device to deal with the lack of the victim's body? Did the cops' failure in finding Arlene mean that they weren't confident of a murder conviction? That all the evidence they had pointed to Fraser and Dick planning to abduct Arlene? Were they confident they could prove abduction and hopeful that they could also prove murder? Hopeful but not optimistic? It was a legal nightmare but it would all come out in the wash when the case

155

eventually came to trial. At which time, Joe Beltrami declared, 'These charges will be contested with the utmost vigour.' Well, with the old trooper on board, they would be, wouldn't they? Guaranteed.

On the 1st of August 2001, in the face of those horror charges, Hector Dick actually succeeded in achieving bail and was released from prison. Those in the know were horrified. Innocent or guilty, the state believed there was a case against Hector Dick as a murderer who was capable of chopping up and destroying the corpse of a friend, a woman. Yet here he was being released to the community, among them.

The court obviously believed that the crimes Hector Dick stood accused of related to one woman only, Arlene, and that no one else was at risk from him. There were those in his home town of Elgin who weren't so sure. They had never trusted the man.

Rumours abounded that Dick planned to shoot off to Portugal as soon as he was free. This was based on him and his wife Irene having booked a holiday there before he was arrested and jailed. The holiday was cancelled as he'd had to hand his passport in on being bailed. His lawyer, George Mathers, went public on the matter, saying, 'It was ludicrous to think this man would have any intention of absconding. He wants to clear his name and has nothing to fear from going on trial.'

The lawyer was only doing his job, of course, but most people who knew the man thought that Hector Dick had a great deal to fear from going to trial. There was less surprise when, two months later on the 2nd of October 2001, Nat Fraser was also released on bail. The conditions that would have secured release for Dick would have equally applied to Fraser – even more so. Nat Fraser stood accused of murdering his wife, a more common occurrence than the dread killings by psychotic strangers that crime fiction features so frequently. Usually, under such circumstances, the suspect is thought to have had very personal reasons for the murder – unlike an alleged accomplice – unlike, in this instance, Hector Dick.

Why would someone help a man kill his wife? Through friendship to the man? That must be some strong relationship. Through fear of the man? Though he coped with jail badly, Hector Dick gave no one the impression that he was scared of Nat Fraser. Fraser wasn't the type of man people feared – unless they thought he would run off with their wives. For money? Hector Dick liked money, that's for sure. All paid killers are deemed to be very dangerous by the state and quite rightly so. If you'll kill once for gain, what's to stop you killing again for gain?

Either way, both men were released and they were told to expect the trial to begin in July 2002. But events were to take a dramatic twist long before then.

13

THREE IN THE POT
APRIL – DECEMBER 2002

'Glenn, there's someone downstairs asking to see you,' said one of my female colleagues, popping her head into the room. It was Friday afternoon and my normal strategy on Fridays was to get away from work sharpish. Some meeting had delayed me and I was keen to get out the door.

'Any idea who it is?' I asked, wondering if it was a five-minute delay I was in for or longer.

'They didn't say,' she replied.

'They?'

'It's two men.'

'They look like coppers,' shouted a male workmate who had overheard the conversation.

'Fuck off, you twat,' I growled, by now utterly fed up with constant jokes and jibes about me and the police.

Downstairs, as I walked through the office, I spotted the two blokes. 'Oh, shit,' I moaned in my head, 'it's them.' It was two Grampian cops I had seen so often before. Every now and then, police would travel south, turn up at my work unexpectedly and ask me to sign some papers. I grimaced a welcome at them.

'Glenn,' said one of the cops, acting all cheerful and handing me a bundle of papers.

'What's this?'

'It's an indictment. A new indictment.'

158

I looked down and started to read the legalese. One phrase jumped out at me, 'CONSPIRACY TO MURDER'.

'You not going to phone your little friend then?' smiled the other cop.

'Fucking right I am,' I spat and went off to call Andrew, my lawyer.

I was in the mire. If I had been worried about facing up to the attempting to pervert the course of justice, this conspiracy to murder charge was in another league. The indictment went on to detail other aspects of the case that applied to Hector and Nat but would influence any court or jury's view of me. Abduction. Dismemberment. Disposal. Removing teeth. Taking away her rings – those bloody rings that had allegedly reappeared in the family's home. I shivered at the grotesque horror of it all.

It was the 26th of April 2002, two days before the fourth anniversary of Arlene's disappearance. I had no doubt that the Grampian cops saw that anniversary as significant and wanted to show some progress was being made around that date. Now the cops had their three accused. This investigation had become personal some time ago and that wasn't going to change now. The cops had their accused but what else did they have?

Andrew was horrified. Then he butted in to say that it had just been on BBC Radio Scotland's five o'clock news bulletin that I'd been charged. The cops had served the indictment on me only a few minutes before but already the media had been advised. Grampian Police were very proud of themselves and they were milking this for every ounce.

The shock of the charges was just too much for me. I had to get my head and nerves settled. So, to cool my heels, I decided to go see my pal David Hilton. As I drove to David's, I passed some local surreptitiously unloading boxes from the back of his car into a lock-up. It was well known that he bought dodgy cigarettes and sold them on at knock-down prices. I had no problem with the bloke's scam but, for once, I thought how ironic it was that he was carrying out his enterprise openly in daylight while I, an innocent man, was facing murder charges.

Sitting with David having a beer, he let me gibber on as good friends do. I shared with him that Andrew and I had been considering suing Grampian Police for wrongful imprisonment. Not long before, he had broken the good news to me that I was to have my legal costs covered by Legal Aid. That was the only bit of good news in this whole saga and I couldn't work it out. I had a few quid, was comfortable, yet the state would meet my expenses. Unlike Nat in his serious assault case, I had truthfully declared all my dosh. But murder cases don't come cheap. The anticipated costs of my defence, in what was to be a highly complex case, spiralled and must have knocked me into qualifying for Legal Aid.

Andrew had declared his opinion that the cops had no evidence strong enough to charge or jail me and, because of this, they had wrongfully arrested and imprisoned me. I was right up for taking them on and we both had a hearty laugh at the prospect of doing so under Legal Aid. But then they dropped the new indictment on me and all bets were off.

Soon after the cops charged me with conspiracy to murder, I met with Andrew who, by then, had had a chance to peruse the charges. He told me what I already knew – that I was in deep trouble.

'Glenn,' he said, 'you must get your papers in order.' It was the most chilling statement I'd heard since this sorry business started. What he meant was to prepare for going to jail. This from the same man who, one week before, was agreeing I should be suing Grampian Police for wrongful arrest and imprisonment. Never mind politics, a week is a long time in life.

The case would now undoubtedly go to trial at the High Court, possibly in Glasgow as Nat's lawyer Joe Beltrami wanted or Edinburgh. There was no way they could raise an impartial jury anywhere in the north-east. In fact, I doubted if they could find fifteen men and women anywhere in Scotland that hadn't read and formed a view about Arlene. So we needed a QC to represent me in the High Court.

We managed to appoint one of the top lawyers in Scotland, Bill Taylor QC. Taylor had made his name by representing Abdelbaset

Ali Mohmed al-Megrahi who was accused and eventually convicted of the 1988 bombing of the PanAm jet over Lockerbie.

I wasn't the only one trying to get the best defence lawyer. Hector Dick had appointed Donald Findlay QC, the handlebar-whiskered, pipe-smoking, Rangers-supporting lawyer who appeared as eccentric as he was excellent in court. Findlay had starred in many of the top trials in Scotland most notably that of Paul Ferris, the baby-faced mobster who was charged with killing Fatboy Thompson, son of Godfather Arthur Thompson. Ferris was also up on a knee-capping charge, an attempted murder charge and a host of others. In the longest criminal trial in Scottish history, Ferris had received not guilty verdicts on all of them.

Nat Fraser, of course, had appointed Joe Beltrami who was one of the few solicitors in Scotland with QC status. But they would also get Paul McBride QC on board. He was a growing force in the courts and, at the time, flavour of the month in big criminal trials.

As ever, formal court hearings were required. The decision was made that the cases would be heard at Edinburgh High Court, which is considered to be the highest court in Scotland. It's a grand old place that has seen as much famous action as the Old Bailey and has that same feel of musty severity and doom about it. Of course, I'd far rather have been going there as an onlooker than an accused.

That first appearance at the High Court was almost an anticlimax. Criminal trials, even controversial ones, are probably more to do with paperwork and procedure than with the cut and thrust of sharp legal minds cross-examining witnesses. In my case, I was in and out in about twenty minutes and I was left absolutely clueless about what had actually happened. Apparently, it's a typical courtroom experience.

Andrew and I spent a great deal of time preparing the case with Bill Taylor. It was due to go to trial on the 31st of May 2002 but, on the 22nd of October 2001, Bill Taylor QC had gone to court and asked for a postponement because he wasn't ready. The postponement was granted and a new trial date was fixed for October 2002. Then Bill advised Andrew that we would have to find another

QC since the pressure of other work was proving too much for him to tackle this complex case.

At first, I was furious, thinking that I'd have to start again with the new QC. As it happened, we managed to instruct Edgar Prais QC, one of the foremost criminal lawyers in Scotland. He's handled cases from acid-throwing crimes of passion to hit contracts to disappearing corpses. A run though Edgar's CV is juicier than any Hollywood plot.

Edgar immediately struck me as quirky, eccentric, a great character and a red-hot lawyer. From the off, we met frequently in Edinburgh, in a little room under the lawyers' library. The meetings would go on for many hours at a time and it really did feel a bit like *Rumpole of the Bailey* – if it hadn't been so bloody serious.

With a further delay in the trial announced, Maya and I went to Ireland for a long weekend in November. It was a short break and a chance to recharge our batteries. At least that's what people thought. In part, it was true because all these delays did nothing but increase our anxiety. I just wanted to get into court now. But, in fact, I was sussing out Ireland for Plan B. I went to companies, chatted about job opportunities, sussed out wages and even had a look at areas to live in. I returned to Scotland knowing that I could run there if need be.

Then I was back in Edinburgh for another meeting and Edgar decided to give me a reality check. 'You know you could go down,' he said, in a matter of fact tone.

'That's confident,' I replied, not wanting to think of jail time for a second longer.

'I mean it, Glenn, this is a complex case.'

'I know but I didn't do it.'

He went off on one. 'You must be realistic. You could go to jail for a very long time, regardless. I know you're innocent but it's not me who makes the decisions. It'll be a jury and, if they find you guilty . . .'

'Don't worry, I'll not be going to prison again.'

'What? What do you mean?'

'If this looks like it's going against me, I'll be out of the country by nightfall.'

'You WHAT?' Edgar Prais gave me what for and he didn't let go. What I had admitted to was planning to break the law and he couldn't stay in the same room with someone with those intentions. So he roared on and on, laying right into me. It was so bad and so clear, I realised I risked losing him as a lawyer and I certainly didn't want to do that. So I tried to tell him I'd been joking. And I convinced him, eventually, thank God. But I hadn't been in jest. I was deadly serious about fleeing the country.

As far as we could ascertain, the scene the prosecution was going to paint would have certain key elements. The first was the interpretation of Nat and me talking in Porterfield Prison visiting room. Since Maya's appeal had been settled, I had spent an enormous amount of my time in libraries and with support groups for deaf and dumb people, trying to understand the process of lip-reading better so I could challenge the cops' evidence.

The forensic lip-reader, Jessica Rees, who had interpreted the tapes for the cops, had a sound heritage. To start with, I'd hoped she had a dodgy reputation that we could have a go at but no such luck. My research certainly made me believe that lip-reading is an approximate art not a science and can be skewed by all sorts of things like accents. With Nat's north-east Scottish twang and my public-school accent, Jessica had two very distinct and contrasting accents to deal with. I wondered if she knew that when looking at the tapes.

Edgar, Andrew and Sarah Livingstone, another member of the legal team, went further. They took the tapes to Deafworks, an organisation near Oxford who specialise in lip-reading among other things. Deafworks interpreted the tapes independently and came up with a highly contrasting transcript. I for one was not surprised.

Where Jessica had read one of us saying 'body', Deafworks read 'bird'. I pointed out that was very likely and, given that Nat and I were talking a lot about women, it could also have been 'boobs' or 'breasts'. Deafworks said that many of the other key words couldn't be interpreted. If Deafworks had been asked by the cops to interpret the tapes originally, I would never have been charged in the first place. It has to be asked how a forensic lip-reader got it so wrong, especially when two men's liberty was at stake. Shouldn't the cops have sought a second opinion from another lip-reading expert, even if it came from someone who wasn't forensically accredited as Jessica Rees was?

The cops also claimed that Arlene had been abducted from her home on the 28th of April and that, some time between then and a day in May – for some reason they changed the latter date several times – she was killed. The beige Ford Fiesta was allegedly used to transport Arlene or her body or both. Given he had admitted having bought the car, that seemed to put Hector in the hot seat. Yet, so far, they still hadn't found the car in question so they'd have no forensics proving that Arlene had been in it – unless they were able to produce a witness, of course.

Arlene's rings were claimed to have been removed from her body and, to avoid giving leads, smuggled back into the house where they were found by her father's second wife. They were found on the 7th of May so all the accused had to do was prove where they were that day. Arlene's parents had already said that Nat had visited the house that day and had used the bathroom where the rings were found. So he had a question or two to answer. Hector Dick had minute-perfect alibis for every day, mainly citing his workers or his wife, Irene, as having seen him or been with him. Of all the dates I had been asked for, the 7th of May was one I was having trouble with. But more crucial in the case against me were my whereabouts on the 28th of April, the day Arlene had disappeared.

I had been in Elgin and even slept in the same room as Nat on the 26th of April in Ian and Jane Taylor's home in nearby Lhanbryde. I left there on the morning of the 27th to visit relatives in Applecross, on a peninsula in Wester Ross in the north-west of Scotland. The cops clearly weren't satisfied with my timings and the prosecution would raise that against me, suggesting that I doubled back to Elgin and was involved in abducting or murdering Arlene.

The cops also suspected that I had taken Arlene's body from Elgin and, on the way to Applecross, I'd dumped it – probably into the deep dark waters of Loch Ness – or buried her in that landscape that's so beautiful but so remote and lonely. We knew this because they had questioned my friends about it.

'What time did you see Lucas?'

'What sort of state was he in?'

'Did he seem agitated?'

'Who did he phone?'

'Did Lucas have a spade in the boot of his car?'

Though my legal team accepted my word, they decided it would be better if we all took the journey together. So, around Christmas and New Year, I found myself in the farthest reaches of Scotland on the highest road in Britain, already deemed to be one of the most dangerous and, during the winter months, at high risk of black ice.

In my car, I had Andrew, Edgar and Sarah Livingstone. The driving took my total concentration.

'Look! Deer!' Edgar said, pointing excitedly at a herd up on the horizon. He hadn't been to that part of Scotland before and the views are spectacular.

But no sooner had he marvelled at some aspect of the scenery than he had his mind back on business. 'You must remember what you said to Hector Dick in that phone call, Glenn,' he insisted. It was the replies I gave to that type of question that my spending much of the rest of my life outside or inside jail would depend on so I'd have to answer as carefully as I could.

'Would you just look at those colours in that field?' Edgar was back to acting the tourist.

'Now, the 7th of May – that could prove crucial, Glenn. Take me through what you can remember of that day.'

I'd start replying when an enthralled voice would burst out with something like, 'Is that the sea I can see?'

And so it went on, with both Andrew and Sarah throwing questions at me as well. 'And you have to tell us everything you did on the day you travelled from Elgin to here, Glenn. Everything.'

A few miles up the road, I pulled over, got out the car and went behind a bush. All the lawyers followed me. 'This is where I stopped for a piss,' I explained. Well they'd said *every*thing.

The thought crossed my mind on how much the three lawyers in my car charged an hour and if any or all of them were charging Legal Aid for their travelling time. And here I was juggling the dodgy driving, their interrogation and acting as their tour guide all at the same time. Around 4.30 p.m. that day, someone noticed the hour and declared that they had better be getting back. Me, I had to be at work hundreds of miles away in Spalding in twelve hours.

This criminal justice malarkey was exhausting and no mistake but at least I had a defence team who were thoroughly prepared. With the calibre of lawyers Nat and Hector Dick had, I expected no less from them.

This was going to be some trial.

14

KICK OFF

JANUARY 2003

Public execution is written all over the old part of Edinburgh that leads down the cobbled street from the castle to Holyroodhouse. Even with the traffic, the shops, restaurants and heaving pubs, you can still feel the old city the way it was. It's no accident that the High Court is right there in its midst.

Edinburgh is a lovely city if you're a tourist. I wished to hell I had been. But I had a murder trial to go to and was sitting in the hot seat.

Yet again, friends and family came through. My ex-wife Anne had called me at home to say that her brother, Ivor, had offered me the loan of his flat for the duration of the trial. Ivor had worked for me for a while in Inverness. A great guy, he was a keen supporter of the SNP, a red-hot Aberdeen fan and a fully paid up member of the Tartan Army. The lawyers reckoned the trial would last six weeks and I didn't fancy hotel food for that length of time. Plus, of course, the accused man pays his own way. Innocent till proven guilty? Absolutely but that'll cost you an arm and a leg then.

The flat was in Dumbiedykes right down at the end of the Royal Mile where they were building the new Scottish Parliament. A row was raging between the politicians and it was splattered over the press how the building was going many tens of millions of pounds over budget. In contrast, Dumbiedykes looked as if it hadn't had a farthing spent on it in decades.

The trial was due to kick off on the 6th of January. Maya decided to come and stay with me for the duration. We were determined to keep the whole experience as normal as possible. Besides this was still part of our honeymoon and we didn't know if it was the last time we were going to have for years.

The very thorough Edgar Prais QC wanted to meet with me on the Saturday before the trial to go over certain details. As Maya and I set off from Spalding, my bloody car burst into flames. Thank God neither of us was hurt but I was hoping to hell it wasn't an omen. Fesa, my employer, bailed us out by loaning us a pool car and off we went early on Saturday morning.

I had driven that road north so many times, usually to the football, to visit friends and relatives or on holiday – in other words, for pleasure. As I drove, I couldn't stop the thought crossing my mind that this could be the last time I'd be doing it for a long time. What had those cops warned me? Six years – ten years – maybe more?

Walking up the Royal Mile towards the High Court, from some distance away, I spotted a crowd congregating at the front of the building. There were TV vans, cameras and men in warm coats with Dictaphones in their hands. The press corps – I hadn't bloody thought about them. I started to shit myself big time. It was bad enough I was in this mess but now I had to deal with it being exposed as widely as the media could reach.

I pulled myself up to my full height, tried to look serious – but not too serious – and went striding towards them with the intention of marching through them. Eighteen stone on the hoof – they just got out of my way.

Nobody tells you what to do in court. I arrived there early for the first day and wasn't sure where to go or anything – an unnerving addition at a time when you're screaming from the ceiling with anxiety. So I asked an official who very politely took me into the courtroom and pointed out where I should sit and so on.

At the High Court, I was walking up the main staircase when I spotted Nat at the top in the company of a rather tasty young woman. 'That's bloody cool,' I thought, 'still able to think of nooky with this lot hanging over his head.' But Nat was that kind of guy. He certainly looked relaxed and was wearing his usual pleasant demeanour.

'Introduce me to your new friend, then,' I said to him with a wink and a nod after we had greeted each other.

'She's not my friend,' he laughed out loud, 'this is my lawyer, Sophie.'

'Bloody hell!' I almost blushed. 'I must be getting old.'

Sophie was a young French woman who had qualified in law in her home territory and was working with Beltrami & Co. to get the right qualifications to practise in Scotland. Although very capable, she was new to Scotland and working in a junior position so I thought it a bit off that someone in a murder case should have that level of representation even if the early part of the proceedings were mere formalities. Of course, it turned out that she was just part of Nat's legal team – his lawyer was Gary McAteer and Paul McBride was his QC.

It was the first time Nat and I had been together since I was originally charged with attempting to pervert the course of justice. But we didn't have much catching up to do. Well, you don't when both of you have been fighting serious criminal charges and those were the last things either of us wanted to talk about. So we did what we normally did and talked about women, football, music and women.

As the time for the start of proceedings approached, I went and took up my place in the courtroom. Nat was already there and we chatted cautiously, totally on edge knowing that we were being watched by everyone in the public gallery and we may send out the wrong signal if we smiled or laughed or seemed too much at ease.

The first I saw of Hector Dick was when he squeezed past to sit between Nat and me just a few seconds before the trial was due to start.

'Morning, Hector,' I said as cheerily as I could.

'Morning, Heckie,' said Nat, using the familiar form of address he had for the man.

'Aye, aye,' replied Hector in that rumbling, douce, Doric accent of his.

'Aye' was the only word I was to hear from Hector during that early part of the trial. In the north-east of Scotland, they use it not only as a greeting but also as a sort of meaningless acknowledgement. You can make an observation to somebody like, 'It's cold in here, eh?' And if they don't want to get into conversation they'd just reply, 'Aye.' So my dialogues with Hector Dick went something like, 'That juror looks as rough as fuck, Hector. What do you think?'

'Aaaye.' This was usually preceded by a sharp intake of breath and a slight shake of the head. Now and then, it was no problem but I knew as well as Hector Dick did that his constant use of that reply was polite for, 'Fuck off and leave me alone.' So I did.

Even sitting as the accused, the procedures of court are intriguing – like the judge, in this instance Lord Mackay of Drumadoon, sitting in his throne-like chair, higher than anyone else, with his long wig, colourful gowns and his clerk or whatever going ahead of him, telling us all to stand in his presence. And we did – just as if it was something out of the seventeenth century.

In contrast, I couldn't believe the way they went about choosing jury members. For a start the pool of folk to choose from is pretty much down to chance. Obviously, they qualify as citizens who don't have criminal records or work at particular jobs but after that who you get is the luck of the draw. The lawyers know what they are about, of course, and seek out certain people they reckon are likely to see the world in a way that will be sympathetic to their case. But it all seemed so haphazard. A few of our jury looked and sounded as if they'd be happier drinking fortified wine on a park bench. When the fifteen were finally chosen, I hoped to hell they would be on our side. Then the evidence started.

As Alan Turnbull QC led the prosecution, I started making notes and kept making them. He started by outlining the case against us, saying that we had abducted and killed Arlene, removed her teeth and jewellery and dumped her body somewhere in Scotland. Those reappearing rings were supposed to have been put back in the house by us and, on the 28th of April, we allegedly removed a coat of Arlene's along with a handbag and a box of her private papers from the house. We were also accused of torching Arlene's car weeks before she disappeared as well as having possession of that beige Ford Fiesta. All three of us were pleading not guilty to all charges, of course.

Elgin lawyer, Loanne Lennon confirmed that Arlene had spoken to her about divorce two months previously and was due to see her the day that she disappeared but she never kept the appointment. Yes, Arlene had been after a substantial financial settlement but she had no idea of Nat's true wealth. The lawyer had advised her how to ascertain his worth legally. So where did that figure of a £250,000 divorce settlement come from? Had someone made it up?

Advocate Depute Alan Turnbull QC asked Ms Lennon, 'Could you contemplate her putting the children off to school one morning and simply walking out on their lives without making any arrangements for their future care?'

'No.'

'Was Mrs Fraser a loving mother to her two children, Jamie and Natalie?'

'Yes.'

I couldn't see how Ms Lennon was qualified to make such judgements about these kinds of aspects of human behaviour – at least not in a court of law. But then maybe I'd been watching too many fictionalised courtroom dramas.

So the scene was set already, it seemed to me. Arlene was a loving mother, which indeed she was, who would never walk away from her kids. She was about to ditch her man, Nat, giving him a motive for murder and, of course, his two pals, Hector and me, might well help him.

Arlene's friend, Michelle Scott, was on next and spoke about their lunch date that never happened. How she had visited Arlene's home at 2 Smith Street at 11 a.m. then again at 1 p.m. Later that night and worried, she had contacted some of Arlene's friends and they had contacted the cops.

171

Nat's QC, Paul McBride, was on his feet asking Michelle Scott about the Frasers' marriage and she had to agree that it was 'tempestuous'. Michelle had been Arlene's confidante for years and I already knew that she hated Nat. Probably with good reason, having only heard Arlene's version of the troubles in their relationship. Anyway, that's what friends are for – seeing things your way.

So far, the proceedings were going exactly as expected.

The next day, Arlene's GP Dr Andrew McPherson was called and told the court how Arlene had had a breast enhancement operation two or three years before she disappeared. He also acknowledged that he treated her for Crohn's disease and that she was required to take the medication or would suffer abdominal pains and vomiting. Nat's lawyer McBride cross-examined the doc on how much the boob job would have cost. About £4,000 was the answer. Did he know where she had got the money? No. What the jury didn't know was that neither had Nat Fraser known where the money came from – so much for Arlene only having £60 housekeeping a week.

Grampian Police forensic scientist Neville Trower gave evidence saying that he had sprayed the house with a chemical agent that makes traces of blood glow in the dark. They had also used every technical trick in the book to find traces of a violent struggle or whatever and had found none. The bold Donald Findlay QC, representing Dick, cross-examined to great effect, making the forensic bod agree with his statement that, 'despite all the scientific skill, technical expertise and wizardry you could throw at this house, you could find not one scrap of scientific evidence to show that any physical harm had come to Arlene Fraser'.

Findlay wasn't kidding. Even after the search at my house, I eventually got some of my goods back in sealed plastic bags marked, 'WARNING Contents have been treated chemically DO NOT HANDLE.' They had been treated for bloodstains and the like – and that was at my house where there was no suggestion in the Crown case that any violence took place. If they did that to my home, what the hell did the forensic boys throw at Nat and Arlene's house?

To me, the lack of forensic evidence at 2 Smith Street still seemed to be a blatantly major flaw in their whole case. Even if it had been someone she knew who abducted her, surely to God Arlene would have struggled? Can we not just all pack up now and bugger off back to our lives?

No. Arlene's mother, Isabelle Thompson, took the stand. She described how it was not Nat who had told her that Arlene had disappeared – she heard the news from her other daughter, Carol. In her opinion, Nat had looked 'normal' in the days after Arlene had gone – he hadn't been anxious and upset like the rest of them. She also spoke about confronting Nat on whether he had done anything to Arlene. Apparently she had asked him if he had done any 'deals' on Arlene. What was she getting at? Hit men? Where had she got that idea? Nat had denied it, of course.

Ian Taylor's wife, Jane, took the stand and talked of Nat leaving a bank statement out in his room when he was staying with her and her husband. Apparently Jane had been annoyed since she suspected he had left it deliberately to show that there was very little money in the account. Jane thought Nat had wanted her to tell this to Arlene.

That's when I decided I'd had enough. What do you do when you are sitting there in the dock? All the journalists try and catch your eye. Trouble is knowing who the journalists are. I kept looking around me at no one or down at my hands but this jury member kept catching my attention. She was asleep – I was sure of it – and not for the first time. She looked hung-over – she'd looked that way every day of the trial. I drew this to the lawyers' attention and the trial was halted. After a while, we reconvened and that jury member was missing. She had been excused any further involvement and the judge announced that she couldn't concentrate for the required two or three hours at a stretch through no fault of her own. So now only fourteen good men and women would decide on our fates. But would that be in our favour or against us?

Arlene's sister, Carol Gillies, told how, exactly one week before Arlene disappeared, she had phoned her at her home in Erskine.

Arlene had said that she was worried because Hector Dick was hanging about outside the house. Why would Hector be loitering outside Arlene's house? What had Arlene to fear from him? Hector Dick often used to visit Arlene either alone or with his wife, Irene. Now Carol's comments were keeping me wide awake and I eyed Hector the pig farmer next to me. As usual, he had that stupefied expression on his mug – half scared, half stupid.

It was Hector Dick's turn for some pressure as the mechanic, Kevin Ritchie, took the stand to tell how he had sold that beige Ford Fiesta to him, on order. In addition to telling how Dick had contacted him to get a car with a boot in a hurry, Ritchie also revealed that he had asked if a car could be identified if it didn't have any number plates. Ritchie claimed to have explained to him about the chassis number on cars.

When asked if Hector Dick had explained why he needed a car, Ritchie had apparently been told that it had something to do with bootleg booze. It was an open secret in the area that Hector was involved in that racket. But then Ritchie recalled that Hector had said that he had been someplace the week before and his car had been recognised. That was a few weeks before Arlene disappeared, when she was scared by Dick hanging around outside her home.

As Ritchie spoke from the witness stand, I took a sly look at Hector Dick next to me. His ruddy cheeks had drained of colour and his fingers gripped and twisted the bottom of his jacket. Things weren't looking good for Hector Dick.

Catherine McInnes was next in the stand. She was Arlene's father's second wife and had been staying at 2 Smith Street after Arlene had disappeared. She swore that the family had thoroughly searched the house in the days after Arlene disappeared, as indeed had the police. Yet, on the 7th of May 1998, almost two weeks later, she had found Arlene's three rings in the bathroom. The rings hadn't been there previously, according to Catherine McInnes who would be backed up by Arlene's mother, father and sister. She would also be backed up by a police video of the house which was shown to the jury where detailed shots of the bathroom revealed no rings.

According to Catherine McInnes, Nat Fraser had been in the house that day and had used the bathroom before she found the rings.

Now it was Nat's turn to sweat.

For the prosecution, Alan Turnbull QC ran through Nat's alibi for the day of Arlene's disappearance, which included being out on fruit and veg deliveries along with a van boy, Grant Fraser, no relative. Grant Fraser swore that Nat couldn't have been in 2 Smith Street between 9 a.m. and 10 a.m., the suspected time of Arlene disappearing. It was looking better – solid I reckoned.

But Nat had phoned a woman, Hazel Walker, that morning by prior arrangement. She agreed that he had phoned her every weekday for the previous week but never again after the 28th of April. Turnbull was skilled in his interview technique, giving out the clear message that Nat had set up the phone conversation as an obvious cover. As for me, I just assumed that Nat had stopped chasing that particular prospect of nooky when Arlene went missing and hoards of cops and media hit the town.

Detective Constable Gordon Ritchie took the oath and gave evidence about the efforts he had made to check if Arlene was still alive. Apparently, she hadn't used her bankbook or those of her kids or claimed welfare benefits. Nor had she been to an NHS dentist or NHS doctor for a prescription for her medication for Crohn's disease. They claimed even to have used Interpol to check all the European medical centres to check if she had asked any of them for her Crohn's disease medicine and said that she had not. I wasn't so sure those checks would be entirely foolproof but the cop's evidence was allowed to stand unchallenged – after all, why would a policeman lie about such a search?

The trial broke for the weekend and I was relieved to get a couple of days off with Maya. We had bought a stack of new things for the flat by way of a thank you to Ivor and I had been relaxing at nights by painting some of the rooms. I have to admit feeling like a right prick when I couldn't work out why the electricity had gone off all of a sudden and had to be taught about electricity cards and buying your power in advance.

Coming back from court every day, done up in one of my best suits, shirts and ties, I felt like a fish out of water. Kids hanging around street corners eyed me up suspiciously and, as I entered his shop, one of the local shopkeepers slyly threw a towel over a display of some cigarettes – obviously dodgy ones. What did they think I was, a copper?

The flat was still an ace idea. Once I had cleared the inevitable media people at the door of the court, one short walk, all downhill, and I felt that I was really getting away from the pressure of the trial.

So far, the evidence had not put the finger specifically on me. But the matters of the videotapes and Jessica Rees's transcript remained unresolved. We still weren't sure if they were going to use that as evidence or not. So I had a relaxing weekend, only now and then worrying about how the week to come was going to put me under the spotlight.

The following Monday morning, I strode up the Royal Mile towards the High Court, bracing myself for a rough time. As we stood up for Lord Mackay to take his place, we were in for a shock. The judge told the jury to go home, saying that legal points had to be debated. He was very apologetic and added, 'I recognise this must all be a bit of a mystery but, unfortunately, in criminal trials, points of law do arise.'

So we were having a day off. You'd think they could have let us know in advance so we could have had a lie in. Mind you, I'd already had a lie in on one morning. The night before, Andrew McCartan had told me that the trial would start later than usual the following day. So I had an extra hour in bed with Maya, a leisurely breakfast and strolled up the hill. When I arrived at the court, Andrew was going ballistic. He had been repeatedly phoning my mobile to tell me to get there. But I turn my mobile phone off when Maya and I have some quality time together. Scotland's highest court, dealing with the most controversial murder trial in a generation, had been waiting for me as I took time with my wife. At least Andrew took the blame and later we had a laugh.

One man who wasn't laughing was Hector Dick. He had sat sullen and silent throughout days in court. A strange bugger, I thought. Here's the three of us caught up in the same tangle and all screaming our innocence. I had no reason to believe that the other two blokes weren't as innocent as I knew I was. At least the three of us should show a bit of solidarity. But, no – Dick just sat there schtum, with an angry scowl on his face most of the time.

Dick had a routine from day one. In the morning, before the proceedings started, he used to go into this small room at the top of the stairs and sit there alone. He'd wait till the very last minute before entering the courtroom then squeeze past me, always insisting on sitting in the middle. At the end of the day, he'd slip out of the High Court on his own without even saying goodbye most times. Yet this was a bloke who had been a close friend to Nat for years.

I didn't know him at all well before the trial. I had only met him briefly on a couple of occasions. After the charges had been brought, I had spoken to him on the phone a few times. So, although I really didn't know him well, my instinct was that he was a sneaky sod who was up to something. We were about to find out just how sneaky he was.

15

JUDAS
JANUARY 2003

Hector Dick stabbed us in the back and so did the Crown.

When the judge announced that Hector Dick and Glenn Lucas were dismissed from the trial, confusion rippled through the court, with few people understanding what was going on. And this Glenn Lucas was among them. He had to tell us to stand down and I was staring at Andrew at the lawyers' table with a what-the-fuck's-happening expression. He smiled widely and waved his arm telling me to move my arse. I went to the public benches and spoke with him there.

'The charges have been dropped, Glenn,' he said still grinning.

'I don't . . .'

'It doesn't matter. You're free.'

'But what about Nat?' I asked.

'He's still in there, unfortunately.'

'Why?'

'We'll find out soon enough.'

Hector Dick hadn't dallied. As soon as the judge made the announcement, he was up and off and out of that room, his gaze now directed at his feet. It was the fastest I'd seen him move since the whole business kicked off. 'Strange bugger,' I thought and not for the first time. However, it turned out that he was not so much strange as self-serving.

When Alan Turnbull QC for the prosecution had been on his feet explaining that he had dropped the charges against the two accused, Lucas and Dick, he simply said it was 'with the intention of calling Hector Dick as a witness against the remaining accused'.

Andrew, Sarah Livingstone and Edgar Prais had all looked at each other and I swear all their eyebrows were raised in exactly the same arched fashion.

'He's turned Queen's evidence,' explained Andrew to me minutes later.

'I know I'm thick, Andrew, but what do you mean?' I asked. This sudden change of events had thrown me totally.

'He'll give new evidence against Nat Fraser,' he explained.

'Why the fuck will . . .' the penny was finally dropping.

'In return for . . .'

'I know, I fucking well know – in return for all the charges being dropped against him.'

'That sums it up perfectly,' continued Andrew with a sad, weary expression wiped all over his face.

'The CUNT,' I hissed.

'Ssshhh,' Andrew hissed, as he motioned over his shoulder at Lord Mackay still resplendent in his throne.

'EVIL BASTARD,' I mouthed. 'How can he get off with that?' I asked my lawyer in an audible whisper. 'Don't jail me for twenty-five fucking years and I'll guarantee you get him – that Nat Fraser. His head on a platter. That's the prick you want, isn't it? Just don't hurt me.' Then louder, 'That bastard Dick might be the one who did it.'

'Yeah,' Andrew nodded in agreement.

'But how?'

'It's the law, Glenn. The law.'

'The law's a cunting ass then!' And it was. It is. I could see it all so clearly. No wonder Dick had moved sharpish out of the courtroom. If he had still been there when I was sussing out what he had done, I would have been hard pressed to stop myself from getting hold of him and giving him a good kicking.

'It's all over for you, Glenn,' Edgar Prais QC was smiling.

'Guess it'll be Blackpool this year for your holidays, Edgar, not the Bahamas?'

He smiled at the jibe and I knew he understood. Edgar is the type of man who, having prepared, wants to go in and do battle – have his joust, his big day in court. Of course, rather than compliment him – not my style – I had to tease him about earning less from the trial than if I had gone the whole length. I'm sure he made the Bahamas anyway.

I looked across the court. Nat Fraser was sitting there wearing a bewildered, incredulous look. I know Nat – know him well. His face was missing its easy smile and his eyes were no longer twinkling and these absences were significant. His expression said that he had just been told by his lawyers what was going down and he couldn't understand it.

Lord Mackay, the judge, was explaining matters to the jury, 'If the Crown decides to withdraw the libel against an accused – in other words, to accept the plea of not guilty – that is entirely a matter for the prosecutor. The court has no role, other than to ensure that what happens is recorded. It is not part of our procedure that the advocate depute should explain in open court why certain decisions are taken.' He then hesitated for a little as if to add emphasis to his next statement, 'It is the Crown's decision and the Court must accept it.'

He was talking to the jury, not to me. But I know, if I had been sitting in that group, I'd be wondering what the fuck was going on. They'd sat for days and heard worrying evidence that seemed to be implicating Hector Dick in whatever happened to Arlene. Now, all of a sudden, he was going to walk free and, worse, he was going to give evidence against his former co-accused.

Let's just imagine for a minute that the pair of them had murdered Arlene and, therefore, both knew enough dirt on the other to have them well done. One guy is sitting there listening to the evidence thinking things are going badly for him so he breaks ranks first and, in return for getting off scot-free, he puts the other one in it. How is that justice?

Even before the trial and all through it, Edgar Prais QC had been predicting something like this would happen. 'Hector's going to throw a wobbly. Hector's going to throw a wobbly,' he'd said on several occasions. I knew what he meant. The man looked ready to crack and, so far, the evidence had piled more and more pressure on him. But he hadn't cracked – he'd crossed the floor.

Lord Mackay was speaking again, warning the jury, 'It would be quite wrong of you to speculate as to why this decision has been taken. I must counsel you to keep an open mind about issues that remain in this trial.'

I couldn't see that happening. Everyone must be wondering what Dick had to say and how he knew anything if he hadn't been involved himself.

Nat's legal team looked as shocked as anyone – more so, in fact. They hadn't known anything about this move either obviously. The whole deal had happened offstage, between the prosecution and Hector Dick's defence team.

Of course, Nat's lawyers were as much in the dark as almost anyone else about what was coming next. But they were about to get a chance to find out since the trial was postponed for a few days till, as is their right with any witness, they took statements from Hector Dick.

'That'll be interesting,' I said to Andrew who nodded in enthusiastic agreement.

A couple of days later, I met with Nat's legal team so they could take statements from me. 'If there's any way I can help,' I offered.

'Thank you but in what way?' one of them replied.

'I don't know,' I said but thought they might know. 'As a witness or something?'

'Thank you, Mr Lucas,' was the response.

I asked them if there was anything I could do for Nat. They didn't seem to know what I meant. And that was that.

After that, I had to go and see a Mr Dickson who had been the procurator fiscal in Elgin. I found the meeting room at the High Court and sat there waiting for him, not really sure why I was there.

What was he going to do? Apologise for my wrongful arrest? Charge me with something else?

Dickson arrived in the room all bustle and hustle and apologised for being late. He chatted on, all friendly-like, about him buying a house. Yet, a very short time before, this bloke had been part of a team who were trying to get me jailed for a long time for something I didn't do. Now he was being friendly. What is that all about? Is it what some folk think of as civilised behaviour?

It felt like Dickson was debriefing me, running over essentially what had happened between me and the cops throughout the whole sorry saga. He was running through interviews I'd had with the cops and so on and then he said, 'Now the 7th of May – that was the first time the police spoke to you . . .'

I butted in. 'The 7th?'

'Yes,' he looked down at his papers, 'the 7th. Why?'

I was rubbing my face in total bloody exasperation. 'The 7th was the day the cops gave me so much grief over – the day they claimed I was in Elgin. The day the rings mysteriously reappeared. That was the fucking day your case tied me in to the whole murder rap. Yet the cops were speaking to me, calling me in Spalding, Lincolnshire, you fucking twat.'

A short while but a long rant later, I stood at the top of the steps leading into the High Court. My face was flushed red, my heart thumping. I had vented all my frustrated anger on the man over the fact that I'd been caught up in that murder case. Some of the names I had called him were just too much. Had I gone too far? Can you get charged for cursing and swearing at a Crown official in a court of law? Right then, I didn't care.

My mobile phone rang. It was a mate from Ireland calling to congratulate me on my acquittal. It was one of many calls I had received from well-wishers around the UK as the news spread. After a few minutes of good natured banter, my pal said, 'Shame about your friend, Nat, though. He's really in the hot seat now.'

'I shouldn't worry about Nat,' I replied. 'He has a full alibi for the day Arlene went missing and there's absolutely no proof that she's actually dead, never mind murdered.'

Standing on the steps of the High Court in the chilly air of an Edinburgh January day, I truly believed what I had said. Of course, I should have added that it all depended on what Hector Dick came out with. We would soon find out.

16

FRIENDS LIKE THESE

JANUARY 2003

Hector Dick edged uncomfortably in the witness box at the High Court, Edinburgh.

'I asked him what had happened to her and he said she was dead,' he started, staring straight ahead, being careful not to look at his friend Nat Fraser. 'He said he had disposed of the body by burning it. He said he had ground up her remains, including her teeth, so there could be no identification through dental records.'

The court was silent. Two or three of the jury looked visibly shaken. Nat Fraser sat in the dock ashen-faced and unsmiling, looking down at his feet.

Dick explained that this confession of Nat Fraser was made while the two men were driving together with no one else present. Nat Fraser had apparently told him the lot.

However, according to his best friend, the accused hadn't confessed to murder – he had paid someone to do it. It cost £15,000 and he paid for it out of a secret stash he had. Dick had asked how Arlene was killed. The answer he said he received was silence but it was accompanied by Nat Fraser's hands miming strangulation.

Alan Turnbull QC, leading the prosecution, was now in full flow. What had happened to Arlene? Nat Fraser had apparently sung like a bird to Hector Dick on that also.

'He said he had been under surveillance but outmanoeuvred police by disposing of the body,' said Dick, without missing a beat.

For two weeks, Arlene's body was apparently hidden under the very noses of the cops and hundreds of civilian volunteers scouring the entire area and while Nat Fraser himself was under constant surveillance.

Was there anything else about that time? Plenty more it seemed, according to Dick. Nat Fraser was no fool. He'd read true-crime books on the only two cases where people had been convicted with no body. He'd read up on them in advance. And he took precautions on the day by going to the house at 2 Smith Street on the pretext of looking for Arlene.

'He told me he had cleaned up, that he'd wiped up,' said Dick, spelling out that Nat Fraser had confessed to covering his tracks. He said Nat Fraser knew that very day that the police would treat Arlene's absence as suspicious and would have their house forensically checked.

What reasons would Nat Fraser have had for killing Arlene?

Jealousy and greed, it seemed. But this had all come out in the weeks before Arlene had disappeared. Nat thought Arlene was going out too often socialising and that she was having an affair.

'He was green eyed on that side of things,' explained Hector Dick. 'He was jealous of Arlene. I recall him telling me he didn't consider she was a good mother and that she was lazy and lay in bed a lot.'

Nat Fraser didn't want anyone else living with his children, according to Hector Dick. And he didn't want to lose money. Before Arlene had disappeared, he had told his pal Hector that a divorce would cost him £86,000. Dick let that comment stand as if everyone understood that no one would want to cough up that amount of cash.

Nat had apparently talked to his friend about people who went missing – it happened all the time and no one bothered or looked for them. He said that he'd spoken to some people who knew about these things.

What about that car – that beige Ford Fiesta? Dick admitted to buying it from mechanic Kevin Ritchie but insisted that, on the night before Arlene disappeared, Nat Fraser had asked him to buy it.

Apparently, Dick had thought that his friend just wanted it to take goods out of his marital home.

Two days after Arlene disappeared, Nat Fraser had apparently told Dick that the car would be coming back and he delivered it to his farm three days after that. Inside, he says he saw some children's clothes and, in the back seat, there was a brown, half-length woman's coat. But the news of Arlene's disappearance and his chats with Nat had worried him so much he decided to destroy the motor.

'I decided I would burn the car,' he explained. 'I then flattened it with a digger and rolled it up so it would fit in a tractor trailer and went to the scrapyard at Elgin.' According to Hector Dick, that was on the 4th of May 1998 and he never saw the car again.

Hands up – Hector Dick admitted that he'd been convicted of attempting to pervert the course of justice over withholding information on that same car and that he'd been jailed for a year for it.

He must have felt bad about going to jail over that car?

Yes he did.

Had he ever discussed it with Nat Fraser?

Of course he had. 'I asked him if he would come clean on the car and his knowledge of it,' said Dick. 'He told me there was no chance and it was my own fault I'd got involved. He said I was in the real world now. He said he had an alibi and he wasn't budging. I was devastated.'

Hector Dick looked down at his feet. His face contorted into a grimace. Was it an expression of pain? Of terror? He answered that question himself, 'It was the first time we had fallen out about it. I was in tears.'

For goodness sake, why had the poor man not spoken out earlier or gone to the authorities?

'Previously, Nat had told me that I could say what I liked and he would just deny it,' Hector Dick said, still looking at his feet. 'That no one could prove anything. He had an alibi and he wasn't budging.'

There you had it. A planned murder, a paid hit man, covering his

186

tracks, hiding the body, destroying it, scattering the pieces and arranging an alibi to cover the day Arlene disappeared. If the jury deemed Hector Dick to be a credible witness, Nat Fraser was a dead man or at least he would be going to jail for a long time.

But, before the end of play that first day, Paul McBride QC, defending, had a chance to get back some ground through cross-examination. 'How many lies have you told to the authorities in the last five years?' asked McBride, having already called Hector Dick a consummate liar.

'Quite a few,' Dick admitted. He had already confessed to lying repeatedly about the car. That's what he meant and that's how it was left.

Things weren't looking good for Nat Fraser.

The next day, Paul McBride QC continued his onslaught on Hector Dick. He raised the issue of Dick having attempted suicide and had the witness agree that it wasn't a cry for help but a deliberate attempt to end his life. In Dick's view, he wanted to end it all and take the pressure off his wife. But McBride wasn't finished, 'Another reason why someone might try to kill themselves is remorse or regret at what they themselves have done. People who, for example, kill other people or commit crimes of a serious nature might be so depressed that they kill themselves.'

Paul McBride QC then tried to turn the tables on Hector Dick by referring to him having been seen outside Arlene's house seven days before she disappeared. He accused Dick of going on a reconnaissance mission. Dick denied it all. Instead, he admitted going to deliver a crate of smuggled booze to Arlene but he left when she wasn't in. He admitted his involvement in the trafficking lark and said he had been warned by the cops that Customs and Excise could easily chase him for unpaid tax – a lot of unpaid tax. And that was yet another worry.

Dick denied having anything to do with the murder of Arlene Fraser, who, he said, was a close friend of his for a decade. McBride wasn't having that either. Hadn't he just given evidence that he had listened to Nat Fraser talking about getting rid of his wife and then of having her murdered and destroying her body? What sort of man can listen to that and not do something? In his own way, Hector Dick admitted to being ashamed. Not good enough.

'You knew full well, during the course of this trial, that you were able to provide a statement to the prosecuting authorities,' Paul McBride accused. 'Putting words into Nat Fraser's mouth that were never said is your way of slithering out of a charge of murder that you know more about than you are prepared to tell us.'

'Not correct,' mumbled Hector Dick.

'Just as you have consistently lied to the authorities over the years,' McBride was going for him straight, 'even when you get off a charge, you are still prepared to stand there, with Arlene Fraser's family sitting in court, and mouth lie after lie after lie when you know the extent of your guilt and involvement.'

'That's not correct,' Dick insisted.

'You are a cold and calculating man and you are a clever man, aren't you?' continued Paul McBride.

'I don't know about that,' Dick replied, so low that it was almost a mutter.

'You think nothing about lying morning, noon and night, you think nothing about making up stories morning, noon and night and you think nothing about obfuscating the truth morning, noon and night.' Paul McBride QC was hammering Dick's credibility. Maybe he too thought the man was on edge – that he'd throw a wobbly when pushed.

He didn't. Hector Dick just denied it all and admitted, 'I don't expect to win any prizes.'

It was the understatement of the whole trial. If the jury believed Hector Dick, they would conclude that Nat Fraser killed Arlene. But they would also have to accept that Dick knew something of the plans in advance, helped by getting a car, then destroyed that car, suspecting it was incriminating evidence and then repeatedly lied to the cops about that car. If the jury believed Hector Dick, they would also have to accept that he heard Nat Fraser's confession to murder and decided to do nothing about it till he himself went on trial. But the jury weren't there to determine if Hector Dick was guilty or not. He was the star witness and he was finished.

Soon, the prosecution turned their attention to motive. 'I remember Arlene telling me that her husband had told her, if she was not going to live with him, she was not going to live with anyone,' Arlene's close friend, Marion Taylor, told the court. It was damning support of a motive, indeed. No one had any reason to doubt Marion Taylor. Like so many others, she had got caught up in this mess simply because she was a close friend of Arlene.

Another friend, Michelle Scott, took the stand. She was the friend who had had a lunch date with Arlene on the 28th of April – the date she didn't keep. Michelle could confirm that Arlene had a 'three-quarters length' fake leather coat that was never found in her house. It had been a chocolate-brown colour, similar to the colour and style of coat Hector Dick claimed to have seen in the beige Ford Fiesta on the day he destroyed the car.

That was the prosecution's case – confession, details and motive. It all hung heavily in the air and caused Nat Fraser's team great trouble. Normally, defence lawyers are reluctant to put the accused on the stand. It's just too risky – they can come across as uncaring or aggressive or juries can simply not like their manner. Of course, there are exceptions to this. One exception is if the defence believes the accused will make a particularly good impact on the jury. Another is if the prosecution case is particularly strong. If the first of these exceptions applies, putting the accused on the stand is an act of confidence. If the second applies, putting the accused on the stand is an act of desperation. Nat Fraser was never going to make a good impression on the jury and the prosecution case wasn't that strong yet he took the stand. It was a poor decision on both counts.

'I loved her and I didn't kill my wife,' Nat Fraser said, from the witness box, 'and I didn't pay anyone to kill my wife.' It was a start that was to give the flavour of his evidence – denial.

Nat Fraser had little to say in terms of helping the jury to an alternative view on what had happened to Arlene. He simply didn't know.

189

Paul McBride QC rattled the questions at his client fast and furious.

'Did you kill your wife?'

'No, sir.'

'Did you arrange for her to be killed?'

'No, sir.'

'Were you involved in her disappearance?'

'No, sir.'

'Did you threaten that, if you couldn't have her, nobody would?'

'No, sir.'

Again and again, 'No, sir' rang through the High Court.

What about the motive? Nat Fraser admitted openly to having what he called a 'festering jealousy', knowing that she was going out with other men. But he never thought he and Arlene would split up. All their married lives, they had fallen out and fallen back in again just as quick.

She was a good mother to wee Jamie and Natalie. He and Arlene had had more good times than bad times.

What about Hector Dick's evidence? What about his best friend saying he confessed to hiring a hit man and disposing of Arlene's body?

'It's rubbish he is coming away with,' Nat Fraser rumbled angrily, 'just lies.'

But Nat Fraser admitted that, in spite of Arlene having been missing for five years, he always believed that she was alive, always 'lived in hope'. Always, that is, until a few days before, when he heard Dick's evidence. Then, and only then, did he believe Arlene was dead.

When Alan Turnbull QC for the prosecution stood up, a special hush went through the court. The dog had seen the rabbit. Now what was going to happen? Turnbull wanted to know if it was true to say that Arlene was a well-liked person around Elgin – that she didn't have an enemy in the world.

Nat Fraser readily agreed.

'But with your marriage problems and a possible divorce, would

190

you agree that you are the only person with a possible motive to harm Arlene?'

Nat Fraser thought hard for what seemed to him an age but was only seconds. 'Yes, sir,' he answered in a low voice.

'The truth is that you have done a terrible thing,' declared Turnbull suddenly speaking louder.

'No, it isn't.' There was no polite 'sir' now. Nat Fraser was rattled.

'You have taken the life of the woman you promised you would live with forever.'

'No.'

'You have taken, from your own children, the life of their mother – all for greed and a wee bit of money.'

'NO!'

'Don't you think it's time to give up this futile hope that somehow you can still avoid responsibility for what you did?'

Nat Fraser just shook his head

'The evidence makes it perfectly plain you were responsible for the death of your wife.'

'No, I wasn't.'

There was more, much more but it was just more of the same. The prosecution had won the joust in a one-sided victory. Nat Fraser had spent many hours in the witness box only to make denials. It was not the best of positions.

The lawyers made their closing statements and Lord Mackay addressed the jury and summed up before the jurors were sent out to try to make some sense of it all.

But what sense did they make?

17

DECISION TIME

JANUARY 2003

Twenty-five years in jail. That's a lifetime. A generation. Twenty-five years in jail for Nat Fraser and no one even knows what happened to Arlene – not for sure. It couldn't be right.

I heard the jury's verdict by eight votes to six – the slimmest majority possible – then Lord Mackay's sentence at work. There had been nothing left for me to do in Edinburgh. They wouldn't let me near Nat anyway. No one thought there was anything I could do to help and, though I wanted to sit through the rest of the trial, I was thoroughly pissed off at fighting my way through the horde of media punters every time I tried to get in or out of the High Court. Besides, I reckoned Nat would be found innocent and acquitted as I had been. Hector Dick had spun a tale straight out of some pulp-fiction novel – even as a layperson I could see that. It was one man's word against another. Hector versus Nat. How the hell it was accepted as sufficient to convict a man to life in prison was beyond me.

When Nat had been sentenced to a minimum of twenty-five years in jail, Arlene's family came out and begged him to tell them where Arlene's body was. I believed they were wrong to see Nat's conviction as being so clear-cut, nor did I think they should take it for granted that Arlene was definitely dead. But I could understand their pain and their need for an answer – an unequivocal answer. I just wasn't sure the trial had given them that.

There was less sympathy in my soul for someone else who was

doing a lot of post-trial talking. Detective Superintendent Jim Stephen had been in overall charge of the case and now he seemed to be luxuriating in some kind of verbal victory dance. Speaking about Nat, Detective Superintendent Stephen announced to the press:

> It is not too late for him to begin to salvage some decency, some humanity. He takes with him to his cell the secrets of that terrible day in April 1998. We will visit him in prison to try to establish the truth of what happened to Arlene.

Are cops always so certain that they've got the right man?

Hector's evidence was tainted evidence, only given to save his own neck. Mostly, I was sick for my friend Nat, one of the gentlest people I'd ever met. That might sound strange in view of the fact that he'd served time for what was undoubtedly a brutal attack on Arlene but that assault was totally out of character and I wasn't the only one who thought that. Even as a kid in the playground, he'd avoided confrontations and fights and this trait had stayed with him through adolescence and into his adulthood. So, it took me days to even begin to get my head round the fact that he'd been found guilty of murder and sentenced to twenty-five years. Once I'd calmed down, I decided it was time to have a long, clear think about what might be rather than what I believed to be.

It must be confessed that, at one point at the High Court, surrounded by the cloaks and wigs and realising what a serious hole I'd landed in, I did start worrying about Nat and Hector. The two of them had been jailed together at Inverness. What sort of plot had they hatched there together if something bad had happened to Arlene? Were they setting me up? You can think you know someone without actually knowing great tracts of what they're about. I wasn't God, just an ordinary bloke. How was I to know what was really going on?

Of course, I pushed those doubts aside preferring to believe my friend Nat would never do such a thing against me. Then my worries were blown totally out of the water when I walked free. Hector had done a deal and ensured that Nat ended up in prison.

Hector was now doing other deals. For days, he was appearing in the press with some other sensational story about him and 'wife-killer Nat Fraser' as they now called him. For all that he looked the sour-faced, gruff sod that he was, he was acting the celebrity – for a price, of course.

Every day, the stories became more farcical. One that seemed to catch the public imagination was about Nat making porn films of him and three women and then proudly distributing copies, free of charge, around Elgin, his small home town. Hector even implied that Ian Taylor, Nat's pal and business partner, might well have been the cameraman since one of his sidelines was taking videos of weddings and the like.

I seemed to remember a conversation with Nat a couple of years back and went on the phone to Ian Taylor for confirmation. I remembered it right. Hector was into porn big time and was known for offering his latest acquisition to the lads. In all the time I had known Nat, sharing the most revealing excesses of our shagging behaviour, he hadn't mentioned porn once. I remember him saying at some point, 'I prefer the real thing to looking at dirty pictures' – much as I do myself.

What was Hector Dick doing? Was it payback time? Or was he just making up stories so that he would get paid? Or was it just because, with Nat safely tucked up in prison, he could say anything? Then Dick went to the papers again, talking about how he had been terrified, at one time, that Nat was going to kill him – how Nat had threatened him and Dick thought he was going to be thrown over a sixty-foot cliff. How he was so terrified that he slept with a shotgun under his bed and, a short time later, a bullet had sped past the cab of his lorry while he was driving.

'My Pal Nat Tried to Shoot Me', he was screaming. It was 'wife-killer Nat Fraser' yet again. Face it, if society believes you murdered your innocent wife, society will believe you are capable of pretty much anything.

'Wait a minute,' I spoke out loud, startling Maya by my side. 'I've heard that story before.'

'What?' I'd startled her from a reverie as she watched TV. If she was typically Russian, then one racial stereotype was right – they were deep buggers but passionate and direct.

'Do you remember?' I started hesitantly then immediately changed tack. 'Did I ever tell you about Hector Dick saying that someone had tried to shoot him?'

She blinked her eyes forcing herself to be fully alert, to give me all her attention. When she's thinking hard you can tell. No need to keep that secret as far as Maya is concerned. 'Eeehh, yes,' she eventually answered.

'Can you remember who he said had tried to kill him?'

'Sure,' she nodded her head, indicating yes and left it at that. These bloody Russians are too literal for my liking.

'Who did he say had tried to shoot him?' I said, pacing each word and feeling half desperate, half tourist abroad as I spoke.

'That man,' she looked to the side and upwards as if seeking inspiration. 'That young man.' It took me all my willpower to stop myself shouting at her to spit it out. 'The mechanic.' Maya pronounced that last word as if it were three separate words. I couldn't hold any longer.

'What was his name?' I stared down at her lovely face, imploring her to come up with the right answer – to speak that name soon so I wouldn't be tempted any more to spit it out and demand to know if that's who she was thinking of. She looked up at me and smiled – one of her big, broad open smiles, the type of unconditional smile a child gives his mummy or her daddy, the kind of smile that, if you ever stop appreciating it, you know you are dead.

'The mechanic – Kevin Ritchie.'

'You beauty,' I roared more than spoke and caught her startled face in my hands and gave her the biggest slobbery kiss I've ever given.

She looked up at me, smiling but questioning.

'I needed that,' I responded.

She just smiled wider, of course, a wicked curl at the end of her lips.

I took her face clasped between my hands. 'I needed to hear you say that name.' My Maya just smiled more. Fuck knows if she understood me at that precise moment in time. The beauty is that she didn't feel she needed to.

Hector Dick had lied – and it wasn't just a passing white lie to get out of an embarrassing situation like we all resort to from time to time. He's front-page news in the best-selling daily in Scotland – in fact, if you think about it in terms of per head of population, one of the best-selling papers in the world. He's up there and he's lying about Nat – lying to me and to the newspaper and to all its readers.

'If he can carry *that* off, he can sit in a court of law and lie his thick head off,' I thought, wrapping my arm around Maya and letting her settle back down to watch the TV and hopefully to forget about my mad turn. Maya did settle and got lost in some TV programme. Me? I started thinking.

Arlene's case had been raised on *Crimewatch*, the BBC TV programme that appeals for info on unsolved crimes. A while after that, Grampian Police's Crimestoppers had a call reporting that there was a Land Rover outside Arlene's house on the 28th of April 1998, the day she disappeared. And it was around 9.30 a.m., the approximate time she disappeared. And wasn't there another one? A neighbour thought they heard an engine noise like a Land Rover at the door of 2 Smith Street that morning? There was one person I knew of who knew Arlene and who drove a Land Rover – Hector Dick.

What had Andrew McCartan said at the end of the trial? 'Leave this alone, Glenn. It could be dangerous.' Andrew told me the story of Scottish lawyer Willie McRae, a radical bloke who was fighting the nuclear industry's dumping of waste and, by all accounts, he was close to winning. That was until he was found dead in his car off the remote A87 in the north of Scotland in 1985. McRae's death was quickly diagnosed as a suicide. Trouble was he had been shot twice and the murder weapon was found many yards from the scene of his death. McRae was known to have been shadowed at all times by MI5. 'These things do happen in Britain, Glenn,' Andrew had said, as he nodded in his sombre, serious way. 'It's only a matter of being aware of them and then taking great care.'

Edgar Prais QC, who was also there and was nodding in agreement, added, 'You never follow advice anyway, Glenn. Never have.'

At the time, I assumed he was describing me but was he advising me to back off? I didn't need that advice now – not after I knew Paul McBride QC had been right in the High Court. Hector Dick was a liar and a jury had jailed a man – OK, he was my friend – for a murder that nobody knew for certain had actually happened. Well nobody that was admitting it.

'Maya,' I rumpled her shoulder softly and she stirred by my side looking up into my face. 'I may have to go away quite a lot in the next wee while.'

'Where?' her voice was breaking, half asleep, half awake.

'Here and there – up north mainly.'

She nodded.

'And those holidays we had planned . . .'

She was wide awake now and staring at me quizzically.

'. . . might have to wait a while.'

She let the comments sink in before replying, 'It's about Arlene, isn't it?'

'Yes, about Arlene.' Though it was also about Nat and especially their kids, Jamie and Natalie. Nat's sister, Lynn, had had to tell them that their father was jailed and would be there for a long time. The children had lost their mother and now their father too – those poor bloody kids.

'You are going to . . .' Maya hesitated, looking for the right word, 'search for her?'

'Yes, in a way. Yes.'

'Are you not scared what you may find?'

'No.'

She looked at me as if I was a child who had come up with the wrong answer to a difficult question. 'Silly man,' she said and she squeezed my hand.

197

'I'm more terrified of doing nothing.'

She looked at me, smiled and kissed my cheek.

'So I'm going to do something.'

She was still looking at me, silent and smiling. 'Quite right too,' she said with deep approval.

18

ARLENE

The music was blaring with the THUMP THUMP THUMP of the bass shaking the wooden floor. In one corner, a group of young women wearing party hats, short skirts and low-cut tops invited every man to kiss the woman decked out in balloons, a tissue paper skirt and sign around her neck that said 'KISS THE BRIDE – LAST CHANCE'. They had been in every pub in Elgin and this was their last stop – the Newmarket Bar. It was where things happened in their town late at night.

Around the long bar, men and women, mostly young, stood in groups, crammed against each other, laughing, drinking, eyeing each other up. Here and there new couplings were being formed – whether for the night or longer no one seemed to care. It was party time.

He was chatting with his mates, shouting above the loud music but still hearing enough to catch the jokes. With his back to the door, he didn't see her come in. Long brown hair, slim and trendily dressed, she was attractive and on her own. She wasn't on a night out but on a mission.

From across the room, they watched her pick her way through the revellers. Unlike them, she seemed sober, serious. When she touched him on the shoulder, he turned and smiled then froze.

Those standing near them turned to watch and listen.

'So what happened to you?' she demanded.

'What you mean?' He was stooping down, their faces close.

'Thought you were staying in?' She didn't look pleased.

'Aye, I was but I just fancied a pint.' He stepped back and threw his arms out to the side, pleading for understanding.

'With them?' She pointed at the guys behind him.

'Aye, with the boys.' He took a sip of his drink.

'Instead of me?' Her voice was rising above the music.

He shrugged.

'Instead of coming round to see me? And what about her?' She pointed at the one woman in the group – a younger woman, in her late teens.

'She's nae with me!' He was shaking his head and shouting now, to make sure he was heard.

'Fucking looks like it to me!' Her voice was becoming a screech as she struggled to be heard over the music.

'She's . . .'

The woman reached out and smacked him hard across the face. His glass smashed on the floor as he grabbed at her arms but he was too late – or too drunk. She hit out again and scratched at his cheeks, yelling, 'YOU'RE NOTHING BUT A USELESS PRICK . . . FUCKING ME THEN NOTHING . . . LIKE YOU CAN JUST DROP ME, YOU FUCKING PRICK . . . WHO DO YOU THINK I AM? . . . A LITTLE WHORE LIKE HER . . . A CUNT LIKE THAT . . . ?'

Somehow he managed to wrap his arms round her body and hold her flailing fists safe by her side but still she kicked and screamed as others watched and grinned. He pulled her over to the side wall of the bar, where there were fewer people and it was dark. 'Please, Arlene,' he pleaded, gasping for breath, 'please calm down.'

This was just one of many scenes involving Arlene that Elgin folk eventually and reluctantly shared with me. Arlene was no angel. And who could blame her? Her marriage was on the rocks, she was young, intelligent and full of energy. Why shouldn't she have a life? But that's not what the High Court was told. All through the trial, the impression was that Arlene's life consisted entirely of being a loving mother and a good housewife. Perhaps the impression people were given of Arlene as a person can best be summed up by a description given to the Crown Office by her family.

Arlene's family, her mother – Isabelle Thompson and her husband Bill – her father – Hector McInnes and his wife Cathy – her sister – Carol Gillies and her husband Steve – have compiled information about Arlene that they would wish to share with you. It is their hope that this information gives an insight into the type of person Arlene was and how she is remembered by them.

ARLENE FRASER
Composed by her family, October 2002

Arlene was born in Elgin on the 18th of August 1964, the second daughter of Isabelle and Hector McInnes who, at that time, was a naval aircraft mechanic. He was posted to Malta in March 1966 when Arlene was a toddler and, after spending fifteen months abroad, the family returned to Elgin in May 1967. They settled in South Lesmurdie and Arlene attended the East End Primary School from August 1969. Out of school, she shared her mother's interest in horse riding, which suited her tomboyish personality.

Arlene's parents separated in 1971 and her father was subsequently posted to Cornwall. She continued to keep in contact with her father and many happy holidays were spent in Cornwall or at her grandparent's house in Edinburgh.

At the age of eleven, Arlene progressed to Elgin Academy. During this phase, typical teenage behaviour emerged. There were many rebellious spells and times when she hated school, often playing truant. Clashes of personality between Arlene and her sister Carol were a daily occurrence! Not surprisingly, she left school at sixteen with no particular academic ambitions or achievements.

Arlene went on to take employment in various short-term

201

positions. Her main permanent job was in a boutique in Elgin called the Time Machine. This work suited her well as her main interest at this age was shopping, clothes, make-up and keep fit.

Arlene only had a couple of steady boyfriends before she met Nat Fraser in 1985. They subsequently got engaged in September 1986 and married on the 9th of May 1987. The couple's first child, Jamie, was born in 1987. Arlene was besotted with her son and, in time, became a very relaxed mother. Jamie was dressed in the trendiest of clothes and Arlene adapted to the role of full-time mother with considerable ease. Natalie was born five years later in 1992. Arlene soon regained her figure after both pregnancies and she always looked good. With her make-up immaculate and dressed in the latest of fashions, the tomboyish look of her younger days was long gone.

She settled into a life of routine and started child-minding other children in the summer. Jamie and Natalie were enrolled in various activities and clubs. Arlene enjoyed driving and would happily take Jamie to Aberdeen on many an occasion to participate in swimming galas. As Natalie loved to sing and dance, Arlene enrolled her in the majorettes. Arlene was very content to build her life around the kids.

In 1997, Arlene announced she was returning to further education and enrolled on a two-year business course at Moray College.

According to other people who knew Arlene well, all of this is an accurate description of her. But it's what the description doesn't say – and perhaps what her family didn't know – that has been omitted.

As a teenager, Arlene would get into loads of rows with her parents as well as having regular run-ins with her sister Carol. On one occasion in her late teens, she ran away from home with her friend Shirley Surgenor. This was no overnight flight to somewhere

ARLENE

just down the road. The pair went off to London for several days. It was Shirley's older brother, Brendan, who was sent south to fetch the girls home. The same Brendan police visited in Lanzarote but who denied knowing Arlene at all. All teenagers have troubles at home but not all run away – and those who do often return, only to run away time and time again.

By all accounts, Arlene saw Nat Fraser as a catch and it was certainly a mutual attraction – Nat looked on her as a beautiful young woman. But Nat Fraser wasn't just handsome and good fun – he was also an entrepreneur with a reputation of making money, lots of money. Some thought he was one of the richest men in Elgin and that would be no mean feat. When they were engaged, Arlene would boast to friends that, 'I'll soon have a chequebook with all Nat Fraser's cash.' Arlene liked money and what it could buy – everyone knew that – but, at times, Nat Fraser would have disappointed her in that department as he was never as rich as people imagined.

Nat Fraser bobbed and weaved, making risky moves and always keen to explore another opportunity. At times, money was tight and the whole family would have to economise. It was a major disappointment for Arlene and a source of friction in the marriage.

Two weeks before their marriage, Arlene nearly called it off because she had caught Nat out, suspecting there was another woman. It was an aspect of his behaviour that never relented and another source of tension. But he wasn't the only one.

Maybe Arlene had thought that, if she couldn't beat Nat, she might as well join him at his own game. For years, she had affairs off and on. At the trial, when Nat Fraser admitted he had a 'festering jealousy' over the thought of Arlene being with someone else, what he didn't say was that he had been plagued by this jealousy for years.

When Arlene first disappeared, everyone else was thinking the worst but Nat reckoned she had just gone off with another man. This wasn't a new thought for Nat although it might well have been for Arlene's family. Well why should they know about Arlene and Nat's private life?

As their marriage deteriorated, Arlene spread her wings and spent a lot of time in Buckie and Cullen, small towns on the coast. Though close to Elgin in terms of distance, such rural communities separated by country miles have distinct identities of their own. An Elgin woman wouldn't be readily recognised on the streets of Buckie or Cullen. These were safe places for Arlene to let her hair down.

As one young local man recounted, 'There's a house in Buckie well known for its parties and drugs. Most of the folk that hang out there are in their early twenties. Arlene was a bit older but she looked good and she was into everything so . . . cool.' The young man refused to be named – as most people who speak of Arlene do. Their reluctance is always for the same reason – they fear the cops.

'It was a few months after Arlene had disappeared,' one Elgin man said, 'these uniformed cops came to my work and interviewed all the workforce. When it was my turn, they asked me if I had ever gone out with Arlene and I told them I had. It was only one night – a year before – for a few drinks. Next I know, they have me down at the police station grilling me for six hours. I wish to fuck I'd kept my mouth shut.' He told all his friends. They kept their mouths shut.

Another man told of when he was caught up in the door-to-door interviews. 'I was in with the wife at the time and the cops were very pleasant. We gave them a cup of tea and answered their questions in every way we could. One cop was chatting, like, and mentioned that they're also interviewing single men since some folk thought Arlene had run off with a bloke.

'The next day, I nipped down to the police station on my own and tells them that Arlene and I had a wee thing going – just a couple of nights in my car, down in one of the industrial estates. Just a bit of fun. You'd think I'd admitted to murdering her or something. They kept me for hours that day then pulled me in the next and every bloody day for a week. Even threatened to tell my wife about me and Arlene if I didn't give them more info. I didn't have more info to give them.'

He told all his pals. His pals stayed silent.

After a short while, Grampian Police could put their hands on their hearts and dismiss the theory that Arlene had run off with a man. It was official – there was no man in her life. The reality? There were *men* in her life.

Nat is my close friend but that didn't stop me finding Arlene attractive and vivacious. When she was in company, I could sense men responding to her, flirting a little, playing those cat-and-mouse games. And that's a compliment, not a criticism.

Go to any community anywhere and you can buy drugs – even big geezers like me who bear more than a passing resemblance to cops can get hold of them without any problems. During the hunt for Arlene, her parents angrily dismissed the suggestion that Arlene took drugs of any sort – well, parents do, don't they?

We know that she was a regular at house parties in Buckie and Cullen where dope, cocaine and ecstasy were consumed regularly. Those around that scene say that Arlene was into most things apart from dope but there's better evidence than hearsay.

During 1997 and the early part of 1998, when Arlene and Nat's marriage was rocky but while they were still living together, she used to be out several times a week. The Arlene I know wouldn't be one for late nights. Even at parties, she would often leave early, becoming tired and ready for bed by 10 o'clock. Then suddenly she started staying out later and later. It got to the point where she was arriving home the next morning while Nat was getting the kids ready for school. 'She'd be full of beans,' Nat said, from his prison cell, 'chatty and rushing around doing things. It just wasn't like her. Even when Arlene had had a full night's sleep, it usually took her a good while to come entirely to her senses. I couldn't understand it.'

The police forensic team had been through 2 Smith Street thoroughly, looking for anything suspicious. They found no sign of a struggle but they did find traces of the drug speed on the kitchen floor. Speed, of course, gives the user energy and makes them talkative. It's also the drug that some rookie doctors take to help them deal with marathon shifts and students use while swotting through the night with no sleep.

One of Arlene's male friends was reputed locally to be a drug dealer. I can't name him because we have no hard evidence but that's what the drug users say. The same man left Elgin a short while after Arlene disappeared – maybe even on the same day – leaving no forwarding address.

The court had made a big deal out of Arlene being a loving mother who would never leave her children. She was a loving mother – of that there is no doubt and I had seen that with my very eyes. But life isn't always easy, loving mother or not. When her relationship with Nat was at low points, Arlene seemed to hit those same low points – no surprise there. Several of her friends remember her saying things like, 'I could just get up and leave' and 'I could walk away from it all' and 'Yes, I could just leave the kids.'

Often, Nat Fraser would turn up with Jamie and Natalie at the chip shop in the nearby town of Aberlour. The staff behind the counter would chat away to the young kids, saying how nice it was they were out with their dad. They recalled that often one of the children say, 'Our mother can't be bothered with us.'

Not that it rates as hugely significant except for accuracy but Arlene hated housework and was reluctant to do it. For most of their married life, even when a full-time housewife, Arlene refused to do any washing or ironing for Nat. Since Nat started work before dawn and always worked late, his mother Ibby had been washing and ironing for him for years. Yet, in the High Court, Arlene was described as 'a good housewife'. It all adds up to feeding those kind of positive images we have in our minds – positive images are just another form of prejudice, albeit positive prejudice.

Again and again, the cops reiterated that Arlene hadn't taken her medication for her Crohn's disease – something, they said, she would never do. Crohn's is an irritable bowel condition that can produce intense stomach cramps, vomiting, low energy and bleeding. The farther north in Scotland you go the more common it is. It is a long-term or chronic condition and can often result in weight loss. However, many Crohn's sufferers go for long periods without any of the symptoms. Some feel so well they are tempted not to take their medication.

ARLENE

The disease also has one other potential symptom – depression. Most people associate depression with feeling down. However, while it often does manifest itself in that way, it can also produce compulsive, rash behaviour – a deep sense that it's time to get rid of everything that's bad in your life. And sometimes that's you or sometimes it's what's around you.

Arlene was consulting a lawyer about divorce. She was also getting an education and forming other relationships. Arlene was already making a new life for herself. Maybe on that day, the 28th of April 1998, she just decided to do it quicker.

Arlene Fraser was no angel and a good thing it was too. Who'd want an angel for a friend or a wife?

19

HECTOR

There was a handful of drinkers and they were all men – older working men, smoking and chatting and keeping one eye on the football match being played out on the TV screen high on the wall. The door swung open and their voices hushed as they all turned to see who was coming through that door. They miss nothing in the Imperial Bar, Elgin.

'Sometimes Hector Dick comes in here, aye,' said one of the younger drinkers. 'But not often and nobody speaks to him. Nae just in here but in the whole of Elgin. Nae after what he's done.'

Almost a year after the murder trial, the people of Elgin told me the same thing again and again. Whatever their theory on Arlene, whatever their view of Nat, they didn't want Hector Dick in their midst.

'Nat Fraser wasn't really my best friend.' Hector Dick's words had rung round the High Court. 'I just used to spend some time with him. He was good company.'

I could fathom out why someone frightened for their life might well turn and tell lies but was there any need for Hector Dick to deny a friendship? What was the point? Did he hope that, by doing so, he could, in the eyes of the people of Elgin, distance himself from Nat and what he'd been convicted of? Too late, Hector, it didn't work.

Hector Dick wouldn't speak to me, of course. So I had to speak to others. That was harder than it should have been.

'Aye, aye, Ian. Chilly night, eh?' It was the boss of one of the small country hotels that are dotted around Morayshire – a nice place. The boss was working behind the bar that night and, typical of a rural area, he knew everyone – or thought he did.

'Aye, it's chilly. Just the night for a wee warmer,' replied Ian Taylor, Nat's former business partner.

'What will you have then, gents,' asked the boss-cum-barman and Ian gave him our order. 'Have you heard how Nat's getting on?'

'Aye, as fine as can be expected,' replied Ian, with typical under-statement given that Nat had started a twenty-five-year jail term. 'Have you seen much of Hector?' he continued.

'That bad bastard? Na, na. He doesn't come in here which is just as well,' replied the barman, suddenly drying a glass with vigour, his tone laden with threat.

'What, is he barred?' Ian was joking.

'Na. Nae barred,' the barman was deadly serious, 'just nae welcome.'

'But he's no' moved away or anything?'

'Na. Hasn't budged. Drives about the town as if he's whiter than white!' The barman was shaking his head, half in amazement and half in disgust. 'He'll get his comeuppance though. One of these days.' The barman put the drinks on the bar then asked, 'Whatever happened to that big dodgy English fucker?'

I edged past Ian up close to the bar, 'How do you do.' I held out my hand to shake. He took it. 'I'm that big dodgy English fucker.'

'How the hell did I nae see you?' he asked, blushing but smiling.

Most other people do see me – I'm hard to miss. That was either a good thing or a bad thing but, in other ways, I wasn't taking chances. Every time I headed north, I tried to change my car and made sure all my family had Andrew McCartan's number handy. I had keyed it in to the quick dial on my mobile. If most of the locals knew who I was, the police certainly would. They knew me well, after all, and, if they nabbed me for any reason, I was going to make sure Andrew was phoned pronto.

Local people have a lot to say about Hector Dick but only in private. This wasn't in an effort to avoid unwanted and over-zealous police attention – it was mainly through fear. The most unlikely hard nut of an individual was scared of Dick. I wondered why.

Hector Dick is from farming stock, born and bred around Mosstowie. Although the north-east of Scotland has rich fertile land that is wonderful for some crops and produces good grass for dairy cattle, farming can still be a precarious way of life. There used to be small farms everywhere in that corner of Scotland but, gradually, they either failed or a generation decided not to follow that way of life and they had to be sold out to the big boys. Not Hector Dick – he was going to survive come hell or high water.

When you speak to Dick, he likes to come across as the wee daft laddie – not very bright, one step behind the leader. But this is just a front. He is as sharp as they come and that's the reason his farm is still going strong and he's going from strength to strength financially. But he almost lost it all before he started – over a girl.

'Come on then,' the young man pulled up her top exposing her breasts.

In the dark, she giggled.

'Beauties,' he mumbled, rubbing her nipples and squeezing her breasts with his big, calloused hands. 'Let's see yer fanny,' he grunted, the urgency in his voice changing his manner from pleading to demanding. With one hand, he hiked up her skirt and started yanking at her pants. No experienced lover, he was rough, uncertain, hurried. But he could be excused – he was young but not as young as she was.

Within seconds, he mounted her, riding her roughly – rutting not making love. But he could be forgiven his clumsiness. Even though he had been working the farm for years and earned a man's wage he was only young – but much older than her. She was still at school – well below the legal age limit. But what did that matter? She was willing to have sex. She'd had sex with other young men so why shouldn't Hector Dick have sex with her too?

At the age of nineteen, Hector Dick was convicted of underage sex with a local girl. At least three other young men were convicted of the same offence with the same girl. I'll not mention her name – she's a grown woman now with a family of her own. Those who remember the incident write it off as being not very serious. The girl had been willing, after all, and the men were . . . well, they were young.

The penalty was light – in keeping with the 'it happens' attitude that was prevalent at the time. These days, they wouldn't have been so lucky. Today, it would have been different. The fact that they were all much older than her and that they knew each other well could raise the possibility that they might have groomed her to participate in their sordid games.

These days, at the very least, the culprits would have found themselves on probation – if not in jail – and on the sex offenders' register, possibly for the rest of their lives. We know a lot more about sex abuse now than when Hector Dick was nineteen. We protect our young folk better too.

The jury at the High Court knew nothing of that aspect of Hector's past.

Sex had always been a big thing for Hector Dick. But money was his other big lust – still is. Sometimes it brought him into dangerous territory.

The old man sat at the table, nodding, half asleep. Jimmy Lauder was in Hazelbank Farm. It was owned by his brother but Willie Lauder had gone into a nursing home and Jimmy was there to check up on the farm.

The farmhouse was silent but, from somewhere behind him, Jimmy heard a creak and just after that his lights went out with a blinding flash. When Jimmy came to, he had a large lump on his head and Hazelbank Farm was on fire. He crawled under the worst of the smoke and made it to the door. Just then, a passer-by stopped and raised the alarm. But it was too late – Hazelbank was gutted. The fire was too much for Jimmy Lauder and, six months after Hazelbank was torched, he died. His assailant was never caught.

Willie and Jimmy Lauder had both lived the hardy life of the north-east farmer all their days. Though still in his early 60s, when

Willie began to show signs that he was getting on – he was a bit frail and his hearing and eyesight were not as good as they had been – he'd reluctantly agreed to go into the nursing home. So, with Jimmy dead and Willie in a nursing home, there was no option for the family but to sell both brothers' farms. They got £200,000 – not a fortune for two lifetimes' work but there would be more than enough to care for Willie for the rest of his days in the nursing home with a bit left over for his relatives. However, someone else had other ideas.

'Hecky, why do you go and visit old Willie Lauder so much,' Nat Fraser had asked.

'Ach, I'm just doing him a good turn,' Dick had replied, 'and, you never know, there might be something in it for me.'

And Nat Fraser wasn't the only person to be asking why Hector Dick was visiting his neighbour Willie Lauder almost every day. Dick wasn't known for his charity – quite the opposite.

A short while later, Hector and his wife Irene invited Willie Lauder to leave the nursing home and to come stay at their farm. He had never felt comfortable in the caring regime of the home and he accepted in a flash, seeing what he thought would be an opportunity to regain some of the independence he missed so much. But Willie Lauder didn't move into the Dicks' farmhouse. They installed him in what Dick called 'the bothy' – an old run-down caravan with no facilities. It was the type of rough-and-ready place that some people might keep free-range hens or use for storage. It was certainly not suitable as a home for an old man. Despite his hardy background, Willie had never had to endure such bleak conditions. He was an accident waiting to happen and it did.

On the 17th of March 1998, Willie Lauder was crossing the yard. Somehow he didn't hear or see the muck spreader reversing towards him. Roger Mustard, a neighbour of Dick who sometimes did some work for him, was driving and he didn't see Willie Lauder either. Four weeks before Arlene went missing, Willie Lauder died in hospital from his injuries. It was a tragedy but there was worse to come.

Not long after Willie Lauder moved out of the nursing home,

HECTOR

Hector Dick had driven him through to a lawyer called Liddle in Forres. Unable to read or write, Willie needed the guiding hand of a trusted friend and, in the lawyer's office, the old man changed his will, making Hector Dick the main beneficiary of his estate and, following Willie's death, Hector Dick found himself £130,000 richer courtesy of the old man.

Soon after he'd overseen the change to Willie's will, the lawyer Hector Dick had taken Willie to disappeared. He was due to attend a formal hearing with Law Society officials who were concerned about some of his business practices. Local people were worried and Willie Lauder's family called for an inquiry. There was none.

A £130,000 windfall would be good enough for most people but not for Hector Dick. He was always trying to make money. He operated as a pig farmer but he also had a coal yard at his farm and he owned big diggers that he would hire out, often with himself as the driver. At one point, he bought a house in one of the most upmarket parts of Elgin and he moved his sister-in-law in to it. He'd boasted to Nat Fraser that, although she was a relation, he still charged her rent. Of course, that wasn't anything too scandalous but then there was the illegal booze.

'It's just a cheap dram,' Dick would say later. 'Nothing big – just a box here and there.'

Everyone in Elgin knew that Hector Dick was the man bringing smuggled booze into the town. Many would buy it from him directly or go through one or other of his contacts. But it wasn't just small-scale deals that were being done in which a number of pubs and clubs made large, regular purchases. Why not? It was top-class booze, properly labelled and so on – it was just that no tax had been paid on it. Two lorry loads of booze were being smuggled into Elgin every week. That's a racket worth at least £300,000 every single week of the year – it was a serious business with some big-time players behind it.

Gangs in the central belt specialise in smuggling in booze on which tax hasn't been paid. But, curiously, while the west of Scotland and Glasgow has the reputation for organised crime, the biggest

213

smugglers of booze and cigarettes can be found in the east, around Edinburgh. Hector Dick had family and social connections in Fife – in the east, near Edinburgh.

The way these teams work means that their local connection, the frontman, gets a percentage of the total value of booze sold – maybe as much as five per cent. For this, they have to take orders, collect the cash and make sure the money is paid to the gang on time. It's a lucrative business for the frontmen – as long as they don't get caught.

Arlene had been gone for over three years and the cops were putting pressure on Nat Fraser and Hector Dick when Nat Fraser observed, 'You're looking a bit worried, Hecky. What's up?'

'They've caught me with the booze,' Dick replied, all sullen.

'Red-handed?' Nat Fraser laughed – everyone knew that Hector dealt in booze and must have been the easiest lawbreaker in history to catch.

'No. Well, aye. They're saying that Customs are demanding money. Unpaid tax. They're saying it'll be at least £175,000.'

'Jesus Christ,' his pal whistled sympathetically.

'Aye, Jesus Christ right enough.'

When it was clear to me that Hector Dick was also being dragged in to the search for Arlene, I made efforts to talk to him on the phone. In one conversation, he repeated the claim about Customs and Excise with that precise figure. It wasn't till after the trial that Nat Fraser and I put these bits of information together. We both agreed that the prospect of losing so much money had seemed to weigh heavier on Hector Dick than the hassle he was getting from the murder squad.

It turns out that Hector Dick has never had to pay Customs and Excise any money for unpaid tax on smuggled booze. Had the cops lied? Or was a deal struck, in the bowels of the High Court, securing Dick's evidence in exchange for the demand for the unpaid tax money going away?

Frontmen in the smuggling rackets tend to trust very few other people to do the business for them. The goods are too valuable – and too tempting – and the amount of money too large to trust anyone else. But Hector Dick did trust one other person – Arlene.

214

'Everyone knew you could buy booze from Arlene,' her friend Patricia Gauld had said in court. As with Hector Dick, selling the smuggled booze didn't seem to be a problem. It wasn't as if it was a big crime, in most people's opinion. It was just the taxman you were cheating. But it was big money. And where there is big money, there are big risks – and not always from the cops.

One week before she went missing, Arlene was on the phone to her sister, Carol. 'That Hector Dick's been hanging about outside for ages,' said Arlene, sounding worried.

Carol heard a long silence as Arlene obviously watched at the window.

Carol doesn't report hearing knocks on the door but, eventually, she heard Arlene sigh in relief and say, 'That's him away.'

'What was that about?' asked Carol.

'I don't know,' replied Arlene and they continued with their conversation. But did Arlene know? Why didn't she let that old friend in? Why did she seem so frightened?

Later, Dick would claim that he had gone there to deliver a crate of smuggled booze and had been surprised Arlene wasn't in. He would have known that that day, Tuesday, was the one day Arlene didn't have college or other commitments. She was likely to be around the house, still in her dressing gown, if he called early enough but not too early. He could have visited at other times, like the evenings or the weekend, but he chose to call when he knew the children were out and Arlene had all day. And what was so important that he hung around 'for ages'? Was it business or pleasure he had in mind?

Arlene Fraser showed one or two of her friends a box full of money. She described it to them as either her 'rainy-day fund' or her 'escape money'. She didn't tell any of them how she had come by it. It certainly wasn't from her housekeeping money or her Family Allowance. There was just too much there.

It also wasn't from selling the odd box of booze for Hector – the 'cheap dram', as he called it. Anyone who knows Hector Dick will tell you that getting his full cut from the sales of the alcohol was of paramount importance to him. Once he'd taken his share and his suppliers had got their cut, there wouldn't have been much profit on the odd box of booze for Arlene and the others who actually sold it on. However, if it wasn't just a box here and there she was dealing in, if she had a range of customers on a larger scale, it could have added up – especially if she had failed to pay Hector all or some of his cut. And, if she hadn't paid him his share of the money paid to her on a big order of booze, all sorts of hell would have ensued. Not only would Hector Dick have failed to get his cut but the big team behind the racket would also be left out of pocket. That's just asking for trouble. Gangs like that don't wait for long and they don't take no for an answer. Nor do they care about smaller fish down the line like Arlene. If they had a deal in place with Hector Dick, they would expect Hector Dick to pay – even if he hadn't been paid himself.

Was that why Arlene was scared that a man she had known as a friend for ten years was hanging around her house? Was Dick there to collect rather than deliver? Had she been avoiding him because of the cash? Had she been avoiding him for so long that she knew he'd be angry? In a town the size of Elgin, she must have known she couldn't avoid him forever. Did Arlene know that, one way or another, her time was running out?

There's another reason.

'He gives me the shivers every time he comes into the shop,' one young sales assistant revealed.

'Since the trial do you mean?'

'Noooo,' she was adamant, 'he's always given me the shivers. It's like he's undressing you every time he looks at you.'

It was clear she didn't like the thought of Hector Dick undressing her. But she's not alone. Many Elgin women have the same feelings about Dick and have had ever since they met him.

In better, friendlier times Nat Fraser and Ian Taylor would laugh at Dick's fantasies of stripping women and particularly at those veterinary fantasies he shared that involved tubes, syringes and sheets of plastic just like the ones he had in his barn.

'I could never quite work out what he was getting at,' said Nat Fraser. 'What were those props about? Doesn't he like women?'

Hector Dick had always sought out Arlene when she was alone right from the start of his friendship with Nat. He'd often arrive during the day when he knew Nat was out at work. Sometimes early in the morning he'd bring her morning rolls and sit with her over a cup of tea while she was still in her nightclothes. Dick would listen to Nat talking about gigs he had with his band then, when he was out and playing, the pig farmer would call round to see Arlene.

It had been a standing joke for years that Hector Dick lusted after Arlene. So much so that he went public to the newspapers after the trial saying, 'Arlene was a good friend, that's all.'

In April 1998, Arlene and Nat were separated, she was pursuing divorce and, like other locals, Hector Dick would have known she was seeing other men. Did he now think that Arlene was fair game?

But she wasn't – not as far as he was concerned. Arlene liked men who had pleasant faces, were quick-witted, dressed well and spent money. Dick in her view was dull faced, slow, dressed in a boiler suit most of the time and was mean with his cash. Hector Dick had no chance with Arlene but did he accept that?

As part of his defence against the rumours that he was lusting after Arlene, Dick cited that his wife, Irene, trusted him alone with her. Whether that's true or not is for Irene to answer. But, in the police hunt for Arlene Fraser, Irene Dick was interviewed around eighty-five times – much more often than almost everyone else. Why?

The cops agreed with the local people – Irene had to know more about her man Hector's comings and goings than anyone else. Whatever they were, they were not revealed in the High Court.

20

NAT

When I decided to do this book, I went to see Nat in jail. 'You're my good friend, Nat,' I started awkwardly, 'you know that?'

He nodded looking worried about what was coming next.

'Will you help me write this book?'

'Of course I will,' he replied instantly.

'But I need to tell you . . .' This was bloody hard, especially in Shotts Prison visiting room surrounded by other prisoners, their friends, CCTV cameras and screws. 'if I find out anything that convinces me you killed Arlene, that's what I'll write.'

'Of course you will.'

'What?'

'You've always been an awkward bastard, Glenn. As corrupt as anyone I know.' He smiled. 'But some things you'll not compromise on. Am I right?'

'Yeah . . .' I said but without knowing where he was going with this.

'One thing is, if Arlene really *is* dead, finding out who killed her?'

'Yeah . . .'

'And the other thing is, if you think it's me, you won't hesitate to say so? Right?'

I let his comment sink in. 'That's what I . . .'

'So where will we start?' He took a sip of his coffee and smiled and that was that.

Leaving the jail later, out into a winter Lanarkshire day, I knew I had to go to a certain place – the place where they knew Nat – and ask them about the man.

'Arlene?' the waitress looked suddenly forlorn, her bright smile withering on her face. 'Arlene must be dead.' I nodded and looked up at her from the table.

'Why can't she be missing?' I wasn't demanding but being as open and as neutral as I knew how.

'A mother doesn't leave her wee ones.'

I'd heard this so often that it was becoming like a mantra. 'Even if she had troubles?'

She nodded her head.

'Are you a mother?'

Another nod. I left it for a second. 'This looks tasty.' I smiled at the waitress, genuinely and easily complimenting her on the food. One of the beauties of a place like Elgin is that so much of the food comes from the surrounding farmland and, in this case, the sea. It's one of the best places I've known for steak or a fish supper.

'It was a real shame, you know . . .' She wasn't leaving the main subject now that I had opened the door. She honoured me. Many of the folk I had spoken to had just walked away. 'Arlene.'

'And what about Nat? Did you know him?'

'Aye,' she laughed, 'Nat was a good laugh. He was always on the go. On my way home from work, I used to see him a lot of nights with Jamie and Natalie. They always seemed to be laughing.' When they did speak of Nat it was always in the past tense as if he was dead and gone already, not just a couple of hundred miles down the road in a prison cell.

'A good father then?'

'Oh, aye, I think so.' She was smiling broadly.

'So do you think he killed Arlene?'

'I couldn't say,' she was picking up dirty dishes from the table next to mine and she was off. When it was time for my next course, another waitress came to my table.

Nat Fraser is too good a friend of mine. You think you know

your friends, make judgements on how they'd behave in certain situations and how far they'd go in others. But this was too big to be driven by what I thought of my pal Nat. I had to ask others from his home town about what they thought of Nat.

'Gentle.'

'Sweet.'

'Never looking for a fight.'

'Always the one way – good.'

'I've known him thirty years and never seen him lose his temper.'

I could go on but you get the point. Those who were willing to be a little critical would come out with comments like, 'A shagger not a murderer.' or 'I wouldn't buy a second-hand car off him but I'd feel safe in his company.'

Nat Fraser is a chancer, a Jack the Lad, a guy who can't keep his trousers on when the talent is good. He'll sweet-talk you with a smile and take you for a ride. I've seen it all but I've never seen him really harm people. Annoy? Yes. Frustrate? Often. Take advantage of? Certainly.

There are two things Nat takes seriously in life – his kids and his music. And they're in that order by a long chalk. Even now in jail, if I ask him what he wants brought in, he'll ask for a string for his guitar or a particular book of music. Well, I can't bring him his children. I'm the one who adds some top-shelf magazines for his entertainment. And that's about it.

Nat Fraser is a man of few appetites. An occasional glass of beer, a few ciggies a day, not big on his grub, likes a good film but no more than once in a while, drives fast when he needs to, though seldom for fun, can hold a conversation about sport but not for long, dresses well but casually and effortlessly, doesn't sit and sink into slushy, mind-numbing TV hour after hour. Few appetites then – but he has one that is overwhelming.

Nat's big weakness is and always has been sex. Women find him attractive and he has never been able to resist. It's a big weakness. The story about him and the Church of Scotland Minister's wife is true. He's had a lover in every coastal town he'd visit with his van on deliveries. In Portsoy, he'd spend half an hour in bed with one and, by the time he reached Cullen a few miles down the coast, he'd be ready for a session with another one. Both of their men folk would be away in the middle of a raging North Sea, fishing for our food in some of the most dangerous waters in the world. He's even done double-ups not just with two drunken friends but with sisters and mothers and daughters.

Is it a terrible way to behave? Maybe but that's a call for each of us to make according to our standards. Me, I don't judge him badly on that one at all. In fact, for years I thought, if there was ever likely to be any violence around Nat, it would involve him getting a battering from some cuckolded husband.

Most men would already be jealous just reading that short summary of his exploits. If they were to be guaranteed that level of success, many men would find it difficult to refuse. Nat found it impossible all his life. Put simply, he loves women and they seem to love him.

Yet it was Nat who wanted to settle down. Arlene didn't. While she might well have boasted to her pals about soon 'getting Nat Fraser's chequebook', of the two of them, she was the one who was all for another few years of light-hearted freedom. It was Nat who persuaded her, eventually, to get hitched. And there lies the start of the contradiction.

Nat Fraser was desperate to settle down but couldn't stop screwing around. Arlene knew that better than anyone but couldn't stop wanting him – she was attracted to that same part of Nat that other women noticed and drove them into bed with him, sometimes just minutes after they met.

It's OK now to say that their marriage was heading for disaster from the start but that was their lives, the only ones they had and they were caught headlong together. Then the second part of the contradiction hits home.

Ever since Nat was convicted for assaulting Arlene, I couldn't reconcile the Nat I knew with the man who had throttled his wife. I hadn't asked him while it was all going on – it seemed he had enough

221

to contend with. But now, in the prison, it was different. 'What happened that day, Nat? That was a terrible thing to do to her.'

His face lost colour – no mean feat for someone whose complexion was already beginning to have that milky jailhouse pallor.

'It was bad,' he ringed his cup with his hands then suddenly stopped. 'Look, Glenn, this is no' easy.'

'I know and I'm sorry. I'm truly sorry but I need to know.'

He nodded and looked to the side as if checking out who might be listening. 'Arlene came home that night – well, that morning – and I tackled her about it later in the day. She'd told me before about men she'd been with and I found that . . .' His voice started to break till he recovered his composure. 'This is fucking difficult, man.'

'We can leave it if you want.'

He shook his head. 'She didn't deny being with a guy but refused to name him. I pestered her, getting angry and burning up with jealousy. And she says, "Want to know who I was with? I'll tell you. I was with the biggest cock in Elgin." She held her hands out to show me the size and smiled at me. Then she says, "Know how I know exactly how big he was? I was gobbling him all night." And she mouthed a blow job, her eyes all laughing. I fucking cracked right up. You know how they say you see red when you're angry? Fuck it – it's true. I just lost the place completely and the next I know I've got her by the neck and she's gone limp and . . . fuck, you know.'

When I left the prison that day, I'd felt I'd wandered into some place I shouldn't have been. I felt dirty, soiled. I'd seen inside the relationship of two good friends. Parts no one else should see but them. Normally. But this wasn't a normal situation. For Christ's sake, where was Arlene?

Some might say that Nat Fraser can dish the dirt but can't take it. They might say he can't stand the thought of his woman leading a life that was just like his. They might say that sexual jealousy is a killer and it can be. It just seemed to me that on that terrible day when Nat throttled Arlene, the air was full of feeling, rank emotion and heated, nasty, face-to-face confrontation. It was bad – very bad – but is it the same as coldly planning a killing?

Hector Dick took old Willie Lauder to see Forres lawyer Alistair Liddle and, there, he changed his will, leaving a substantial sum to Dick. When Liddle then disappeared, the cops were worried that he may have been killed. In fact, he turned up in Cornwall where he'd been picking berries for a living. He was looking in much better health than he had been before and he had a fresh-faced young woman as his partner. But, before all that transpired, it wasn't Dick the cops hounded over Liddle's disappearance but Nat Fraser.

Nat was interviewed several times as the suspected murderer of Alistair Liddle and the cops accused him of having dumped his corpse in the Moray Firth off Findhorn. This was long before the people of Elgin began to feel that Arlene's disappearance was much more than a case of her having gone off somewhere – this was murder. Nat had no connection with Liddle. The cops had feared the worst had befallen the lawyer only to come across him by accident.

A TV programme on fruit-picking in the south of England had shown one worker who seemed worryingly familiar to some Scottish viewers. Though now several stones lighter, fit and suntanned, some north-east folk thought they recognised the man as Liddle. It was him all right. He had gone off to create another life for himself and he looked as if he was very happy with the way things had turned out. He returned to Scotland to face the music over the questions about possible irregularities in the accounts relating to his former legal practice. And this was the man the local cops believed had been murdered.

In some ways, what happened with Alistair Liddle anticipated Arlene's disappearance. The two had many things in common. The man had his professional worries and he was unhappy at home but he seemed to be going about his business as normal. The cops quickly concluded that he must be dead. Then they interviewed Nat Fraser as a suspect. Why they did so remains an unexplained puzzle which can only lead us to conjecture.

Nat Fraser's easy-going style, popularity, cheeky manner and fondness for women didn't always act in his favour. There were people, mainly men, who thought him too big for his boots and took pleasure in seeing him in trouble.

Grampian Police, like all police forces even to this day, consists mainly of male officers. Had the cops already decided that Nat Fraser was the culprit behind Arlene's disappearance even before they had any evidence? When Arlene went missing, did they put a circle round Nat's name and his name only even before they suspected something untoward had happened to her?

21

DEATH AND THE DETECTOR

2003

'Here's to freedom!' Andrew lifted his drink and we clinked glasses.

'And how about to justice?' I suggested.

'Now that would be something worth toasting,' he smiled.

While other lawyers would have ended contact with their client on the day he was acquitted from court, Andrew McCartan had stuck by me, helping in my search to understand how Nat Fraser had ended up in jail and giving what assistance he could in tackling the puzzle of what exactly had happened to Arlene.

We were sitting in a bar in Aviemore, close to his office. It was the first time we had actually been together since the High Court although we had continued to talk on the phone several times a week. I'd frequently suggested that I'd take him out to lunch but, as ever, it had taken an age to arrange a mutually convenient time. Andrew was worth a lot more than a lunch.

'You know,' he said, between mouthfuls of food, 'approximately 20,000 people go missing in Scotland each year.'

'Twenty fucking thousand?' I knew it was common but that made it feel like an epidemic. 'That's what? Almost sixty a day.'

He nodded his head and swallowed before he replied, saying, 'Most come back in a short time apparently.'

'What? Within hours?'

'A couple of days maybe. But the longer they've gone the less likely it is they'll return.'

'Like Arlene you mean?'

'Maybe like Arlene, maybe not.'

'So . . .' I stopped eating and looked at him closely. 'you don't think I'm entirely fucking crazy then?'

'Never have,' he said as he smiled one of his little smiles.

'The police do though?'

'Ah yes, the self-congratulating police.'

We didn't know it then but the cops' chest-beating was going to get worse. Later, the murder inquiry team would be given the Grampian Police Chief Constable's Award. And then Detective Superintendent Jim Stephen, who led the investigation, would be awarded the Queen's Police Medal in the Queen's Birthday Honours List. Grampian Police would also win other awards directly tied to the case including, somewhat bizarrely, a Scottish PR Award.

'They aren't half crowing about Nat's conviction, are they?' I was being polite. I felt angry that all the public were being shown was that Grampian had got their man. Lives had been affected, in some cases irreparably, folk had been falsely accused, it had cost some families a great deal of money and there were still so many unanswered questions – but none of that seemed to matter.

'It's their right,' sighed Andrew, before changing the topic. 'How's the family?'

It wasn't the normal polite question as between friends. My daughter Zoë lived down in Croydon and she had had her problems. She and her boyfriend had had a wee baby and they were planning on getting hitched. But then he left and started acting like a right cold bastard – a love-struck, doting dad one minute and the next he's playing hard ball, trying to take all their dosh, refusing to pay a dime towards the little one's care and even demanding a DNA test. A couple of times on the phone, I had threatened to give the prick a right good bashing. Of course, I later discovered my phone was bugged at that time but nothing came of it – obviously our modern cops still aren't interested in domestics.

But me being charged brought other problems to Zoë's door. She had suddenly found herself almost friendless during the trial but, after my acquittal, the so-called friends started to reappear. My mother, at her age, had also found her Christmas cards a bit light on numbers and now could never phone anyone without wondering if some copper was listening to the conversation.

'Fine, just fine,' I replied to Andrew's question about my family.

'No more threatening letters?' he asked.

'Yeah, another one last week – tame compared to the others.' I'd received a few death threats and so had the work. Also, someone had sent my boss copies of the *Press and Journal*, the newspaper that serves the north-east of Scotland, every time there was big coverage of the investigation or case.

'Cases like this do bring out the nutters, Glenn. But they'll give up after a while.'

I nodded. It didn't bother me if the sad souls wanted to waste their lives scribbling threats – as long as they kept it to written threats. If they came near me or mine, that would be a different matter and I'd let them have it. Whatever it took.

A while before, I had been doing a bit of business in Norfolk and realised I was close to where Tony Martin lived so I looked him up. Martin was the farmer jailed for shooting a burglar dead and wounding his accomplice. Some people had made his case into a bit of a cause célèbre over the lengths you can go to when protecting your home. That wasn't my issue and I certainly never intended to get myself fixed up with a loaded shotgun but I was curious about him.

Rumour had it that he no longer lived in his home but in a wheelless car on his farm. When I saw him, he certainly looked scruffy enough for that to be true. He was also renowned for being a total loner so I expected short shrift but, in fact, he chatted with me.

Maybe it's because we come from similar backgrounds, I don't know, but we chatted about public school and how prison was just like those regimes, even down to the perpetual threat of violence. Martin hated jail, it seems, not because of the basic facilities but because of the people and the wardens ordering him about. However, he seemed to have hated school even more.

Tony Martin didn't hesitate when I asked what most people would want to ask him – would he shoot a burglar now if the same circumstances occurred? Yes. End of story – no doubt at all.

Before I had been arrested, I would never have thought of going to see Tony Martin. But now I sought out people like him and others, lawyers and the like, involved in our justice system. Being charged by the cops changes lives, that's for sure.

The threatening letters, constant jibes from some colleagues – some funny, some deadly serious – about being a murderer, the price my family paid and the occasional press coverage suggesting that maybe I wasn't so innocent after all made me take action in another way.

'At least they know I'm telling the truth,' I said to Andrew, holding my arms out and with an expression that I hoped looked like total innocence spreading over my face.

'When has that ever mattered,' Andrew joked.

A short while before the visit to Tony Martin, I had taken a lie-detector test. It was carried out by a bloke called Bruce Burgess who was deemed to be one of two experts in the UK on the American standard of polygraphs. Bruce actually does a lot of work in the USA where, unlike Britain, the lie-detector test is accepted in court as evidence. One of his other roles is carrying out the tests on the TV show *Trisha*, where feuding couples are accusing each other of screwing around.

Bruce read up about the trial and the police investigation and then devised the questions which were all about Arlene being murdered, Arlene's whereabouts and so on. I passed and emerged a certificated truth-teller – at least as far as the case was concerned.

I knew that when Nat had been charged with murder he had suggested to his lawyers that he should take such a test. They dismissed the suggestion, saying that it had no status in Scots law but that wasn't his point. Where there remains a great deal of mystery about Arlene's whereabouts and the cops are saying that it was murder, people form opinions about her and about the part we played or didn't play in it. It's very hard to persuade people otherwise. The lie-detector test might help. Though for Nat in prison, it's now too late.

'Any word about the Legal Aid being sorted?' I asked Andrew.

He shook his head, 'They take a long time, Glenn.'

'Is that deliberate you think?'

'Probably,' and he smiled again.

I had asked Andrew for all my papers from the investigation and trial and he was quite willing to hand them over but he had been told that he should hang on to everything till his Legal Aid claim for my case was checked, cleared and paid. This was all fine and well but I saw them as my papers – a huge part of my life – and maybe they'd contain some information that would help the Fraser family. Who knows? Yet the delay had been going on for months with no sign of it ending. I had the distinct impression that they didn't want me to get my hands on my files.

'I'll be driving within the speed limit after this,' I laughed. 'Must remember to be a good boy.' I was heading to Elgin and took the view that I would get lifted for any minor infringement of any law. In one of my first visits up there, a cop car had sat all night in my hotel car park and followed me around all day. Now they were being less watchful but still attentive.

'You sure you want to keep on looking into this mess, Glenn?' It was the first time that Andrew had questioned my actions.

'Bloody right! If the cops are still trying to link me with a hit man, what am I supposed to do?'

A few months earlier, a friend of mine from Newquay called me quite shaken. He was a successful businessman and a millionaire, someone who had never had involvement with the cops in his life – till he met me. The cops had called to say they were coming to interview him but didn't say what it concerned. Two plain-clothes officers had turned up at his office. Of course he agreed to see them, always being willing to help the police. Over four hours they grilled him about me. Now this is a bloke I might have an occasional phone chat with but, due to the distance from Lincolnshire to Newquay, we only meet now and then.

The cops wanted to know about my movements, how often I was down in Devon and Cornwall and whether I had any other connections there. Then they came out with those names again – Finnegan and Legg. Once the names were spoken they kept at them, time after time. It was the missing link in the case. If Hector Dick was to be believed, a hit man had been hired to kill Arlene and that hit man had never been traced. The cops were still looking for him and quite right too, if they really believed that story, but the sods still thought I was the man who organised the hit. Acquittal or not, I wasn't out of this yet as far as Grampian Police was concerned.

'I know, Glenn, but you're getting in deeper and deeper.' Andrew was giving me all his attention now, his drink pushed to the side. 'You're tackling a big team here.' He meant the police.

'But every week there seems to be something new, something exposed,' I pled and he nodded in agreement. 'I mean what about this Grampian copper who is claiming that he had complained about how the case was being handled shortly after Arlene disappeared?'

A serving policeman, David Alexander, had just appeared in court charged with being in someone's garden without permission. He claimed that Grampian Police were trying to ditch him and had been ever since he was involved in the squad hunting for Arlene. Having complained about how the investigation was being handled, he was transferred out to a smaller, less demanding posting in spite of his having high marks in his assessments. That's all he was saying at this time but I told Andrew I was hopeful he might say more.

'I know,' replied Andrew, 'but you have to remember that he has a lot at stake here – his job, his pension. It will be risky for him to speak out.'

'But what if he loses his job? He'll have nothing to lose after that.'

'Maybe, but he still has to live in Elgin and, if he spills the beans, the local constabulary aren't going to take too kindly to him.' I got his point but it was so frustrating.

Off the record, police officers had said that, from very soon after Arlene had disappeared, Nat Fraser's name was the only name in the circle. They also said that some cops had complained about this, saying they didn't even know if there had been a murder – never mind being sure of who the murderer might be. These cops were moved out pronto and replaced with others who didn't question the strategy – so the cops said but it was always off the record. Their wishes for anonymity had to be respected. But, if only one – just one – would make the claim publicly . . .

'I can't just sit still, Andrew,' I concluded in utter frustration. 'God knows what might happen if I just do nothing.' We were gathering together our things and getting ready to leave.

'You are beginning to annoy powerful people, Glenn,' Andrew said as we stood beside our cars in the car park.

'I know,' I said, 'but that's the way it's going to have to be.'

We shook hands and moved towards our cars. Andrew turned and said, 'Take care, Glenn. Take very great care.' Then he drove away. It was to be the last time I would ever see him.

On the 8th of October 2003, on a deserted road around 1.50 in the morning, Andrew McCartan's car spilled down an embankment. Hours later, he was officially declared dead in Ninewells Hospital, Dundee.

On the way to Andrew's funeral, I took a detour to visit the site of the crash on the A9, near Calvine in Perthshire. The road was level with a good surface and, at the point where his car left the road, it was straight. The official reason for the cause of the crash was that the car had run over a rock at speed. Minor landslides or rolling stones are quite common in some parts of the Highlands. The side of the road was level and grassed and had ditches at either side to catch loose debris. I walked up and down several times, checking and rechecking. There were no rocks on the road that day I was there.

Later that day at his funeral, one of Andrew's friends revealed that Andrew had also been receiving death threats over the Arlene case. Death threats because he was representing me. Death threats because he wouldn't run with the pack. Death threats because he believed in justice.

How could I give up now?

Shortly after Andrew's death I engaged John Macaulay, a top Glasgow crime lawyer. In our first meeting, I told him I wanted to pursue action on a number of points:

- to have all my legal papers from the investigation and trial passed to me in their entirety;
- to pursue my rights to find out if my phone had ever been tapped, if so, why and whether it was still being tapped;
- and to demand from the Crown why I had been charged and imprisoned, only for me to be acquitted.

John Macaulay is a big man, strong voiced and polite. I can imagine him making an impact in the court. He listened to my list and smiled, 'That'll shake them up.'

I smiled back. 'Are you sure you want to go through with this?'

'Absolutely. I'm determined.'

I thought of Andrew slowly dying on that lonely country road late at night – it was the very thing he feared. Some time ago, he'd told me about lawyer Willie McRae. He was found dead on another lonely Scottish road. There was a bullet in his head and, many yards away from his body, lay a gun. OK, there was no bullet and there was no gun for Andrew – just a car crash that, at best, seemed like extremely bad luck and, at worst, appeared very sinister – but he too had met his end, just as he feared, on that lonely country road. There was no going back now.

'It may produce disappointing results,' John cautioned.

'I'll take my chances,' I replied.

But I wasn't to be disappointed. Not disappointed at all.

22

THE UNDERBELLY
2004

'There were two sets of almost identical rings,' Nat Fraser said to me from across a table in Shotts Prison visiting room.

'Arlene's rings?' I asked. 'I don't understand.'

'Our house was broken into in . . . emm . . . 1996, I think,' said Nat, still looking dapper and comfortable in spite of his surroundings. 'A stack of stuff was taken including those three rings. They were her wedding rings and that so they had to be replaced.'

'And Arlene wanted exactly the same rings?'

'More or less,' said Nat, 'they came as a matching set, that and a solitaire diamond necklace she always wore. She wanted them to match the necklace.'

'So, strictly speaking, at the time Arlene disappeared . . .'

'there was another set of identical rings around some place,' he finished my sentence anxious to get his point across.

A few tables down, a father in a red prison-issue sweatshirt was playing with his toddler son on the table. His wife beamed at them from the other side of the fixed table – she wasn't allowed to get close to her man. Nearby, I noticed an unsmiling screw keeping a very keen eye on them. The wee boy wasn't allowed too close to his dad either, in case he had some dope hidden in his clothes.

'Why didn't you mention this at the time, Nat?'

'I did,' he protested. 'I'm sure I did but I just didn't think it was that important.'

Those were the rings that had reappeared in the bathroom at 2 Smith Street ten days after Arlene had disappeared. Discovered by Arlene's father's second wife, Cathy McInnes, the family and the cops swore the rings hadn't been in the house before. Cathy also swore that Nat had been in the house that day and had used the bathroom. They were the same rings that the prosecution had described as 'most compelling evidence' at the murder trial – the very rings that seemed to swing the jury to convict Nat.

Now, after the event, it was probably too little too late. I left the jail for that dreary drive to the motorway and into Glasgow to see my lawyer, John Macaulay. He had phoned me with good news – my legal files or rather boxes had arrived.

Andrew McCartan might have been a great guy and a good lawyer but it seemed to me he couldn't organise paperwork. Later I'd learn that few lawyers can.

'I've found two interesting documents already,' said John with a smile. 'About those rings.'

Nat and Arlene's son, Jamie, had been interviewed several times at great length by the police. Although he was just a young boy at the time, the notes of one early interview ran to one hundred and eighty pages. And, in there, was a particular gold mine or maybe a ring of fire.

Jamie had been adamant that the rings had just been lying in an ashtray. He didn't know how long they'd been there but he was definite where they had been. Arlene was known to be quite careless about where she laid things down so that wouldn't be unusual for her – out of the mouths of babes . . .

The defence team for Nat had, of course, precognosed Jamie – that is interviewed him to find out what he knew about certain events, before taking a statement from him. The notes of that session were only a few lines long and had no mention of any rings.

Later, in that treasure chest, we'd find a police note confirming that a formal identification of the rings was made but not until the 27th of April 2001, almost three full years down the line. What the hell was that about?

Also, weeks after the house was meant to have been thoroughly searched by the cops, a separate forensic team and the family, another ring was found on a window ledge and an earring was discovered elsewhere. During most of that time, Arlene's parents and their spouses as well as her sister, Carol, had lived in the house. Yet they didn't spot these items which could have proved so crucial. Did they overlook the rings in the ashtray? If so, who moved them to the bathroom and why?

In early statements when most people thought Arlene had run off, some of her friends stated that she never wore her rings when she went out.

'It might put the men off,' Arlene would laugh.

Another said that, since she had fallen out with Nat big time in January 1998, she never wore the rings at all. All that suggested the innocent Jamie was quite right to say that the rings were lying in an ashtray. As expensive as they were, that's how Arlene treated things – a bit disorganised, a wee bit absent-mindedly.

The rings matched the diamond solitaire necklace that Arlene wore all the time but the necklace was never recovered. The cops, the prosecution and Hector Dick implied that the murderer had returned the rings to avoid them being used to identify her remains or his culpability. If this was the case, why did he not do the same with the expensive necklace? Everyone also associated that necklace with Arlene.

It felt like our first big breakthrough. I guess the prosecution had laid so much emphasis on the so-called 'appearing rings' in case the jury found Hector Dick to be an unreliable witness. If the jury had known the full story, would they have still convicted Nat?

There was also a much more sinister implication about the paperwork we had found. The prosecution knew all about Jamie saying that the rings were found in an ashtray. Yet they didn't reveal that to the court. They did, however, use evidence from Cathy McInnes who said that they suddenly appeared in the bathroom on the same day as Nat had used that bathroom.

Had the prosecution knowingly presented evidence that they

knew might well be false? We wouldn't have to wait much longer to find the answer.

Soon we had identified certified statements from three independent witnesses who had seen Arlene after the day she disappeared from her home. All of these witnesses were available and willing to give evidence. None were called.

In a statement about something else entirely, a copper, one of those involved in arresting me, made a long contribution on how, in his view, sightings of the missing person wasted time in an investigation and, to back this up, he referred to another case. The policeman's words explained to me why each of those who say they saw Arlene felt as if, from day one, the cops didn't believe them and came back again and again to badger them to change their minds.

A friend of Arlene, Mary Brown, stated how Arlene had affairs with other men and constantly argued with Nat. There was more. Arlene took Mary into the bedroom at 2 Smith Street one day, removed a grey box from a unit drawer and from underneath a pile of papers, pulled 'a huge wodge of money'. Arlene said it was her 'rainy-day money'.

'Does Nat know it's there?' Mary had asked.

'No and don't tell anyone,' Arlene had instructed.

The box held even more interesting tricks. 'Why have you got two passports?' asked Mary.

Arlene smiled and opened both. 'This one here is my rainy-day passport,' she had said, with a grin. Mary Brown then looked at the two open passports. Both had Arlene's photo in them. She then noticed that one was in Arlene's own name but the other, the one she referred to as her 'rainy-day' passport, bore an entirely different name although she can't remember what the name was.

Grampian Police only ever recovered one passport – the one in Arlene Fraser's name.

Before the cops searched the house, they asked Nat if he had any money there. He told them about various plants including one behind a vent where approximately £500 was stored. The vent had been loosened and they found no money there. Other sums of money mentioned by Nat were found but the cops never found any 'wodge' of cash in a grey box in a bedroom unit drawer.

Around the time of Arlene's disappearance, Mary's fifteen-year old daughter, Tina, started taking drugs and would try to score at two different addresses in Elgin. One night, she revealed to her mother that she had often met Arlene at those same houses and that Arlene was buying and taking drugs.

Mary Brown had told all of this to the police. Some time after she gave her formal statement, she was visited by two CID officers who bluntly called her a liar and said that they could 'prove' Arlene hadn't taken drugs. They never did explain how they could 'prove' that but they went on to question Mary again and again about the secret money and the two passports.

The police and the prosecution had this and similar evidence but none of it was revealed to the jury at the High Court. Nat's defence team also had this information and didn't use it either.

In one police search on the 30th of April, two days after Arlene's disappearance, a PC Leith Morgan found her pink towelling dressing gown hanging up behind the bathroom door. In the pocket of the dressing gown he found two condoms, unused.

I had known fine well that, for months, Arlene and Nat had had no sex life with each other. It worried me further that normally condoms would be kept by the bed, within easy reach, but Arlene had these two in her dressing gown. Was this so the kids wouldn't find them or had she kept them from Nat? Had she been expecting company and was ready to receive him?

The cops had videoed every room in the house on the 29th of April, the day after Arlene had disappeared. The purpose of the video footage is to slowly cover every angle of every room so that everything can be checked later for significant objects present or absent – like 'appearing rings'. The video evidence was missing from the legal files. Not only that, the first copy was found to have become corrupted and was unusable so a second video had to be filmed. How does a video get corrupted and why was it missing from my box of tricks? That first so-called corrupted video was never seen by the court and nor was it made available to the defence team. Why not?

What was most often missing in those legal papers was content. Hector Dick's alibi for the 28th of April was precise and comprehensive. Yet, early on in the investigation, the cops were saying off the record that Dick was responsible for Arlene's disappearance. That alibi needed checking and rechecking. Dick would state that, at different times throughout the day in question, either Ian Gordon, a worker and friend, or his own brother, James Dick, were in his company. Nat's legal team had interviewed them both but the reports that they produced of those interviews amounted to only a few lines with nothing definite that the defence could use. It was, therefore, no wonder that, when Hector Dick turned Queen's evidence, all the defence could do was to call him a liar. I'm sure they were right in that but they had no ammunition to prove it.

The treasure chest of legal papers was revealing new and essential information every time we looked at it. I began to look forward to meetings in John Macaulay's basement office, just knowing something new would be revealed. But it was time to reach out a bit.

'Do you recognise this woman?' I held the photograph of Arlene up. It was the same one they had used in the police posters.

'Very nice and all, sir, but no,' the Garda sergeant behind the desk in one of Dublin's largest cop shops was polite and helpful.

'She's missing,' I started to explain and he interrupted me.

'Oh, I'm sorry. Is it your missus?'

'No, a friend . . . well, a friend's wife but she's also a friend.'

He was nodding his head sympathetically.

'She went missing in 1998.'

'That's a long time ago, sir.'

'Yeah, a long time. But the Scottish cops were meant to have circulated her details all across Ireland – all across Europe actually.'

Now he had a quizzical look on his face.

I assumed his confusion was down to the fact that the police don't usually put as much effort into tracking a missing person. 'Would you have records going back to then?'

'I doubt it. I can look but it might well be boxed in the cellar – seeing how long it's been.'

I decided to give the sergeant a summary of why I was asking.

He nodded, 'You know how many missing persons notices we get a day? Scores of them. To be honest all we do is file them. Some of them don't even make it to a file.'

I was to get the same response in police stations all across Ireland – in the north as well as the Republic. In Belfast they even went further, adding, 'Missing persons! Do you know what else we had to deal with back then? Loyalist feuds, revenge kneecappings and all that. We would have just binned a missing person report.'

Eventually, I got hold of a high-ranking officer in the Republic.

'In 1998,' he explained, 'in fact, till the last couple of years, our information systems were, to be blunt, bloody useless. Even if somebody had bothered to check, they would be very unlikely to find anything that matched – even if they were in one of our jails.'

'So if she looked just the same but had changed her name?'

'Och, no chance we'd trace her.'

'Was . . .' I was nervous about this and watched out the window as a cop wagon sped past, wondering where it was going. 'Was it the same across Europe? Better? Worse?'

'Some were slightly ahead of the game, some even worse than us but it was all pretty inadequate.'

'What about Interpol?' I asked. Grampian cops had claimed they had used Interpol to try to trace Arlene throughout Europe.

'Where do you think that shower get their information from?' he asked before answering his own question, 'Us, of course.'

A British passport in a false name but with your own picture can get you anywhere. This was even more true in 1998 when, before the tragedy of 9/11, borders across Europe were practically wide open. A wodge of money, especially sterling, could get you anything – even the medication you need for your Crohn's disease. You just show your passport with your new name in it to the doctor – a private one, of course. With money and a passport in 1998 you could go anywhere. Anywhere at all.

It was beginning to look to me as though Arlene was missing. For a while, I'd fallen into thinking of her as abducted, such is the power of the law and the media. But they didn't know any of this. At least those who did kept it well quiet.

John Macaulay had been busy while I was away.

Elgin folk's reticence over Arlene was understandable. For the past six years, they had the press ready to print almost any word or little snippet of gossip around Arlene and Nat. The good folk of Elgin didn't want to get caught up in that. But maybe they'd talk to a lawyer, confidentially.

John agreed to place an advert in the *Northern Scot* newspaper, requesting information on the case and mentioning, in particular, the beige Ford Fiesta that the cops had stated was used in Arlene's abduction. It was a bold move that created a buzz. At first, we didn't reveal that I was behind the move. The newspapers up north had written me up as someone determined to prove Nat Fraser innocent. However, what I really wanted was simply the truth. People do believe almost everything they read in the papers and knowing that I was behind the ploy would have tainted the nature of the calls we received.

Within hours people started to call John's office.

- The Ford Fiesta was seen being driven by Hector Dick in Elgin the day after Arlene disappeared.
- The Ford Fiesta was seen being driven by Ian Gordon, Hector Dick's worker and the essential corroborator of his alibi, at the Fiddochside Inn, Craigellachie, about a week after Arlene disappeared.
- The Ford Fiesta was seen being driven by Hector Dick in Keith.

The list just went on and on and, importantly, it cast doubt on Dick's evidence in the High Court that Nat Fraser had been in possession of the car from the 28th of April to the 1st of May. All we needed now was some proof, especially about that car. John Macaulay went north.

'Unless Hector Dick is going through a time warp, it is not the Fiesta the police are looking for,' said Douglas Williamson, the managing director of Williamson's scrap merchants.

'Why not?' asked the procurator fiscal from Edinburgh, as they sat in the interview room at Elgin police station in January 2003.

Douglas Williamson told him straight, just as he had told the cops time and time again. Hector Dick had lied and lied about that beige Ford Fiesta till he admitted that he had bought it and disposed of it. But was he telling the whole truth? Even after Dick admitted getting the Fiesta, he changed his mind no less than three times about how he disposed of it. Eventually, at the High Court, he had sworn that he had burned the car, then crushed it and delivered it to a local scrapyard. He meant Williamson's. All this had happened on the 4th of May 1998, according to his evidence. If that was true, some of our callers had to be mistaken about sightings of the car. But was it true?

In his statement supporting the evidence he gave in court, Dick had said he remembered the date very well since it had happened on the same day he had sold Williamson a large metal, stainless steel tank. Douglas Williamson remembered that tank very well because it was the first one of its kind that he had handled and he had originally sold it to Hector's brother James. He had been amazed at their ingenuity. They transported fish waste as fertiliser from Fort William. When they used open containers they lost a lot through spillage. The tank would stop that and save them money. Bright men.

Douglas Williamson keeps good records. He could show that he sold James Dick the tank on the 4th of July 1995 for £1,000 plus VAT. There was a tank within the tank – a stainless steel inner section that would be no good for the Dicks so Williamson agreed to give them money back on it if they returned it to him. Hector Dick delivered the stainless steel tank back to Williamson's on the 14th of September 1995. In his statement to the cops, he said he had delivered the remains of the Fiesta on the same day as the tank. He stated that day to have been the 4th of May 1998 – two and half years later.

Hector Dick lied about the disposal of the beige Ford Fiesta. The murder squad were told this by Douglas Williamson in November 1998 when he gave them a formal statement. He repeated this to them several times and again in January 2003 when Hector Dick had turned Queen's evidence.

Williamson was called to the High Court to give evidence. He was sitting in the witness room with some cops when that same Edinburgh procurator fiscal came to see him. 'Because of the way things have progressed, you will no longer be required,' the PF said.

'Are we free to go to lunch then?' Williamson asked, not quite catching his drift.

'You are no longer to be called as a witness and we no longer require you,' said the PF, walking out of the room.

The Crown sent Williamson away, knowing he had evidence that would prove Hector Dick to be a liar. As Douglas Williamson drove home to Elgin, Hector Dick was holding the attention of the High Court and saying what a terrible wife murderer Nat Fraser was.

John Macaulay had bothered to find and speak with Douglas Williamson. The good man was quite clear that, every time he mentioned some facts that didn't fit with their case, both the cops and the prosecution weren't interested.

He had also tried his hardest and given them a place to look for Arlene. Believing that Arlene was dead and her body had been dumped, Williamson pointed out that Hector Dick had a licence to dump asbestos on a disused quarry site in Wellbank near Dundee. The asbestos has to be double-wrapped and enclosed for safety and, as long as the paperwork is in order, no one checks the loads. As soon as the load is dumped into the landfill site it is immediately buried under one and a half metres of rubble. A body could easily be wrapped in the middle of one of the large bundles and it could then be safely and secretly dumped in the massive quarry. No one goes near to check the asbestos – it's too dangerous. They just fill the hole in.

The cops ignored that too.

But now it's your turn. Who do you believe? The cops? Let's have a look at the cops.

23

THE COPS

2004

'You're not going to find what you're looking for.' The voice on the other end of the phone line was male, deep, educated, confident and with a ring of authority.

'How do you know what I'm looking for?' I asked, intrigued. Always intrigued.

'Whatever they think goes against their case has been removed and destroyed – a long time ago.'

'Who by?'

'Cops.'

'How do you know?'

The bloke had refused to give his name. 'I just know,' he said and hung up.

At one point, I had been thinking of changing my phone numbers and going ex-directory to avoid the crank calls I'd been getting in addition to the death-threat letters. I decided not to – if cranks might call so might someone useful. They had but anonymously again.

Not all the letters were from cranks either. It didn't look like a death threat. They are often written in green ink and the name and address on the envelope spelled out in large, unwieldy capitals or clumsy, childlike joined-up writing. This one was neatly typed just like the single sheet of paper that was inside.

No date, no name, no address – just a postmark from the Aberdeen area – and no 'Dear' but right into it.

> Mr Lucas,
> It seems to be widely accepted within Grampian Police that you are
> not going to give up on your quest to clear your name and that of
> your co-accused Nat Fraser in connection to the Arlene Fraser case.
> I take it that you understand that as many obstacles as possible will
> be put in your way to both stop and discourage you in your quest
> for the truth.

My arse twitched with nervous fear. This opening sounded like the
beginning of a threat. Polite. Decent English. But there was
something about the tone. How wrong I was. The letter went on to
list points that its writer thought I may find interesting.

> You are being discreetly watched while on your visits to the Moray
> area.

No surprise there since the cops hadn't exactly made a secret of it.

> It is known that Hector Dick did commit perjury on the witness
> stand during the trial.

Now the writer had my attention. Although they hadn't spelled
out the details, the only way they could know for sure about Dick's
perjury was by reading all the legal papers and knowing about
Douglas Williamson's evidence – evidence that was never presented
to the court or the public.

> Witnesses who gave statements as to the possible sightings of
> Arlene Fraser on or after the 28th April were 'persuaded' they were
> mistaken.

I knew that but I only learned it after the trial through a great deal
of muck-raking.

Witnesses gave statements that Mr Dick suspected either his wife
or his daughter of having an affair with Mr Fraser in 1997/98.

Now this was news to me. I knew that Irene Dick would often make
comments of a sexual nature about Nat but had just written that off
as banter. There was nothing in my trial papers to say that Hector
actually suspected an affair. Whether that was true or not, all those
statements should have been included. Where had those statements
gone? Statements that suggested Hector Dick had an additional
motive for putting Nat inside. Not just saving his own neck but
jealousy.

The lip-reading evidence was not used in court as it was deemed
inaccurate and would have greatly weakened the prosecution case.

Bingo. I'd found a report by a Professor A. Q. Summerfield of the
Medical Research Council Institute of Hearing Research, Notting-
ham, who tested Jessica Rees's lip-reading skills. In a test involving
820 words, she got 55% correct. More worrying was that she
introduced 224 words that had never been said. That about took
care of her transcript of the conversation between Nat and me in
the visiting room of Porterfield Prison, Inverness, and her allegation
that we were talking about 'chopping up bodies'. It was pure tosh
and I knew it but how had the writer of the letter known that the
lip-reading had been inaccurate? The letter-writer must have seen
the same reports I had managed to get my hands on.

There were three separate witnesses who gave statements to the
effect that they saw Hector Dick driving a Ford Fiesta car in the
Elgin area between 09.00 and 10.00 on the 28th April 1998. These
statements have subsequently disappeared.

This was new and very worrying information. If it was accurate, it
meant that Hector had been driving the car the cops allege was
used in abducting Arlene at the time she was known to have

disappeared. Was that why, in the early days, they were saying, albeit privately, that Hector did it? But, if that was the case, why hadn't the cops acted on it. Hector Dick said to both Nat and me, on separate occasions, that he had something over the cops. Was this what he meant? Was whatever he had on the cops used to pull these statements linking him to the car that the cops reckoned had been used in Arlene's disappearance? Is that what had happened?

> Mr Dick was given immunity from prosecution on VAT fraud in connection to the sale of duty free alcohol.

We had already worked that one out – a mere £175,000 starting figure, according to Hector Dick. But what I liked about this line was the phrase 'duty free alcohol'. Precise and accurate not the 'bootleg booze' that other people might call it. The letter-writer had to be in the law-and-order business.

> If you had not been acquitted along with Hector Dick, he was prepared to implicate you in the 'crime' by claiming Mr Fraser told him of your involvement.

The letter ended abruptly, leaving me with a shiver running down my spine. How close had I come to spending twenty-five years in jail for a crime I hadn't committed? A crime no one had proved had actually happened? Just as the letter-writer had written, Arlene's disappearance was not a crime but a 'crime'. What did the inverted commas hint at?

Was the writer a cop? Or maybe a lawyer in the prosecution service? Or possibly somebody from that part of officialdom who would really know what goes on backstage in a murder case like this? Whoever they were they had hit the mark on so many points and had information that had never been put in the public domain in spite of the millions of words that had been written about Arlene.

'The language is right,' said John Macaulay in his office, with the letter held in front of him again, reading it for the umpteenth time.

I'd shown the letter to one other trusted contact, someone else who was used to such correspondence, who also knew about language. He had said it was a cop who had written the letter and now I was waiting for John's assessment.

He read down another couple of paragraphs. 'Some of the phraseology is straight from the police vocabulary. The formality of the terms is also typical. And the writer certainly knows aspects of the case that only the investigating team, the prosecution and now, of course,' he looked up and smiled, 'we know for sure.' John went quiet, still looking at the letter.

'Do you think a cop wrote it?' I asked, unable to hold myself back.

He looked up as if startled, 'Oh, in my opinion, it was undoubtedly written by a police officer.' He offered a slow smile in my direction. 'Undoubtedly.'

John Macaulay isn't just one of Scotland's foremost lawyers he is also a former policeman.

Information on the cops was coming in from strange and diverse directions. A journalist contacted one of Nat's relatives. He had attended a broadcast appeal for Arlene to come home not long after she'd disappeared. Nat had led that appeal and every major media organisation was present. Once Nat had left the building, the police let it be known to all the gathered journalists that their main suspect was, indeed, Nat Fraser. No wonder the media had given him such a bad time from the off. But it had been bothering this particular journalist for years and, now that Nat had been jailed for life, it was bothering him even more.

Then a letter arrived for Nat at Shotts Prison from a guy he'd been friendly with while they were both doing time in Porterfield Prison, Inverness. Nat had been serving his eighteen-month sentence for the assault on Arlene. One of the senior staff at the jail had approached this guy, promising him favours and extra privileges if he could spill some dirt on Nat. 'We'll even not notice that dope you smoke,' said the screw with a wink.

Again the con had done nothing until, a few years later, when

Nat was sentenced to twenty-five years. The con had smelled a rat back then in Inverness. Maybe it was an even bigger rat that got Nat convicted?

All that these people wanted to do was help. They sensed that there had been a set-up and they didn't like it. And none of them asked for anything in return – not even a thank you.

'I'm not anti police you know.' I was back again, sitting across the fixed table from Nat Fraser in Shotts Prison visiting room. Ever since we had been secretly filmed in Porterfield Prison, I was always wary about where we sat. But the staff at Shotts seemed more laid-back than most. They were efficient but they also treated prisoners and visitors alike with some decency, some respect. I was beginning to relax in that place.

'No?' Nat laughed. 'You could have fooled me!'

'I know I fucking sound like it but I'm not.'

'What are you then? A big fan.'

'I'm anti corrupt cops.'

'Is that not the same thing?' he was smiling, laughter in his eyes.

It struck me then how well he was coping with this. If it had been me tucked away for twenty-five years, I'd have been crawling up the walls and howling at the moon. But not Nat Fraser.

'I'm sure the majority are just honest men and women trying to do a good job.'

'Aye, aye, I'm sure you're right,' he was nodding, not joking anymore. I knew that he agreed with me.

'It's just I wish some of the bastards were braver. I wish they'd speak out when the knew evidence was being destroyed or witnesses badgered or deals struck with perjurers or that lies were being told in court.' My temper had risen and my hands were gripping on to the table in front of me, my knuckles shining chalk white. I wonder what Jessica Rees would have made of this little scene.

'Relax, man,' Nat coaxed. 'Relax. You'd think it was you in prison, not me.'

'In some ways, I'm in prison too,' I blustered before quickly returning to our normal topics of women, music, football and women.

Nat Fraser had formally appealed against his conviction, of course. The whole process seemed to be dragging on and on and the Crown, the judge and Nat's legal team were blaming it on the complexities of the case. Inevitably, the delay meant that there would be speculation in the media about what he would use for his appeal. Someone whispered to a newspaper that Nat's son Jamie would be giving key evidence and, of course, the headline was full of moral outrage. How dare he exploit his son? That kind of thing. But none of the media had been near Jamie for years and didn't realise that he is now a confident, handsome, intelligent seventeen-year-old who wants to speak out and has important things to say.

Both Jamie and Natalie still stay in the family home and are looked after by Nat's mother, Ibby. They are close to their dad and miss him – just as they miss their mother. Jamie and Natalie don't see their dad as a murderer. Just as, if their mum did deliberately disappear in 1998, they don't see her as uncaring. Unlike Arlene's parents and sister, they haven't embraced the easy answer the High Court gave them in January 2003. And they don't think like headline-writers. It's their mum and dad after all and they love them both.

Writing about Jamie appearing at the appeal, the journalists rightly pursued the cops for a comment. They couldn't do so officially, of course, because an appeal was outstanding but, unofficially, one was quoted as saying, 'If that's all they've got, we've nothing to worry about.'

It's a battle, in other words. The cops don't want Nat Fraser out of jail even if he's innocent. They are not after the truth, they're after victory.

Detective Superintendent Jim Stephen, who led the case, made a statement a short while after the trial ended. In it, he said, 'I can assure Arlene's family and the community in Elgin that our inquiry will continue until we find out what has happened to Arlene.' Months after his conviction, Nat received a visit from Detective Superintendent Jim Stephen. It was a short meeting and Nat struggled to stay polite. What do you expect when you ask an innocent man where the body of his victim is? Jim Stephen hasn't been back to see Nat again.

There was another line in that letter I got from the anonymous cop.

> There are a number of senior officers who seem to be rather worried as to the contents of a book which is to be published by you.

Let's hope he's right and they're not disappointed. Let's hope they act on the underbelly of this case, the parts that were never revealed.

Someone has already acted. In December 2004, David Alexander, now a former constable with Grampian Police, stood in Elgin Sheriff Court and made a statement in which he claimed that those 'appearing rings' were removed by a cop during an early search of Arlene's house, stored in his desk drawer at the station and then secretly returned to the house at a later date.

Some might dismiss Alexander's statements, saying he had reasons to feel bitter towards Grampian Police. He had been found guilty of a minor breach of the peace charge and had had to resign his post. He had earlier claimed that, having been involved in the Arlene case, he was transferred out after he had raised concerns on how the investigation was being handled. He had lost his career and possibly the respect of his community and he had ended up with a criminal record. Wouldn't he have grounds to be bitter?

David Alexander was a former soldier with an exemplary record. He was also the top student in his year at the Scottish Police Training College, winning the Baton of Honour. As a serving police officer, he had an excellent record – that is, till he was shunted out of the hunt for Arlene.

Alexander hadn't just made the claims about the rings, he had complained that the police had decided, early on, that Arlene had been murdered and that Nat Fraser was the killer despite the fact that they had no evidence of either. Like all good cops, he didn't think that was the right way to go about any investigation.

251

In Scotland, people are meant to be taken to trial within less than four months after being charged. In David Alexander's case, trial was delayed for over fifteen months. This was a most unusual situation when such a minor charge was involved. The delay made sure that the pressure stayed on Alexander and he wasn't allowed to speak out till after Nat Fraser had been tried and convicted. A coincidence? What do you think?

David Alexander is voluntarily helping with Nat Fraser's appeal. More will emerge when that appeal is convened. Let's hope that he names names. What is a police force if it doesn't deal with those within it who break the rules?

All we need is one more cop to speak out – one more or maybe two. Now wouldn't that be a happy day for honest cops everywhere?

24

MURDERED OR MISSING?

FEBRUARY 2005

'You want me to take him?' asked Maya, hovering above us.

'No, we're OK,' I replied with a smile, 'Aren't we, old chum?' And we are. He isn't heavy and I continue speaking down the phone to John Macaulay, discussing yet another sliver of information that casts doubt on what happened to Arlene and on Nat Fraser's conviction. Well, he wouldn't be heavy. He's my five-month-old son, Andrew.

It suddenly occurs to me that, as I've waded into and through the very public sadness of my good friends, Arlene and Nat, my life has been blessed. Maya and I, we're the couple they tried to stop and they lost. We're a love story. Arlene and Nat? Well, I suppose theirs is another kind of love story.

Work is good, the family are healthy, Falkirk Football Club are top of the league and Maya, Andrew and I are together. At times, it stops me in my tracks. I'll be writing to Nat Fraser or talking to young Jamie and think, 'What right have I to feel so good about life?' Then Andrew was born and the first congratulation card to pop through the letterbox was from Uncle Nat. The same Nat who writes every week, is learning computer skills and Spanish and works at pottery, sending his artefacts out to his friends. A holiday camp, you think? Would you go on holiday in the exclusive company of murderers and heroin traffickers to a resort you'll only ever leave when they allow you?

I'll be on the phone to Jamie and he'll suddenly start enthusing about playing the drums and how he prefers jazz, the excitement and enthusiasm clearly buzzing through him, and, in a shy voice, he'll mention girlfriends. And young Natalie – she's growing big now and she's good looking. She and her pals discuss their pop-star favourites as they move in sight of taking their tentative steps into womanhood.

Life goes on. It really does.

But life changes as well. My old dear has altered for good. She was a country lass from the far north of Scotland, a serving Wren during World War II, a Royal Marine major's wife who had to cope with him being away and in danger most of their married life. She's an old Tory, into charity work and Maggie Thatcher is her hero. She's been a law-abiding, conservative citizen all her life. She still is. Except now she doesn't say 'police' she says 'Gestapo', the worst insult she can give. She says it quietly without rancour but she'll never see the police in the same light again. She wonders if she had been wrong about them all these years.

But her life also goes on. It will take more than cops behaving badly to stop her in her tracks.

Arlene's mother, father and sister – how they must grieve. You can feel their pain every time the media goes to them for yet another comment. No doubt, they'll be queuing at their doors to hear what they have to say about this book. No doubt it will be angry. I'd be angry if I'd lost my daughter. But who should they be angry with? That's my point – my only point. In my own way, I'm trying to help – and it's them I'm trying to help as much as anyone else.

But, in the meantime, I'm sure their life goes on. I hope their life goes on.

Maya, me and our young Andrew. We chose Andrew as the perfect name. He is the patron saint of both Russia and Scotland, countries we both love. It is also the name of an eccentric, quirky man I met one night in a police station in Elgin. Andrew McCartan, the lawyer who saved me from a life inside, the man who stood by me in spite of the death threats. Andrew McCartan who was left dying on that lonely country road just the way he feared. The man who gave me the chance of this life with Maya and his namesake, Andrew.

Life goes on even after a death.

What of Arlene? I'll never stop looking for her. But I like to think that, on the morning of the 28th of April 1998, she took her 'wodge of cash' and her 'rainy-day passport', climbed into a boyfriend's car and sped away. I like to think that she breezed through an airport someplace flashing her passport under her new name. I like to think that, right now, she's lying on a beach in some sunny land and she's happy.

Until I know otherwise, Arlene isn't dead for me.

I like to think she's missing.